Studies in Elizabethan and Renaissance Culture II

General editor: Dr. Marcia Vale
Advisory editor: Professor W. A. Armstrong

ENTERTAINMENTS FOR ELIZABETH I

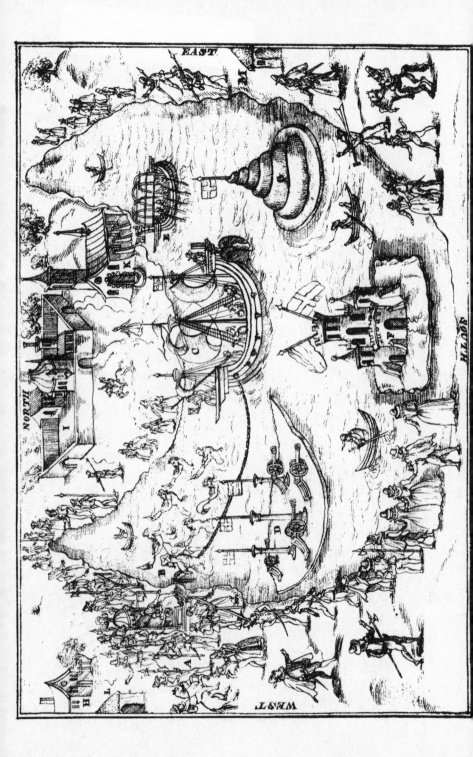

ENTERTAINMENTS FOR ELIZABETH I

JEAN WILSON

D. S. BREWER · ROWMAN & LITTLEFIELD

© Jean Wilson 1980

Published by D. S. Brewer an imprint of
Boydell & Brewer Ltd, PO Box 9, Woodbridge IP12 3DF
and Rowman and Littlefield, 81 Adams Drive, Totowa, N.J. 07512,
U.S.A.

First published 1980

British Library Cataloguing in Publication Data
Wilson, Jean
  Entertainments for Elizabeth I. – (Studies in Elizabethan and
  Renaissance culture; 2).
  1. Masques.
  2. English drama – Early modern and Elizabethan, 1500–1600.
  3. Elizabeth I, *Queen of England* – Drama.
  4. Pageants – England – History.
  I. Title II. Series
  822'.3'080351 PR1253 79–41809
  ~~ISBN 0-85991-048-2~~

US ISBN 0-8476-6820-7

Also in this series

THE GENTLEMAN'S RECREATIONS
*Accomplishments and Pastimes of the
English Gentleman 1580–1630*

ed. Marcia Vale

Printed and bound in Great Britain by
REDWOOD BURN LIMITED
Trowbridge & Esher

Contents

FOR NORMAN AND GAWAIN
WITHOUT WHOM THIS WOULD HAVE BEEN WRITTEN
SEVERAL YEARS AGO

Preface

This book builds unashamedly on the work of earlier students in its field, but is a first attempt to present an accessible selection of the different types of entertainment offered to Elizabeth I, which may be of interest both to those who study sixteenth-century literature, and to those who are interested in the English antecedents of the Jacobean court masque. I hope that it may lead to a rather higher value being placed on these products of Elizabethan court culture than has hitherto generally been the case.

My specific debts are mentioned in the footnotes, but I owe a general debt to my teachers, and in particular to Professor J. A. W. Bennett, FBA who supervised the dissertation of which this book is a very incidental product. I am also most grateful to Christopher Hogwood for the help and advice he gave me on the music for the entertainments, and to Professor Thomas P. Roche for discussing the topic with me and making some very helpful suggestions. I am grateful to Professor Harry Evans, of Douglass College, Rutgers University, for helping me with some of the Latin translations. Any errors are, of course, my own.

My gratitude must also go to the staffs of the Crossroads Nursery school in Princeton and the Millington Road Nursery School in Cambridge, without whom I would certainly never have completed this.

Introduction

1. The establishment of the regime

When Elizabeth I came to the throne in 1558, the rejoicing was rather at the advent of a new hope than at any assurance of the political stability which we can in retrospect see that she brought. The previous one hundred and fifty years had been ones of violent instability, marked by civil war, recurrent rebellions, and more recently by repressive and confusing changes in religious allegiance. Elizabeth herself was the last direct representative of the third generation of a new regime that had only the most tenuous of claims to the throne, but that had so rigorously exterminated rival claimants as to leave that throne open to large numbers of the nobility if the immediate line failed. Her most probable successor was the Scottish Catholic Queen of France. Elizabeth was all that stood between England and civil war or foreign domination.

Her brother had died a child; her sister, after a pathetic, infinitely extended false pregnancy, barren. That sister had further proved as pathetically incompetent as a ruler as she was in her emotional life, flouting the advice of her Parliament and the wishes of her people to marry Philip of Spain, thus subordinating English interests to Hapsburg designs, and embarking on a sustained policy of religious persecution unique in the country's history. To those who hailed her as their saviour Elizabeth's course of action seemed clear, were she to ensure her right to that appelation: she must marry suitably, whether a native nobleman or a foreign prince, and devote herself to the business of producing enough sons to secure the succession, leaving the government of the country to her consort and her Council. The premature deaths of her siblings had shown the necessity of producing an heir, the example of her sister the inconceivability of a woman's ruling successfully.

Elizabeth refused to accede to these expectations, and the early years of her reign were marked by a mounting dread of the uprising to replace her with Mary Stuart which must surely come. Mary had returned to Scotland in 1561, following her widowing. In 1568 she fled to England, and in 1569 the revolution came: an astonishing anti-climax. The main body of the rebels dispersed without meeting the forces sent to suppress them; the only encounter (between Lord Hunsdon and the forces of Leonard Dacre) was little more than a minor skirmish. It was not until the failure of this rebellion, and the ineffectiveness of the Papal Bull of excommunication of 1570, that the Elizabethan regime began to regard itself as established, and the beginnings of the cult of Elizabeth are generally placed, probably correctly, in the early 1570s.[1] Roy Strong ascribes at least part of its genesis to 'the wave of popular feeling for the Queen which swelled after the defeat of the Northern rebellion of 1569 and more especially after the Papal Bull of excommunication issued in 1570',[2] but this is only a partial explanation of the inception of the peculiar and idiosyncratic cult of Elizabeth at this particular time. The years between 1558 and 1570 are perhaps best seen as years of transition and establishment in which the nature of the Elizabethan regime was being formulated and accepted.[3] The defeat of the Northern rebellion suddenly presented the country with the fact that the regime was stable and defined: that England would probably not be involved in another round of civil war, would probably not be ruled by any consort of Elizabeth. Elizabeth's government was not a caretaker waiting for her husband or her son to take over, but a regime in its own right, with its own character. After 1569 rebellions gave way to plots, and after 1569 the pressing need for Elizabeth to marry became less and less loudly expressed. It is as if in the early 1570s her subjects suddenly saw Elizabeth clearly and saw her whole, and so could begin to find an imagery in which to express that vision.

In the years since the publication of Frances Yates's seminal article, *Queen Elizabeth as Astraea*,[4] she and her pupil Roy Strong have described and elucidated the cults surrounding Elizabeth I and her European contemporaries. Their works, together with that of E. C. Wilson, who first identified and ennumerated the multifarious *personae* ascribed to Elizabeth, and John Nichols, whose monumental anthology has provided the basis for all subsequent criticism,[5] bring before us a world of elaborate and esoteric cults, in which each aspect of the queen was turned, in Strong's word, into an 'icon', a devotional image upon which the beholder might meditate. But while the scholarship extended in describing the details of the cult, the events in which it was expressed, and the meanings and ancestry of the images in which it expressed itself, is unrivalled, only limited attempts have been made to go further: to explain and explore what this imagery tells us of how the Elizabethan courtiers saw themselves and their relationship to their queen, or why they chose this particular imagery to express themselves.

2. *The problem of the female monarch*

The most important fact about Elizabeth I was her sex. The formula for proclaiming a new ruler is 'The king is dead, long live the king'. When it runs instead, 'The king is dead, long live the queen', uneasiness is generated; the female monarch is an anomaly, usually resolved by marriage to an acceptable consort who wields effective power while the queen regnant settles down to the queen's traditional occupation of producing a male heir.

The concept of the ruler has always been – in Western European society at least – an essentially masculine one. The imagery of Jonson's *Oberon* encapsulates the associations and resonances of the concept of 'the king':

> '*Sylvan* This is a night of greatness and of state,
> Not to be mixed with light and skipping sport:
> A night of homage to the British court,
> And ceremony due to Arthur's chair,
> From our bright master, Oberon the fair,
> Who with these knights, attendants, here preserved
> In fairyland, for good they have deserved
> Of yond' high throne, are come of right to pay
> Their annual vows; and all their glories lay
> At feet, and tender to this only great
> True majesty, restored in this seat;
> To whose sole power and magic they do give
> The honour of their being, that they live
> Sustained in form, fame and felicity,
> From rage of fortune and the fear to die.
> *Silenus* And may they well. For this indeed is he,
> My boys, whom you must quake at when you see.
> He is above your reach, and neither doth
> Nor can he think within a satyr's tooth.
> Before his presence you must fall or fly.
> He is the matter of virtue, and placed high.
> His meditations to his height are even,
> And all their issue is akin to heaven.
> He is a god o'er kings, yet stoops he then
> Nearest a man when he doth govern men,

To teach them by the sweetness of his sway,
And not by force. He's such a king as they
Who're tyrant's subjects, or ne'er tasted peace,
Would, in their wishes, form for their release.
'Tis he that stays the time from turning old,
And keeps the age up in a head of gold;
That in his own true circle still doth run,
And holds his course as certain as the sun.
He makes it ever day and ever spring
Where he doth shine, and quickens everything
Like a new nature; so that true to call
Him by his title is to say, he's all . . .

The SONG, *by two fays.*

1st Fay	Seek you majesty, to strike?
	Bid the world produce his like.
2nd Fay	Seek you glory, to amaze?
	Here let all eyes stand at gaze.
Both	Seek you wisdom, to inspire?
	Touch then at no other's fire.
1st Fay	Seek you knowledge, to direct?
	Trust to his without suspect.
2nd Fay	Seek you piety, to lead?
	In his footsteps only tread.
Chorus	Every virtue of a king,
	And of all in him we sing.'[6]

Power, both temporal and occult; sustaining strength; likeness to the sun as a source of light and fertility; wholeness: these are all the attributes of kingship, and all masculine in their associations. The king is 'immortall, perfect, masculine', woman 'imperfect, mortall, foeminine'.[7] Jonson's king is active, he strikes, amazes, inspires, directs and leads; a woman is traditionally passive, retiring, a follower – her virtues are Womanhood, Shamefastnesse, Cherefulnesse, Modestie, Curtesie, Silence and Obedience.[8] These virtues are not compatible with kingship. The woman is traditionally powerless, weak, unstable as the moon, incomplete except when joined to a man, created after man, and responsible for his fall. The female king must be a self-contradiction.

When, either because she was not content to hand the government over to a consort, or because she captured the imagination of her people, the queen was indeed regnant, some system of imagery had to be devised which would reconcile her sex with her status. This was not usually accomplished by changing the sex of the ruler (although Queen Christina of Sweden, in her dislike for her own sex, and her late adoption of male dress, seems to have attempted it). The most common pattern for the formulation of such imagery seems to be to take some sphere in which the domination of women is acceptable, and to present the ruler's public role in terms of that sphere. Thus Catherine the Great of Russia presented herself as a blue-stocking, a philosopher, a patron of and worthy companion to men of intellect and fine feeling, transforming the Russian Court and Empire into her *salon*. Victoria became the Mother of her people and her Empire, the world a cosy parlour in which as 'Angel in the House' she could reign supreme. Elizabeth II is presented, in terms more appropriate to the 1930s than to the 1970s, as the Squire's Lady of the Global Village, opening Parliaments as though they were bazaars, and presiding over Commonwealth countries as though they were Committees.

That it should even today be necessary to devise a formula to make a female monarch acceptable indicates how deep the fear of such a figure is. She is 'dangerous' in Mary Douglas's sense of the word, combining two apparently irreconcilable categories, femaleness and rulership, and as Douglas points out, such cross-categoric figures are always subject to taboos and restrictions, in an effort to place them within a protective bound, and are often given a specific imagery in order to make them comprehensible to those with whom they deal, and to themselves.[9] This sense of power, danger and mystery attached to the female monarch may explain why Elizabeth I and Victoria have captured the public imagination as male sovereigns have not, and it certainly goes far to explain the precise nature of the cult which surrounded Elizabeth.

3. Early celebrations of Elizabeth

During the early years of her reign there were, of course, celebrations of Elizabeth, and an imagery attached to her. Her coronation procession[10] was unchanged in manner and general content from previous royal entries, consisting of allusions to the queen's illustrious ancestors, and demonstrations of the nature of the political regime expected of Elizabeth: the 'Seat of Worthy Governance' in the 'nether end of Cornhill' represented Elizabeth supported by Pure Religion trampling on Superstition and Ignorance; Love of Subjects trampling on Rebellion and Insolence; Wisdom trampling on Folly and Vainglory, and Justice trampling on Adulation and Bribery – the virtues those of the sovereign, the vices those of the people, which the sovereign's virtues would repress. When Charles V visited London in 1522 he had been greeted by his noble ancestor Charlemagne, and a dumb-show on the theme 'Blessed are the peace-makers',[11] and the reception of Philip of Spain on his marriage to Mary Tudor in 1554 had included four famous Philips (of Macedon, of Rome, and two of Burgundy), and a dumb-show of Orpheus (Philip) taming the wild beasts (the English, generally hostile to the marriage) by his music (eloquence and tact).[12] But the manner of Elizabeth's viewing of the shows put on for her, and of one show in particular – a pageant obviously intended to refer specifically to her – was markedly different from reports of previous royal behaviour.

The crucial show was at the Little Conduit, and represented two hills, one 'a decayed Commonweal', the other 'a flourishing Commonweal'. From the valley between them emerged Time, leading his daughter Truth, who offered the Queen an English Bible. From the first Elizabeth had been anxious to listen to the speeches that accompanied the pageants, and careful to show gratitude for, and promise to heed, their advice. As she first saw the pageant at the Little Conduit, she immediately asked its meaning, and was told that 'there was placed Tyme. "Tyme?" quoth she, "and Tyme hath brought me hether"', thus explicitly identifying herself with the Truth that Time was to bring forth. When Truth offered her the English Bible she not only took it, but kissed it and clasped it to her bosom, so that those beyond earshot might witness her enthusiastic acceptance.

In doing so she was making a political statement. The acceptance of the English Bible represented an acceptance of Protestantism: an assurance to her subjects that her regime would reverse the changes of her sister's reign, and stop its persecutions; that she responded to London's invitation to be the Truth of Religion whom Time had brought forth, and transform the decayed Commonweal into a flourishing one.

Specific political allusion was not new in such pageants, as an unpleasant incident connected with Philip II's entry in 1554 shows. The pageant at Gracechurch Street included a representation of Henry VIII handing a book labelled 'Verbum Dei' to Edward VI.

> . . . hereupon was no small matter made: for the bishop of Winchester . . . sent for the painter, and not only called him a knave, for painting a book in King Henry's hand, and specially for writing thereupon 'Verbum Dei', but also rank traitor and villain, saying to him that he should rather have put the book into the queen's hand (who was also painted there), for that she had reformed the church and religion . . .

according to the pure and sincere word of God indeed . . . That it was the Queen's majesty's will and commandment, that he should send for him: and so, commanding him to wipe out the book and 'Verbum Dei' too, he sent him home.[13]

What does seem to have been new was Elizabeth's seizing upon the political allusion as an occasion for an important political action, her recognition of the importance of the public entertainment for the purpose of popular propaganda, and her adeptness at theatrical extemporization to serve that purpose – although the extemporization may have been only apparent, since Elizabeth's early query as to the nature of the pageant suggests that she knew quite well what it was. There is also evidence here of her recognition of the need for an imagery to present herself to the people in her eagerness fully to identify with the matter of the pageant: it is not just that Time, bringing in Elizabeth, allows Truth to come forth, which would have been a possible reading of the pageant, but Elizabeth eagerly identifies herself as Truth. All these factors were to be important in the development of her cult.

Another pageant in the coronation show represented Deborah the judge, and restorer, of Israel: and it is this lady, together with Judith and Esther, who is perhaps most typical of the imagery surrounding the queen during the early years of her reign.[14] Their last appearance seems to have been at Norwich in 1578, in a rather old-fashioned if spectacular entertainment, much hampered by rain.[15] The associations of these figures are essentially religious – all were protectors of the children of Israel in times of desperation: Deborah when they were menaced by the Canaanites, Judith when they were beseiged by the Philistines, and Esther during the Babylonian captivity.[16] All were responsible for preserving the people, and thereby ensuring the continuance of true religion. None of them is a virgin, and only Deborah can truly be described as a ruler – she was a prophetess who judged Israel – Judith emerged from her widowed seclusion to kill Holofernes, and returned to it, and Esther was queen only as Ahasuerus's wife. The appropriate image for Elizabeth during the early years of her reign was felt to be a married woman who preserved her people and their religion.

4. Pageantry as counsel

The precise significance of court pageantry is complex. At the most obvious level, it is a compliment to the monarch for whom it is presented, but the events of Elizabeth's coronation procession already suggest that compliment is not its only function, and that Elizabeth in her attention to, and exploitation of, the occasion, was recognising further dimensions. In coronation processions, and processions to welcome newcome foreigners, in particular, what is being presented is not an image of the monarch's rule or foreigner's visit as it is (it has as yet no character) but as the presenters would like it to be. The difference between retrospective panegyric and respectful persuasion is clear if one compares a late celebration of Elizabeth, such as Cranmer's prophecy at the end of Shakespeare's *Henry VIII* (written a decade after her death), with her coronation procession. Shakespeare (or Fletcher) shows what, after her reign (particularly in the nostalgia generated by the rule of James I[17]) seemed an appropriate early public view of her (it is set in the context of the christening procession):

This royal infant – heaven still move about her! –
Though in her cradle, yet now promises
Upon this land a thousand thousand blessings,
Which time shall bring to ripeness: she shall be –
But few now living can behold that goodness –
A pattern to all princes living with her,
And all that shall succeed: Saba was never
More covetous of wisdom and fair virtue
Than this pure soul shall be: all princely graces,
That mould up such a mighty piece as this is,
With all the virtues that attend the good,
Shall still be doubled on her: truth shall nurse her:
Holy and heavenly thoughts still counsel her:
She shall be lov'd and fear'd: her own shall bless her;
Her foes shake like a field of beaten corn,
And hang their heads with sorrow: good grows with her:
In her days every man shall eat in safety,
Under his own vine, what he plants; and sing
The merry songs of peace to all his neighbours:
God shall be truly known; and those about her
From her shall read the perfect ways of honour,
And by those claim their greatness, not by blood . . . (V.iv.17–38).

The coronation pageants deal in no such certainties. Only if Elizabeth relies on Pure Religion, Love of Subjects, Wisdom and Justice, will she succeed in suppressing their opposing vices in her people, which are dangers to her rule. Deborah the judge and restorer of Israel is there not as an image of the queen's rule, but as an example for her to follow, or rather, as an image of the queen's rule as it is hoped it will be. Truth the daughter of Time is not, until the Queen herself makes the identification, Elizabeth, but the Protestant religion, represented by the English Bible, which alone can transform England from a decayed to a flourishing Commonweal.

5. *The message of pageantry*

The audience of a pageant, and of the later Elizabethan entertainments and Jacobean masques, might be described as threefold: the prince whom it honours, the public who view it, and the participants themselves. To each, the image presented is different. The prince is shown himself not only as he is (as a compliment) but as he should be – as, indeed, he ideally is. Thus in the passage from Ben Jonson's *Oberon* quoted above (pp. 3–4) what is presented is not a simple compliment to James (although it does compliment him) but an invocation of the true king who is the reality behind the shaky, slobbering figure on the throne, and also what comes very close to an exercise in sympathetic magic: a hope that the quasi-religious ambiance of the masque, with its ritual dancing and singing, may somehow, by invoking the image of the king-who-is, and who-should-be, in connection with James, invoke it in him, so that he becomes what he is presented as being. The masque itself serves as a vindication of the reality of the ideal vision: the gods and goddesses, mythical queens and fairy kings who by magic visit the court absorb the spectator prince into their number, and into the vision of the masque. Seated at the perfect point for viewing the masque, he is its cynosure, both perfect witness and perfect participant, the completion of the physical arrangement of the theatre, the completion of the action of the masque.

For the public that views the pageant or masque, the position is somewhat simpler. What they are being shown is an image of their country, as embodied in its elite. In that sense the masques and pageants are exercises in public relations, on the lines of the Moscow May-Day parades, or, perhaps more precisely, of Leni Reifenstahl's film about Hitler's Nürnburg rally, *The Triumph of the Will* (1934). Reifenstahl's Nürnburg is as artificial a creation as the Albion of Jones and Jonson, the decorated London of Elizabeth's coronation. It is a reassuring spectacle of the greatest in the land, richly dressed, and enjoying themselves. The thrill and element of self-congratulation aroused by the spectacle must be the same as that evoked in the British crowd at the sight of the Queen attending Ascot, or the American on the night of the presentation of the

Academy Awards. Some of the implications of these public-relations exercises are still the same. The sight of a lavishly-dressed and apparently leisured upper-class informs the people (and visiting foreigners) of the wealth of the land that can support so rich an elite; the speeches that they hear tell them what they want to know: that Hollywood film stars are ordinary, nice, modest people who give time and money to charity and weep when thanked; that Charles I, despite all appearances to the contrary, loves his people (*Salmacida Spolia*, 1640). But for the attentive observer the masque is more complex. Society can only be maintained against the threats of the anti-masque by a harmonization as conscious, hard-sought, and artificially-created as the spectacle which proceeds before him. In this, the dance with which the masque concludes is crucial. For not only the court spectators who are invited to dance by the masquers are absorbed into it, but, by implication, by their presence, the other spectators also; and not only them, but all those whom they represent: the entire population of the realm. They are witnesses of a mythological event, and, just as the presence of supernatural beings validates the ideal vision presented of the ruler, so the presence of the spectators provides further assurance of its reality: they are witnesses of the supernatural events both in the sense of validating spectators and proselytizing converts.

They may also be being assured that the good that they wish from the ruler is being expressed to him. This is particularly true of events like the coronation procession, with its pleas, hopes, and advice. And it is clear that Elizabeth recognized this – her bravura gestures, her grateful thanks, show as much. That the masques, pageants and entertainments were recognized as propaganda is indicated by the speed with which they were described in print,[18] so that not only the immediate spectators, but the country as a whole, might learn of the miracle of sumptuousness, harmony, and meaning which had been performed at Court, in London, or in a house in the South of England,[19] where they could not view it. The wider audiences who bought these accounts might read them and know that all was well with a country whose court was so evidently rich, leisured and harmonious.

It is sometimes difficult to believe that all the participants felt a similar level of idealism. At times, the steps of the Masque dancers might seem to be not so much expressions of Platonic harmony, as means of climbing the ladder of promotion. While the oft-repeated tale of Christopher Hatton's gaining the Queen's favour because of his excellent dancing and appealing legs seems to be a slander on one who proved selflessly loyal to the private, and a competent servant to the public, Elizabeth, it is nevertheless true that both Elizabeth and James (especially the latter) were susceptible to attractive young men, and appearance in a masque or tilt, with the fetching costumes these exercises entailed, was a good way of catching the royal eye and the dubious pecuniary and social advantages which went with it. When Robert Carey wished to regain Elizabeth's favour in 1593 after a marriage which she opposed, he did so by appearing in a tilt:

My father wrote me from Windsor that the Queen meant to have a great triumph there, on her coronation day, and that there was great preparation making for the course of the field and tourney. He gave me notice of the Queen's anger for my marriage, and said it may be, I being so near, and to return without honouring her day, as I ever before had done,[20] might be a cause of her further dislike, but left it to myself to do what I thought best. . . . I came to court, and lodged there very privately, only I made myself known to my father and some few friends besides. I here took order and sent to London to provide me things necessary for the triumph: I prepared a present for her Majesty, which with my caparisons cost me above four hundred pounds. I came into the triumph unknown of any.[21] I was the forsaken knight that had vowed solitariness, but hearing of this great triumph thought to honour my mistress with my best service, and then to return to pay my wonted mourning. The triumph ended, and all things well passed over to the Queen's liking. I then made myself known in court, and for the time I stayed there was daily conversant with my old companions and friends.[22]

The motives of some masque-participants were doubtless cynically solipsistic. Bacon, who wrote masques and speeches for Essex to use at the Elizabethan Accession Day Tilts, takes a wry view of them:

'These things are but toys, to come amongst such serious observations. But yet, since princes will have such things, it is better they should be graced with elegancy, than daubed with cost.'[23]

But such world-weariness is not to be assumed on the part of all the participants. Others, like Anne of Denmark, simply loved dressing-up and parties. The intelligent participant was aware however of the full resonances of the occasion; that they were engaged in a ritual in which they presented themselves to and for themselves, as they really were: the essential difference between masque and theatre is that the masque is truly occasional, has, in a sense, no meaning apart from its single performance, and that no actors are involved. *Hamlet* does not change its status as drama with a change in the principal player: it means as much, or as little, whether Garrick or Gielgud plays the prince. But the masque takes its meaning from the identities of its participants: in *Oberon* it is not that Oberon and his legendary knights represent Prince Henry and the British courtiers, but that they *are* Prince Henry and the British courtiers, and (perhaps more importantly) that Prince Henry and the British courtiers are Oberon and his knights. In *Oberon* all the promise of, and hopes centered in, the young prince are affirmed in his absorption into the heroic legendary history of Britain and of Europe (for Oberon is the protector of Huon of Bordeaux in the Charlemagne romances). And *Oberon* has a yet more immediate political meaning. The growing discontent with James's rule had led to the fixing of the hopes of court and country upon the young prince, who, it was confidently expected, would usher in a new golden age such as they seemed, in retrospect, to have enjoyed under Elizabeth. Henry himself seems to have been conscious of these hopes, allying himself with those survivors, such as Sir Walter Ralegh, who seemed to epitomize that age. The mere name 'Oberon' links him with the Fairy Queen cult of Elizabeth – Oberon was king of the Fairies – and the unnamed knights who accompany him to do homage to James, and to state his claim to be the next inheritor of Arthur's seat, may be the Arthurian knights, and Huon of Bordeaux, who are the traditional inhabitants of Fairyland, or they may be the more recently-dead knights of Elizabeth's glorious court, at present abiding with her in 'Elizium', but ready to return when her true successor, in spirit, as well as in lineage, shall ascend the throne:[24]

> 'Look! does not his palace show
> Like another sky of lights?
> Yonder with him live the knights
> Once the noblest of the earth,
> Quickened by a second birth,
> Who for prowess and for truth
> There are crowned with lasting youth,
> And do hold, by Fate's command,
> Seats of bliss in Fairyland.'[25]

Oberon represents the public acceptance by James of his heir, but it was Prince Henry's masque (New Year 1611), and in it Henry makes statements about the sort of regime he intends to institute – a return to the Elizabethan Golden Age. There is despite all the praise for James quoted above (pp. 3–4) a certain ambiguity in the wording of the masque; the stress is on the homage due to the throne of

Arthur and its inheritors, including the present incumbent, rather than to James himself identified with Arthur,[26] and the ambiguity becomes more marked in the dance:

> Stand forth bright fays and elves, and tune your lays
> Unto his name; then let your nimble feet
> Tread subtle circles that may always meet
> In point to him, and figures to express
> The grace of him and his great empress;
> That all tonight that shall behold these rites
> Performed by princely Oberon and these knights,
> May without stop point out the proper heir
> Designed so long to Arthur's crown and chair.[27]

This speech is followed by the song 'Seek you majesty' quoted above (p. 4). The focus for the dances should be James, but 'Arthur's proper heir' must be Henry, and the song might as well be an eulogy of him as of James, an eulogy of the king Henry will be. Within two years Henry was dead.

In their pageants, jousts and masques, the courts of Elizabeth and the Stuarts formulated their imagery for dealing with themselves and with their situation in relation to the ruler and to the country. From Elizabeth's coronation procession to the pathetic masque *Salmacida Spolia*, in which Charles I and his court vainly danced in an attempt to preserve national harmony and hold back the coming darkness of civil war,[28] it is a complex exercise in propaganda and pious hopes, platonism and pleasure.

6. Elizabeth's consciousness of her cult.

Although Jones and Jonson were fully aware of all these aspects of the masque and pageantry,[29] it seems doubtful that James or Anne of Denmark ever fully grasped them. Elizabeth however, showed from the start that she was conscious of the implications of court spectacles, and prepared, anxious even, to participate. Where James merely sat, Elizabeth answered back, entering into the mythological games played, and showing her consciousness of her multiple mythological and real *personae* and relationship to the action being presented to her. She was a full participant, as James never was. From her acceptance of the role of Truth at her coronation, to the last years of her reign, she never ceased to participate in, comment on, and assess these entertainments. In 1600 she took part in the celebrations for the marriage of Henry Somerset to Anne Russell.

The masque afterward represented eight muses in search of the
ninth (Elizabeth) to dance with them to the music of Apollo. Mary
Fitton begged the Queen to participate, and Elizabeth asking what
she represented, was told 'Affection'. '"Affection", said the Queen,
"is false"'.[30] It was a sour comment – on the marriage of one of her
Maids of Honour, to which as the reign progressed she became
more and more violently opposed,[31] on the treachery of the Earl of
Essex, in disgrace and confinement over his unauthorized return
from Ireland, perhaps even on Mary Fitton herself, to be dismissed
from the court the following year after the disclosure of her affair
with the Earl of Pembroke. But Elizabeth joined the dance.

It was not only on public occasions that Elizabeth participated in
the acted mythology of her court. Once again, Carey's autobiography
is revealing. His first interview with her after his marriage was
decidedly unpleasant:

> Our first encounter was stormy and terrible, which I passed over with
> silence. After she had spoken her pleasure of me and my wife, I told
> her, that she herself was the fault of my marriage, and that if she had
> but graced me with the least of her favours, I had never left her nor her
> court; and seeing that she was the chief cause of my misfortune, I
> would never off my knees till I had kissed her hand, and obtained my
> pardon. She was not displeased with my excuse, and before we parted
> we grew good friends.[32]

Robert Carey was one of Elizabeth's closest relatives, twenty-seven
years her junior, the youngest son of Henry Carey, Lord Hunsdon,
younger child of Mary Boleyn, and Elizabeth's cousin – perhaps her
half-brother, since Mary Boleyn had been Henry VIII's mistress
after her marriage to William Carey: Robert was thus possibly
Elizabeth's nephew.[33] The Careys were close to Elizabeth
throughout her reign, Hunsdon being made a baron at the time of
her coronation, a member of the Council in 1561, and Lord
Chamberlain in 1583, a post he held until his death in 1596. One of
Robert's sisters, Lady Scrope, attended Elizabeth on her deathbed,
and it was she who interpreted the signs made by the Queen after
she had lost the faculty of speech.[34] Robert had been brought up in
and around the court, and knew the Queen from his earliest
childhood. In view of all this, the exchange between him and the
Queen, in which he virtually claims that he had married on the
rebound from Elizabeth, seems *outré*, if not distasteful. But it is not
simple flattery; Elizabeth was no fool, and Carey's last encounter
with her had been to tell her through his father that he did not trust
her, which she obviously found amusing:[35] she was unlikely to value

flattery in one so blunt. What this exchange represents is rather a restoration of the right order which has been broken by Robert's unwary marriage.[36] Carey shows that he knows the relationship which a courtier should have with his Queen, but boldly puts the blame on her, in an ambiguous answer in which the terms of the love-game played out between Elizabeth and her courtiers are made to cover the fact that Carey has obtained neither preferment nor employment at Court. The ostensible disappointment is that of the rejected suitor who, receiving no sign of encouragement, has gone elsewhere in despair, but the answer is in fact that the Queen has given him no help in his career, and has therefore little justification for criticizing his marriage. The charade of the knight/mistress relationship permits Carey to speak to his Queen with a frankness inadmissable if it were not expressed in terms of courtly metaphor, and the Queen is 'not displeased' with this reply.

7. Classicism & medievalism in the cult of Elizabeth

The most fully-explored aspects of the cults of Elizabeth have been the classical ones elucidated by Yates and Strong – the Queen as Astraea, as the Vestal Virgin, and as mistress of a restored Constantinian empire.[37] Yates has shown how the identification of Elizabeth as Astraea, the fruitful virgin who presided over the Golden Age, and will return to restore that age, and who was identified, in an interpretation of Virgil's *Fourth Eclogue*, with the Virgin Mary, was exploited throughout the later years of her reign, and how references to this cult abound in the portraits and in the properties used in the tilts and entertainments. Less attention has perhaps been paid to the romance material with which this classical imagery is associated.

The cult of Elizabeth as Astraea and as the imperial Virgin is essentially classical in its inspiration, as are references to her as a Vestal Virgin. Granted this, one would expect the cults surrounding her to be classical in their imagery and practices: that the medium chosen for her celebration would be the Imperial Triumph, perhaps as it is used in *Albion's Triumph* for Charles I, and as Strong suggests may have been intended in the famous picture of *Queen Elizabeth Carried in Procession*.[38] That such a neo-classical imagery and frame of reference was available is shown, not only in later material such as Jonson's *Masque of Queens*, which provides abundant references on which a cult of Elizabeth might have been based, but in Campion's lyrics celebrating the late Elizabethan court:

What fair pomp have I spied of glittering ladies,
With locks sparkled abroad, and rosy coronet
On their ivory brows, tracked to the dainty thighs
With robes like Amazons, blue as a violet,
With gold aglets adorned, some in a changeable
Pale, with spangs waving taught to be moveable?

Then those knights, that afar off with dolorous viewing
Cast their eyes hitherward, lo! in an agony,
All unbraced, cry aloud, their heavy state rueing:
Moist cheeks with blubbering, painted as ebony
Black; their feltered hair torn with wrathful hand;
And while astonied stark in a maze they stand. . . .
But stay! now I discern they go on a pilgrimage
Towards Love's holy land, fair Paphos or Cyprus.
Such devotion is meet for a blithesome age;
With sweet youth it agrees well to be amorous.
Let old angry fathers lurk in an hermitage;
Come! we'll associate this jolly pilgrimage.[39]

Even here, however, the classicism lacks the purity of Poussin or
Claude Lorrain, as it does in Campion's more famous lyric:

When thou must home to shades of underground,
And there arrived, a new admired guest,
The beauteous spirits that engirt thee round,
White Iope, blithe Helen and the rest,
To hear the stories of thy finished love
From that smooth tongue whose music hell can move:

Then wilt thou speak of banqueting delights,
Of masques and revels which sweet youth did make,
Of tourneys and great challenges of knights,
And all these triumphs for thy beauty's sake.
When thou hast told the honours done to thee,
Then tell, O! tell how thou didst murder me.[40]

The trappings and references are classical, but the actions
performed, the imagery, are from the romances. The despair and
self-destructiveness of the knights, the idea of love's pilgrimage, the
hermit as the man retired from love, are all medieval conventions,
contrasting with the classical figures of the ladies, the Cytherean
object of the pilgrimage. In 'When thou must home' the lady is
envisaged going to a classical afterlife, to Hades rather than to Hell
(there is a suggestion in the word 'home' that the lady may be a Fay
– Proserpina is the 'fairy queen' in another of Campion's lyrics,
following the tradition of *Sir Orfeo* and Chaucer's *Merchant's Tale*).

The companions she will have there will be classical beauties, but the life of which she can tell is an idealized medieval one – masques, revels and tournaments at which she presided, and which were held for her sake. The poem could be written about Elizabeth herself: certainly it encapsulates the atmosphere of the celebrations of her at her court, and the attitudes her courtiers assumed while they were thus celebrating her.

This mingling of classicism and medievalism is typical of the court poetry of the Elizabethans. The frame of reference is classical, but the conventions applied to it medieval: the ethos expressed in the poems is chivalric. The terms of chivalry – 'knight', 'lady', 'curteous' – are constantly recurring. Sir Arthur Gorges, a member of the Sidney circle, frequently uses chivalric imagery, and has what seems a typically medieval attitude to the classical gods and heroes with which his poetry deals, treating them as figures out of a romance. Paris is the 'Troyan knight', and Gorges's two poems about Dido are expressed throughout in the vocabulary of the romances:

> O Venus graunte of grace
> to ayde her case
> That in thy son hath right;
> And thow proud Archer learne
> thy brother stearne,
> To lyve a loyall knyght.[41]

In *Orchestra*, Sir John Davies describes Antinous's lovemaking in terms of a romance wooing:

> The Courtly love *Antinous* did make,
> *Antinous*, that fresh and jolly knight,
> Which of the gallants that did undertake
> To win the Widdow, had most wealth and might,
> Wit to perswade, and beautie to delight:
> The Courtly love he made unto the Queene,
> *Homer* forgot, as if it had not beene.[42]

Antinous here is a medieval figure, with all the qualities that recommend a medieval knight. He is rich and strong, beautiful and intelligent; a hero from Marie de France:

> Li autres du un bachelers
> Bien coneü entre ses pers
> De prüesce, de grant valur,
> E volenters feseit honur:
> Mut turnëot e despendeit
> E bien donot ceo qu'il aveit.[43]

Philip Sidney, who was adopted by the Elizabethan chivalric cult as its posthumous patron, and out of whose circle much of this neo-chivalric writing came, makes particularly striking use of its conventions in *Astrophil and Stella*, which can be read as as clear an exercise in Chaucerianism as Spenser's *Shepheardes Calender. Astrophil and Stella* is courtly and chivalric both in the story it relates and in its habitual modes of expression. The situation (interestingly close to that chosen by Walerian Borowczyk for his 1971 exercise in neo-medievalism, *Blanche*[44]) is that of the young man in love with a lady married to an unworthy husband. In the sonnet in which he puns upon Stella's married name, Sidney makes Astrophil accuse the husband of being both a fool and a miser (xxiv): the archetypal terms of abuse for the *jaloux*. The attitude of the lover to his lady is presented as that of an inferior to a superior. Stella may not be Astrophil's superior in rank, but she is superior in that she is the Lady, and he, by virtue of his love for her, the servant. This is frequently emphasized in the way that Sidney makes Astrophil refer to her. She is his 'dear captainess' (lxxxviii); 'Phenix Stella' (xcii); his 'Sun' (xcviii); 'princess' (cvii). He asks for her attention as if it were an immeasurable boon:

> Alas, if from the height of Virtue's throne,
> Thou canst vouchsafe the influence of a thought
> Upon a wretch, that long thy grace hast sought,
> Weigh then how I by thee am overthrown. (xi)

He describes his love for Stella in terms which make it clear that he regards her as far beyond his reach:

> The reins wherewith my rider doth me tie,
> Are humbled thoughts, which but of reverence move,
> Cur'b in with fear, but with gilt boss above
> Of hope, which makes it seem fair to the eye. (xlix)

The abject humility of the lover, the assumption of trembling fear in his approach to the lady, are reminiscent of the humble romance-lover of the middle ages.

The degree of Sidney's absorption in the romance-tradition is emphasized in a contrast between his ideal of beauty as exemplified in Stella and the anti-romantic ideas of non-courtly writers such as Shakespeare. Stella is a conventional medieval heroine, and described in conventional terms. In one of his more baroque sonnets (ix) Sidney attributes to her the gold, white and red beauty of the ideal romance heroine, an ideal of beauty which the Queen was held to epitomize.[45]

Shakespeare is fully conscious of the traditional romance-beauty, as is shown in sonnet cxxx, where he mocks both himself for loving a woman who is not, by accepted standards, beautiful, and those writers who etherialize a human being into a goddess. This ideal of beauty, although it is identical with that of the romances, may of course merely reflect a prevailing fashion for blondes, but it does seem to be a direct continuation of the medieval ideal as it was reflected in the romances and lyrics, and Puttenham, for instance, is consciously archaising in his presentation of the Queen's beauty, as phrases such as 'so white as whales bone' show.

Sidney's imagery and modes of thought in *Astrophil and Stella* are consistently chivalric. Even when he uses classical allusions, he uses them in a medieval way. In sonnet xiii the pagan gods are presented as medieval knights:

> Phoebus was judge between Jove, Mars, and Love,
> Of these three gods, whose arms the fairest were:
> Jove's golden shield did eagle sables bear,
> Whose talons held young Ganymede above:
> But in vert field Mars bare a golden spear,
> Which through a bleeding heart his point did shove:
> Each had his crest – Mars carried Venus' glove,
> Jove in his helm his thunderbolt did rear.
> Cupid then smiles, for on his crest there lies
> Stella's fair hair, her face he makes his shield,
> Where roses gules are borne in silver field.
> Phoebus drew wide the curtains of the skies
> To blaze these last, and sware devoutly then,
> The first, thus match'd, were scantly gentlemen.

Mars carrying Venus' glove is in accord with the chivalric practices of Elizabeth's court, even if hardly so with classical mythology. The well-known miniature of George Clifford, Earl of Cumberland, as Queen's Champion, shows him wearing her glove in his hat, and one of Essex shows him wearing her glove on his arm[46] (gloves of course remained a relatively cheap personal keepsake until the beginning of this century).

The vocabulary in which Sidney describes Astrophil's love and Stella's attitude to it is that of *amor cortois*. Astrophil sorrows, complains, and begs Stella to show pity, grace or mercy:

> And yet she hears, yet I no pity find;
> But more I cry, less grace she doth impart. (xliv)

He plays on the chivalric and aesthetic meanings of the word 'grace':

> Muses, I oft invoked your holy aid,
> With choicest flowers my speech to engarland so
> That it, despised in true but naked show,
> Might win some grace in your sweet grace array'd. (lv)

This is the vocabulary of the Chaucerian lover. The Squire is inspired by his

> hope to stonden in his lady grace (GP88);

Aurelius, rejected by Dorigen, asks her,

> Is ther none other grace in yow? (FT999)

and when Criseyde visits the sick Troilus

> Lo, the alderfirste word that him asterte
> Was, twyes, 'Mercy, mercy, swete herte! (III.97–8).

Sidney shares the 'partial, prejudiced and ignorant' historian's[47] admiration for the king who 'showed his undaunted behaviour by marrying one lady when he was engaged to another':

> Of all the kings that ever here did reign,
> Edward named Fourth, as first in praise I name;
> Not for his fair outside, nor well-lined brain,
> Although less gifts imp feathers oft on Fame . . . .
> Nor this, nor that, nor any such small cause,
> But only for this worthy knight durst prove
> To lose his crown, rather than fail his love. (lxxv)

This is ideal knightly behaviour. How far Sidney was from admiring in fact those who were prepared to abandon their political responsibilities in the cause of love is shown by his reaction to Elizabeth's proposed marriage to Alençon.[48]

This neo-medievalism, particularly the blending of classical subjects with medieval treatments, might seem to be merely a continuation of the traditions made so familiar by Seznec. An examination of a mid-century anthology such as Tottel's *Miscellany* (1557) argues against this. The spareness of the imagery, the privateness of most of the work, the celebration of quiet and intimate moments, while not best characterized by C. S. Lewis's 'drab', is nevertheless a strong contrast to the bravura of Sidney and his contemporaries. The classical references are absent, as is the lavish and rather stereotyped emotionalism. There is a cynicism, a toughness, in the attitude to love which is absent in Elizabethan court poetry. The Elizabethan poets were rejecting the works of their immediate predecessors in favour of a return to their own interpretation of medieval poetic conventions.

Nor was the neo-medievalism confined to poetry. Strong has pointed out the existence of a first Gothic Revival in architecture, as the fortified dwelling which had become a country house became a fairy-tale castle:[49] the castle's watch-towers became fantasticated banqueting houses at Longleat, or, as at Hardwick, the towering walls of the four-square keep remain, but are executed in glass. In dress, too, he remarks the spiky gothic lines of late Elizabethan costume,[50] as though the conventions of medieval church building were applied to the architectural construction of clothes. And he sees the Elizabethan triumph in the art of miniature as related to the earlier importance of manuscript-illumination.[51]

8. Elizabeth as a supernatural being

The Elizabethan court, centered on a woman who, because of her sex, was inferior to all her ministers and servants, had to find some means of compensating for this inferiority and devise a means of presentation of the queen which would equate her iconographic position with her actual position as head of both Church and State. The most obvious way of doing this was to translate her into a goddess, as in the *Rainbow Portrait,* or the allegorical picture by the monogrammatist HE of *Queen Elizabeth taking the Golden Apple from Juno, Venus and Minerva,* or into some other supernatural being. The most astounding of these *personae* was the Virgin Mary, for whom the English had always felt a special devotion, whose cult had often found chivalric expression,[52] and whose removal, together with Roman Catholicism, from the English religious scene, left a gap which, as a virgin-queen, Elizabeth was ideally qualified to fill. The strain of Mariolatry in Elizabeth's cult is welded by Ralegh with the courtly neo-medievalism in his version of *Walsingham*:

As you came from the holy land
Of Walsinghame
Met you not with my true love
By the way as you came? . . .

Such an one did I meet, good Sir,
Suche an Angelyke face,
Who lyke a queene, lyke a nymph, did appere
By her gate, by her grace.[53]

Here a traditional ballad is adapted so that Elizabeth (the
queen/nymph dichotomy is familiar in celebrations of her, notably
in Spenser's Gloriana and Belphoebe) is associated with the most
famous of the English Marian shrines: that she is met on her way to
it may suggest that she is going to take it over.

The transformation of Elizabeth which underlay all the others,
which contributed to the neo-medievalism of the court culture, and
which provided a basis for a rationalization of her relationship to her
courtiers was to the Lady of a romance, and especially to a
Fairy-Lady. The *mores* of *amor cortois* demanded that, until marriage
at least, the Lady should be, whatever their relative social status, the
superior of the lover, and there was very little danger, after the early
years of her reign, of Elizabeth accepting one of the many knights
who offered her their devotion, and thus reducing her status, as her
sister had reduced hers by her marriage to Philip of Spain. The
celebrations of Elizabeth as Goddess, as Fay, as Virgin, and as
Lady, do not begin to occur with any frequency until the mid-1570s,
when the regime was firmly established, having weathered both the
Northern Rebellion and the Ridolfi Plot, and having been confirmed
by the wave of popular feeling for Elizabeth that rose in response to
these rebellions. The *Princely Pleasures* at Kenilworth of 1575, which
signal the beginning of the cult of Elizabeth as a supernatural Being,
also represent Leicester's final throw in the marriage-game which he
had been playing for the first sixteen years of the reign. Elizabeth
was forty-two; since the cause for which her ministers and
parliament urged her, with ever-mounting desperation, to marry,
was to produce an heir and thus secure the succession, unless she
married soon there would no longer be any point in urging her to do
so, as she would be past the age of child-bearing. She could not be
felt to need a husband to remove the weighty reins of government
from her incompetent feminine hands. When the Kenilworth
entertainment failed to achieve its object, even Leicester realized
that he would never become Consort, and in 1578 he married Lettice
Knollys. The Alençon marriage negotiations provided a brief
resurgence of the hope that Elizabeth would marry, but she was
already thought to be too old, and Alençon was given the hint in the
show of *The Four Foster Children of Desire*[54] that his pretensions were
in vain.

To emphasize her unfading youth and beauty by making her into a supernatural or preternatural being was of course an obvious way of complimenting the aging Queen. The Fay was the most convenient of these characterizations, since it bore the closest relationship to the true situation at court. Fairy mistresses, though ever-young and never-changing, were not immortal, although they might live for a very long time. Fays were mistresses of companies of loyal knights, and lived in an ideal world like 'Elizium' – a land of dead, or seemingly dead, heroes. It was from 'Elizium' that Arthur had returned under the guise of Elizabeth. To many Elizabethans it did seem as though they were living in a new golden age. Peace was reasonably assured internally, and for the first time since the days of Henry V England was winning external military success. There was frequent reference throughout the reign to the Virgilian 'iam redit et Virgo', a phrase which in Eclogue IV heralded the return of the Golden Age, and was regarded in Christian times as a prophecy of the coming of Christ. Elizabeth thus became, in such references, the Virgin who begins the classical golden age, and the Virgin who bears Christ, and therefore brings true religion.

The idea behind pastoral is the return of the Golden World. The Banished Duke and his followers, living in a forest, close to the pastoral world of the shepherds

> live like the old Robin Hood of England . . . and fleet the time carelessly, as they did in the golden world (AYLI I.i.110–125).

The implication of the many pastoral presentations of Elizabeth is that the Golden World has returned with her. The month for the Eclogue celebrating the Queen in *The Shepheardes Calender* is not chosen arbitrarily; April is a spring month and the month of innocent love. Perdita, a goddess both of youth and of chaste love is

> Flora,
> Peering in April's front (WT.IV.iv.2–3).

The Golden Age is an age of pastoral innocence and perpetual spring, and so the choice of April for the eclogue identifies it with the Golden Age. The stanza which describes Elizabeth dressed in spring flowers shows her through its imagery as the Virgin Queen of an innocent pastoral age:

> See where she sits vpon the grassie greene,
> (O seemly sight)
> Yclad in Scarlot like a mayden Queene,

And in ermines white,
Vpon her head a Cremosin coronet,
With Damaske roses and Daffadillies set;
Bayleaues betweene,
And Primroses greene,
Embellish the sweete Violet. (SC, April, 55–63)

The flowers are all ones associated with virginity, as they are in
Perdita's speech in which the violet is compared favourably to the
goddesses of marriage and of unchaste love:

O Proserpina,
For the flowers now, that, frighted, thou lett'st fall
From Dis's waggon! – daffodils,
  That come before the swallow dares, and take
  The winds of March with beauty; violets dim,
But sweeter than the lids of Juno's eyes
Or Cytherea's breath; pale primroses,
That die unmarried ere they can behold
Bright Phoebus in his strength, – a malady
Most incident to maids; bold oxlips, and
The crown-imperial; lillies of all kinds,
The flower-de-luce being one! (WT.IV.iv.116–127)

Here the fact that Proserpina lets the flowers fall as Dis abducts her
shows that they are associated with the innocence of her life on
earth. Elizabeth's contemporaries might even go so far as to create
an artificial spring as the appropriate setting for her visit to them:

Here I will conclude with a conceit of that delicate Knight Sir Francis
Carew, who, for the better accomplishment of his Royal Entertainment
of our late Queen Elizabeth of happy memory at his house at
Bedlington, led her Majesty to a cherry-tree, whose fruit he had of
purpose kept back from ripening, at the least one month after all
cherries had taken their farewell of England. This secret he performed
by so raising a tent or cover of canvas over the whole tree, and wetting
the same now and then with a scoop, or horn, as the heat of the
weather required; and so by withholding the sun-beams from reflecting
upon the berries, they grew both great, and were very long before they
had gotten their perfect cherry colour; and when he was assured of her
Majesty's coming, he removed the tent, and a few sunny days brought
them to their full maturity.[55]

Sir Francis's exercise is of course mainly designed to provide
Elizabeth with an unusual gastronomic treat, and one which

displays his skill as an arboriculturalist, but the prolongation of Spring is also a delicate compliment to her – it has remained to provide the fitting season for her entertainment; wherever she goes, it is Spring.

9. *Elizabeth & Arthur*

To the Elizabethans it seemed that Arthur had come back in the form of Elizabeth, and that she had brought with her some of the atmosphere of that Golden World from which she had returned (Arthur was traditionally believed still to live on as a 'king . . . crownid in Fairie',[56] and the Queens who remove Arthur to Avalon in Malory include at least one Fairy Lady – Morgan le Fay, Arthur's half-sister). Since the time of Henry II, dubious claims to the English throne had been reinforced by an appeal to an Arthurian millenarianism, of which the Tudor cult, intensified as it was by their Welsh origins, is the best known.[57] The death of Arthur, Prince of Wales, eldest son to Henry VII, allied with the scepticism of some historians under Henry VIII, had brought about an abeyance of the cult, and it was not until the neo-medievalism of the latter half of Elizabeth's reign that it came to reflorescence. The fact that Arthur was visualized, probably due to the influence of Malory, as living in an idealized high-gothic setting (as he still is) encouraged the incorporation of the returned-Arthur element into Elizabethan pastoral and the identification of the golden age with the age of Arthur.[58]

Elizabeth's sex belied any direct identification with Arthur, but the Fays so often associated with the Arthurian legend provided a convenient image with the necessary resonances. Sometimes Fays are Ladies of the Lake (the Lady of the Lake appears in the Kenilworth entertainment as a Fay associated with Arthur), and a footnote to the April Eclogue of the *Shepheardes Calender* suggests that Elizabeth may well be being addressed as a Fay more often than is generally recognized. Referring to the lines,

> And whither rennes this beuie of Ladies bright, raunged in a row?
> They bene all Ladies of the Lake behight, that vnto her goe.

EK writes,

> Ladyes of the Lake be Nymphes. For it was an olde opinion amongste the Auncient Heathen, that of euery spring and fountaine was a goddess the Soueraigne. Which opinion stucke in the myndes of men

not manye years sithence, by meanes of certaine fine fablers and lowd
lyers, such as were the Authors of King Arthure the great and such
like, who tell many an vnlawfull leasing of the Ladyes of the Lake,
that is, the Nymphes. For the word Nymphe in Greek signifieth Well
water, or otherwise a Spouse or Bryde. (SC, notes to the April
Eclogue).

It seems at least possible on the basis of this statement in a book that
was extremely popular and influential in the period that when
Elizabeth is referred to as a 'Nymph', as in

Who like a queen, like a nymph did appear,

the image is of a Lady of the Lake, and not necessarily of a classical
Nymph – or that it is at least another example of the fusion of
classical and romance so typical of Elizabethan court writing.

10. *Elizabethan Tilts*

Identifying Elizabeth as they did with the Lady of Romance, it was
natural for her contemporaries to attempt to honour her in an
appropriate fashion. At court this was done in the numerous jousts
held in her honour, especially in the series of Accession Day Tilts.
These Tilts were

first begun and occasioned by the right vertuous and honourable Sir
Henry Lee, Master of her Highnesse Armorie, and now deservingly
Knight of the most Noble Order [of the Garter], who of his great zeale,
and earnest desire to eternize the glory of her Majestie's Court, in the
beginning of her happie reigne, voluntarily vowed, (unlesse infirmity,
age, or other accident, did impeach him) during his life, to present
himselfe, at the Tilt, armed, the day aforesayd yeerely, there to
performe, in honour of her most sacred Majestie, the promise he
formerly made.[59]

They continued throughout Elizabeth's reign, and the celebration of
the Queen's Accession became so fixed a habit that it continued well
into the reign of James I, along with the celebrations for James
himself.

Jousting was a popular sport in the sixteenth century both in
England and on the Continent, and is not in itself evidence of any
tendency to see events in terms of medieval romance on the part of
those who practised it. Although artillery had rendered both the

heavily-armed knight and the archer obsolete, the fact that the skills of knight and archer continued to be practised as sports is no more evidence of a tendency to archaize than is the continued sailing of yachts for sport in a period when powered shipping is used for all practical purposes. It is true that as a spectator sport jousting is only slightly superior to baseball and infinitely inferior to cricket, and that it had virtually ceased to be practised by the mid-seventeenth century. In England it was replaced under Charles II by horse-racing as the spectator, and sailing as the participatory, sports of the court. But Sidney's evocation of a joust – probably, since there are French spectators, *The Four Foster Children of Desire* – makes it clear that jousting had its aficionados:

> Having this day my horse, my hand, my launce
> Guided so well that I obtain'd the prize,
> Both by the judgement of the English eyes,
> And of some sent from that sweet enemie *Fraunce*;
> Horsemen my skill in horsemanship advaunce;
> Towne-folkes my strength; a daintier judge applies
> His praise to sleight, which from good use doth rise;
> Some luckie wits impute it but to chaunce;
> Others, because of both sides I do take
> My bloud from them, who did excell in this,
> Thinke Nature me a man of armes did make . . . (xli)

The real attraction of the jousts was not necessarily the sporting contest, but the pageantry which surrounded it: as though in American football matches the routines of the cheerleaders and general razzmatazz became more important than the game, and the main attraction for the spectators. But the jousts in honour of Elizabeth do seem to have been linked with the world of romances. George Peele's *Anglorum Feriae*, which depicts the Accession Day Tilts of 1595, provides evidence of this in its descriptions of several of the combatants:

> South Hampton ran
> as Bevis of South Hampton that good knighte
> has justed in the honor of the day
> and certes Bevis was a mighty man
> valeant in armes gentle and debonaire . . . (227–231)

> In bases and caparisons of cost
> came three redoubted knights and men at armes
> Olde Knowles his of springs gallant Cavaliers
> and such they showed as were K. Arthures knightes
> he whilom used to feast at Camilot. (261–265)

The tilting regulations drawn up by John Tiptofte, Earl of Worcester, for Edward III were revived in 1562 – in other words, Elizabethan jousts were run on the same lines as those of the years when jousting was at its most popular in England, and which marked the foundation of the Order of the Garter,[60] and not on the pattern of later jousts from which most of the danger had been removed (this was especially true of the jousts of the sixteenth century after Henry VIII had been nearly, and Henri II of France actually, killed in jousting accidents, both through the failure of their opponents to lower the point of the lance, so that the kings were struck on the face through the visor).[61] Since the Elizabethans (correctly) connected the Round Table with Edward III's formation of the Order of the Garter, it is possible that the choice of Edward III's tilting regulations was made in the hope of conforming as closely as possible to the imagined standards of Arthur's court.

The connection between the practices of Arthur and his knights and those of the Elizabethan knights is one that is frequently made by Sir William Segar, artist, herald, and historian of chivalry (he progressed from Portcullis Pursuivant in 1585 to Garter King of Arms in 1603). In his *Honor Military and Ciuill* (1602) he gives the supposed regulations of the Round Table and a code of conduct for an Elizabethan knight, and they are remarkably similar (pp. 55, 60ff.). He describes the ceremonies for creating and degrading knights which he dates at 500 A.D., pointing out that this is the time of Arthur (p. 58). He defends, in surprisingly reasonable tones, the probable basis in truth for the stories of King Arthur and other romances (p. 58) – a repetition of an argument which he had advanced a decade earlier in *The Booke of Honor and Armes* (?1590). Throughout Segar's books the times and ceremonies of Arthur and his knights are used as a standard by which to measure the ceremonies and practices of other orders, especially those of his own day. A major object of the books, besides a scholarly and critical interest in the history of knighthood and knightly customs,[62] is to glorify the Chivalry of the reign of Elizabeth. Most of *Honor Military and Ciuill* is taken up with describing the various jousts and tournaments held in her reign, and Segar has no doubt of the inspiration of these displays of prowess:

> Queene Elizabeth, a Prince of so great magnanimitie and wisedome, as by imitation of her most noble and princely vertues, the Court of England both for Armes and learning hath in her reign excelled all others.[63]

Elizabeth ennobles her courtiers; makes them more chivalrous.

The love which they feel for her is one which benefits both parties.
Elizabeth is glorified by the deeds of her knights, and the knights are
given a motive for performing virtuous actions. This concept of the
Beloved as a source of good in the lover is central to the doctrine of
amor cortois. The knight did not perform glorious and noble actions
merely to win the love of his lady; rather the love he felt for her,
working as an ennobling force within him, compelled him to perform
noble deeds. Like Chaucer's Troilus he might say,

> Yet mot I nede amenden in som wyse,
> Right thorugh the vertu of youre servyse. (III.1287–8)

Spenser articulates the ideal version of the relationship between
Elizabeth and her knights when he makes Guyon describe his
relationship to Gloriana:

> She is the mighty Queene of *Faerie*,
> Whose faire retrait I on my shield do beare;
> She is the flowre of grace and chastitie,
> Throughout the world renowned far and neare,
> My liefe, my liege, my Soueraigne, my deare,
> Whose glory shineth as the morning Starre,
> And with her light the earth enlumines cleare;
> Far reach her mercies, and her prayses farre,
> As well in state of peace, as puissance in warre. (II.ix.4)

Gloriana is both Guyon's mistress – 'my liefe' – and his feudal
overlord – 'my liege'; his ruler – 'my Soueraigne' – and his beloved –
'my deare'. He loves her and is inspired by her, but does not aspire
to her. His service is that of a lover, but not that of a suitor. She is his
lady, and his inspiration, but he hopes for no closer relationship. But
she is his inspiration not only as his Lady, but as the Head of the
Order of Knighthood to which he belongs. She not only evokes the
aspirations to self-ennoblement which drive the knight to undertake
quests, but directs what those quests should be, apportions them to
the knights, and ensures that the Order of Maidenhead is a force for
good, upholding right moral values and protecting the weak and
distressed. It is a commonplace of Spenser criticism that the Fairy
Queen's Annual Feast, like the Iberian Jousts in the *Arcadia* of Sir
Philip Sidney, is an idealized picture of the Elizabethan Accession
Day Tilts, and that Spenser has modelled his depiction upon
Arthur's feasts in Malory, in which the feast is not only a celebration
of Arthur and the Round Table (and usually of some feast in the

Christian Calender) and an occasion for adventure, because of the
Quests which start at it, but also an opportunity for those in need of
aid to appeal to the Round Table for help in redressing their
grievances:

> I deuise that the Faery Queene kept her Annuall feaste xii[64] dayes,
> vppon which xii seuerall dayes, the occasions of the xii seuerall
> aduentures hapned, which being vndertaken by xii seuerall knights,
> are in these xii books seuerally handled and discoursed. The first was
> this. In the beginning of the feast, there presented him selfe a tall
> clownishe younge man, who falling before the Queen of Faeries desired
> a boone (as the manner then was) which during that feaste she might
> not refuse: which was that he might haue the atchieument of any
> aduenture, which during that feaste should happen, that being
> graunted, he rested him on the floore, vnfitte through his rusticity for a
> better place. Soone after entred a faire Ladye in mourning weedes,
> riding on a white Asse, with a dwarfe behind her leading a warlike
> steed, that bore the Armes of a knight, and his speare in the dwarfes
> hand. Shee falling before the Queene of Faeries, complayned that her
> father and mother an ancient King and Queene, had bene by a huge
> dragon many years shut vp in a brasen Castle, who thence suffred
> them not to yssew: and therefore besought the Faery Queene to
> assygne her some one of her knights to take on him that exployt.
> Presently that clownish person vpstarting, desired that aduenture:
> whereat the Queene much wondering, and the Lady much gaine-
> saying, yet he earnestly importuned his desire. In the end the Lady
> told him that vnlesse the armour which she brought, would serue him
> (that is the armour of a Christian man specified by Saint Paul v.
> Ephes.) that he could not succeed in that enterprise, which being
> forthwith put vpon him with dewe furnitures thereunto, he seemed the
> goodliest man in al that company, and was well liked of the Lady. And
> eftsoones taking on him knighthood, and mounting on that straunge
> Courser, he went forth with her on that aduenture: where beginneth
> the first booke, vz.
>
>   *A gentle knight was pricking on the playne. &c.*
>
> The second day ther came in a Palmer bearing an Infant with
> bloody hands, whose Parents he complained to haue bene slayn by an
> Enchaunteresse called Acrasia: and therefore craued of the Faery
> Queene, to appoint him some knight, to performe that aduenture,
> which being assigned to Sir Guyon, he presently went forth with that
> same Palmer: which is the beginning of the second booke and the
> whole subiect thereof. The third day, there came in, a Groome who
> complained before the Faery Queene, that a vile Enchaunter called
> Busirane had in hand a most faire Lady called Amoretta, whom he
> kept in most grieuous torment, because she would not yield him the
> pleasure of her body. Whereupon Sir Scudamour the louer of that
> Lady presently tooke on him that aduenture . . .[65]

How like this idealized picture the Accession Day Tournaments might be is shown by the speech in the Ditchley Manuscript in which a hermit introduces a company of homely people, no better than shepherds, and their leader, a 'clownishly clad' knight.[66]

Elizabeth was the mainspring of *virtu* in her court. She inspired her knights to perform noble deeds for her glorification. The Accession Day Tilts were a public affirmation of loyalty and nobility: the display of what the Elizabethan court considered to be its best qualities. Sir Henry Lee's intention to 'eternize the glory of her Majestie's Court' has already been noticed: Frances Yates's summary of his intentions is probably an accurate one:

> It would seem to have been a part of Sir Henry Lee's plan for the Accession Day Tilts that their imagery should build up, in terms of chivalrous romance, the political and theological position of Protestant England.[67]

To this extent the Tilts were a courtly equivalent of the tableaux mounted by the cities to welcome Elizabeth – with the proviso that the Tilts seem not to have been used for admonition and advice:[68] nothing touches them of the discontent being voiced in Parliament at the end of the reign. The Tilts express the relationship of Elizabeth to her court, country, and world: private pleas and grievances could only be minor, and certainly not critical, ones – like Carey's attempt to win the Queen's favour by his appearance as an unknown knight – and wholehearted self-seeking, like Leicester's Kenilworth Entertainment, was doomed to failure and received with displeasure. The Tilts were not merely private Court occasions, but public displays. The citizens of London and any visiting foreigners might go to them and be reassured that the Court of England and its Queen were as brilliant and noble as the characters in the romances that were imitated in these ceremonies. While the admission price of one shilling put the Tilts into the luxury bracket as entertainment, it did not render them, nor were they intended to be, exclusive, and it is noteworthy that Sidney includes townspeople among those who comment on his jousting, although their comments show a lack of appreciation of the finer points of the sport.

The jousts were in fact primarily ceremonial, rather than sporting, occasions. The Elizabethan court managed to combine ceremony and recreation as no other, except perhaps the Stuart with its masques, has done. The costumes were elaborate and expensive; a foreign visitor records that the attendants of the knights whom he saw were

disguised like savages, or like Irishmen, with their hair hanging down
to the girdle like women; others had horses' manes on their heads,
some came driving in a carriage, the horses being equipped like
elephants, some carriages were drawn by men, others appeared to
move by themselves.[69]

The jousting disguises which appear in contemporary romances –
Artegal's at the tournament for Florimell's girdle, or those of the
competitors at the Iberian Annual Jousts in *The Countess of Pembroke's
Arcadia* – are scarcely more elaborate than those worn by
Elizabethan knights:

> . . . there entred from the other side,
> A straunger knight, from whence no man could reed,
> In queynt disguise, full hard to be descride.
> For all his armour was like saluage weed,
> With woody moss bedight, and all his steed
> With oaken leaues attrapt, that seemed fit
> For saluage wight, and thereto well agreed
> His word, which on his ragged shield was writ,
> *Saluagesse sans finesse*, showing secret wit. (FQ IV.iv.39)

Sidney's description of the Iberian celebrations is, indeed, generally
accepted as a description of an Elizabethan tilt, with Philisides as
Sidney and Lelius as Lee, and while both Frances Yates's
identification of it as the Accession Day Tilt of 1581, and Maurice
Evans's as *The Four Foster Children of Desire*[70] seem perhaps rather
hopefully specific, there is no doubt that it evokes the feeling of, and
refers closely to, such occasions:

> . . . the manner was that the forenoon they should run at tilt, one after
> the other, the afternoon in a broad field in the manner of a battle, till
> either the strangers or that country knights won the field.
>   The first that ran was a brave knight, whose device was to come in
> all chained, with a nymph leading him. Against him came forth an
> Iberian, whose manner of entering was with bagpipes instead of
> trumpets; a shepherd's boy before him for a page, and by him a dozen
> apparelled like shepherds for the fashion, though rich in stuff, who
> carried his lances, which though strong to give a lancely blow indeed,
> yet so were they coloured with hooks near the morne that they prettily
> resembled sheephooks. His own furniture was dressed over with wool,
> so enriched with jewels artificially placed that one would have thought
> it a marriage between the lowest and the highest. His impresa was a
> sheep marked with pitch, with this word, 'Spotted to be known'. And
> because I may tell you out his conceit (though that were not done, till

the running for that time was ended) before the ladies departed from the windows – among whom there was one, they say, that was the Star whereby his course was only directed – the shepherds attending upon Philisides went among them and sang an eclogue; one of them answering another, while the other shepherds pulling out recorders, which possessed the place of pipes, accorded their music to the others' voice. The eclogue had great praise. I only remember six verses, while having questioned one with the other of their fellow-shepherd's sudden growing a man of arms and the cause of his so doing, they thus said:

Me thought some staves he miss'd: if so, not much amiss;
For where he most would hit, he ever yet did miss.
One said he brake across; full well it so might be:
For never was there man more crossly crossed than he.
But most cried, 'O well broke'; O fool full gaily blest:
Where failing is a shame, and breaking is his best.

Thus I have digressed, because his manner liked me well; but when he began to run against Lelius, it had near grown (though great love had ever been betwixt them) to a quarrel. For Philisides breaking his staves with great commendation, Lelius, who was known to be second to none in the perfection of that art, ran ever over his head but so finely, to the skilful eyes, that one might well see he showed more knowledge in missing than others did in hitting, for with so gallant a grace his staff came swimming close over the crest of the helmet, as if he would represent the kiss and not the stroke of Mars. But Philisides was much moved with it while he thought Lelius would show a contempt of his youth; till Lelius (who therefore would satisfy him because he was his friend) made him know that to such bondage he was for so many courses tied by her, whose disgraces to him were graced by her excellency, and whose injuries he could never otherwise return than honours.

But so by Lelius' willing missing was the odds of the Iberian side, and continued so in the next by the excellent running of a knight, though fostered so by the Muses as many times the very rustic people left both their delights and profits to hearken to his songs, yet could he so well perform all armed sports as if he had never had any other pen than a lance in his hand. He came in like a wild man, but such a wildness as showed his eyesight had tamed him, full of withered leaves which, though they fell not, still threatened falling. His impresa was a mill-horse still bound to go in one circle, with this word, 'Data fata secutus'. But after him the Corinthian knights absolutely prevailed, especially a great nobleman of Corinth, whose device was to come without any device, all in white like a new knight (as indeed he was) but so new as his newness shamed most of the others' long exercise. Then another, from whose tent I remember a bird was made fly, with such art to carry a written embassage among the ladies, that one might say, if a live bird, how so taught; if a dead bird, how so made? Then he who hidden, man and horse, in a great figure lively

representing the Phoenix, the fire took so artificially as it consumed the
bird and left him to rise, as it were, out of the ashes thereof. Against
whom was the fine frozen knight, frozen in despair; but his armour so
naturally representing ice, and all his furniture so lively answering
thereto, as yet did I never see anything that pleased me better.[71]

Shakespeare's *Pericles* evokes the entry of such knights before the
tilting and the presentation and interpretation of their shields by the
lady in whose honour the tilt is held:

(Enter a Knight; he passes over, and his Squire presents his shield to
the Princess.)
Simonides Who is the first that doth prefer himself?
Thaisa A knight of Sparta, my renowned father;
And the device he bears upon his shield
Is a black Aethiop reaching at the sun;
The word, *Lux tua vita mihi*.
Simonides He loves you well that holds his life of you.
(The Second Knight passes.)
Who is the second that presents himself?
Thaisa A prince of Macedon, my royal father;
And the device he bears upon his shield
Is an arm'd knight that's conquered by a lady;
The motto thus, in Spanish, *Pui por dulzura que por fuerza*.
(The Third Knight passes.)
Simonides And what's the third?
Thaisa The third of Antioch;
And his device a wreath of chivalry;
The word, *Me pompae provexit apex*.
(The Fourth Knight passes.)
Simonides What is the fourth?
Thaisa A burning torch that's turned upside down;
The word, *Quod me alit, me extinguit*.
Simonides Which shows that beauty hath his power and will,
Which can as well inflame as it can kill.
(The Fifth Knight passes.)
Thaisa The fifth, an hand environed with clouds,
Holding out gold that's by the touchstone tried;
The motto thus, *Sic spectanda fides*.
(The Sixth Knight (Pericles) passes.)
Simonides And what's the sixth and last, the which the knight himself
With such a graceful courtesy deliver'd?
Thaisa He seems to be a stranger; but his present is
A wither'd branch, that's only green at top
The motto, *In hac spe vivo*.
Simonides A pretty moral;
From the dejected state wherein he is,
He hopes by you his fortunes yet may flourish. (II.ii.16–46)

The knight's device and armour often bore a reference – as in *Pericles* – to his state. Sir Henry Lee was particularly fond of this type of allusion. One of his suits of armour (presumably a late one) was ornamented on the pauldrons with the device of an eagle rising to the sun – implying that Lee renewed his youth by gazing on Elizabeth.[72] At the Accession Day Tilt of 1590, when Lee handed over to George Clifford, Earl of Cumberland, as Queen's Champion, his trappings were directly related to the fact of his impending retirement, as Peele recounts:

> Mighty in arms, mounted on puissant horse,
> Knight of the crown, in rich embroidery,
> And costly fair comparison charg'd with crowns,
> O'ershadowed with a wither'd running vine,
> As who should say, 'My spring of youth is past',
> In corselet gilt of curious workmanship,
> Sir Henry Lee, redoubted man-at-arms,
> Leads in the troops . . . (*Polyhymnia* 20–27).

Other knights' suits and trappings might relate to their devotion to Elizabeth, or to their names. Christopher Hatton had a suit of armour engraved with Es, and another engraved with Tudor roses and true-love knots. Leicester had a suit engraved with the ragged-staff badge of his family.[73] In the jousts of 1595 a combatant called James Skydmore (or Scudamore) punned on his own name and referred to *The Faerie Queene* in his device:

> Le Scu d'Amour: The armes of Loialtie
> lodg'd Skydmore in his harte and on he cam
> and well and woorthily demeande himselfe
> in that daies service . . .'[74]

James Skydmore's impresa was presumably the same as the shield of Spenser's Scudamour:

> On which the winged boy in colours cleare
> Depeincted was, full easie to be knowne,
> And he thereby, where euer it in field was showne. (III.xi.7)

Other imagery recurred from tilt to tilt, and seems to have been central to the Elizabeth-cult. Roy Strong examines the crowned pillar which features in both the Accession Day Tilts and the Ditchley Entertainment,[75] and the armillary sphere was obviously also a key image for both the Queen and her champions. It, or an astrolabe appears in a book in Elizabeth's hand in the Royal collection;[76] Elizabeth wears it as an ear-ring in the *Ditchley Portrait* (National Portrait Gallery), and on her right sleeve in the *Rainbow Portrait* (Hatfield House); it is embroidered on the sleeve-linings and hat-brim of George Clifford, Earl of Cumberland, in Hilliard's portrait of him as Queen's Champion (National Maritime Museum), and it is embroidered, together with true-love knots, on the sleeves of Sir Henry Lee in Antonio Mor's early portrait of him (National Portrait Gallery). This is dated 1568, and suggests that Lee was already formulating the Elizabeth-cult by then, even though there is no definite record of his appearance in a tilt before 1571, and the emergence of the fully-developed Elizabeth-cult is usually placed in the early 1570s.[77] The armillary sphere probably refers to Elizabeth's aspect as Astraea, possibly to Astraea's period in heaven as a constellation, and sign of the Zodiac, from which she has returned as Elizabeth.

Strong argues that the Accession Day Tilts came to be presented as separate incidents in a continuous romance[78] – presumably on the lines of the numerous Pentecost celebrations in Arthurian romance. Certainly surviving records indicate a consistency of characters and a constant basis in romance. The Ditchley Manuscript contains several challenges for jousts by Sir Henry Lee, written for himself and for other knights. In 1590 Cumberland, about to be designated Lee's successor, came into the tilt in white (the colour of the new knight), and accompanied by Uther Pendragon and Merlin, with obvious reference to the youthful King Arthur,[79] and in the speeches that accompany him he is referred to as 'Red Dragon' – the badge of Arthur was often taken to be the Red Dragon of Wales, and it is of course a Tudor badge (being, for instance, rather intrusively present in that part of King's College Chapel, Cambridge, built by Henry VIII). In 1593 he repeated this Arthurian motif by coming to the tilt as 'the Knight of Pendragon Castle'.[80] On other occasions three knights defended the cause that Love is worse than hate and that 'ther is a Ladye that scornes Loue and his power, of more virtue and greater beawtie then all the Amorous Dames that be at this daye in the world'; and some wandering knights came before the Queen accompanied by a Black Knight, who had tilted the year before, spent the intervening year with a hermit, and now returned 'in new habite'.[81]

Philisides in Sidney's fictional joust arranges for shepherds to sing explaining his device. This is itself related to events in the Tilts (but it is impossible to say whether based on, or the inspiration for, them). At Lee's retirement in 1590 Robert Hales sang a lyric set by Dowland:

His golden locks time hath to silver turned
O time too swift, O swiftness never ceasing!
His youth 'gainst time and age hath ever spurned,
But spurned in vain; youth waneth by increasing:
Beauty, strength, youth, are flowers but fading seen;
Duty, faith, love, are roots, and ever green.

His helmet now shall make a hive for bees;
And, lovers' sonnets turned to holy psalms,
A man-at-arms must now serve on his knees,
And feed on prayers, which are age his alms:
But though from court to cottage he depart
His saint is sure of his unspotted heart.

And when he saddest sits in homely cell,
He'll teach his swains this carol for a song, –
'Blest be the hearts that wish my sovereign well,
Curst be the souls that think her any wrong.'
Goddess, allow this aged man his right,
To be your beadsman now that was your knight.[82]

It was not only in fiction that the Tilts became the occasion for great art – this is, deservedly, one of the most famous of Elizabethan lyrics, and may be by Lee himself. Certainly the role of the knight-turned-hermit, a motif blending strands from Arthurian romance (the hermit who was in his youth an inland man and has retired to make his soul[83] appears in Malory as Sir Baudwin of Britayne),[84] Raymond Lull's *The Order of Chivalry*,[85] and neo-platonic love-religion, in which the helmet as a beehive is a motif,[86] was one which Lee assumed from then on, with the refinement that the object of his devotions was the same in retirement as in activity, and he makes his soul through his contemplation of Elizabeth, a theme made explicit in another lyric probably by Lee:

Times eldest sonne, olde age, the heyre of ease,
Strengthe foe, loves woe, and foster to devotion,
Bids gallant youthes in martial prowes please,
As for himselfe hee hath no earthly motion,
But thinks sighes, teares, vowes, praiers and sacrifices
As good as shewes, maskes, justes or tilt devises.

Then sit thee downe, and say thy *Nunc demittis*,
With *De profundis*, *Credo* and *Te Deum*,

Chant *Miserere*, for what now so fit is
As that, or this, *Paratum est cor meum?*
O that thy Saint would take in worth thy hart,
Thou canst not please hir with a better part.

When others sing *Venite exultemus*,
Stand by and turn to *Noli aemulari*;
For *quare fremuerunt* use *Oremus*,
Vivat Eliza for an *Ave Mari*;
And teach those swains that lives about thy cell,
To say Amen when thou dost pray so well.[87]

But the Hermit was not a figure appropriate to the Court: at least appropriate only on visits to the Court, as Lee seems to have used it for his appearances at the Accession Day Tilts after his retirement. He was essentially a figure of the countryside, of pastoral, an educator of the shepherds amongst whom he had chosen to withdraw. His place was not at court celebrations, but in the Entertainments presented to Elizabeth at the great country houses she visited on her progresses, and with which this book is principally concerned.

11. Elizabethan Progresses

The English Court had traditionally been peripatetic, moving from one royal household to another according to the season; a practice which has its last vestiges in the Queen's traditional Christmas at Sandringham, Ascot week at Windsor, and summer at Balmoral. However, national unrest and a more centralized administration had resulted in the earlier Tudors restricting themselves almost completely to the scatter of royal households and hunting lodges around London. The Elizabethan progress was both a return to the earlier wider journeyings (although never to disaffected areas: there was no equivalent of her namesake's 1977 visit to Northern Ireland) and innovative in that in place of the descents, in places where no royal property existed, on great religious foundations for harbour for the king and his train, Elizabeth descended on the great houses of the nobility and gentry – which might, of course, be the same place.

The purpose of the progresses was three-fold: it was desirable for the Court to remove from London during the summer, partly because of the insalubriousness of the city during the hot weather and partly because of the plague; the tours round congenial areas of the country and visits to families, many of whom were her relatives (like the Hunsdons) or friends (like the Norrises), provided the Queen with what amounted to a summer holiday, and the progresses were invaluable as public-relations exercises on the part of Elizabeth and her administration. That Elizabeth was fully aware of this aspect is shown by the care she took to exercise her enormous personal charm on these occasions, as when she calmed the Recorder of Warwick in 1572:

> . . . she called Mr. Aglionby to her, and offered her hand to him to kiss, withall smyling, said, 'Come hither, little Recorder. It was told me that you would be afraid to look upon me, or to speak boldly; but you were not so fraid of me as I was of youe; and I now thank you for putting me in mynd of my duety, and that should be in me.'[88]

Theseus's practice in *A Midsummer Night's Dream* seems based on that of Elizabeth:

> . . . what poor duty cannot do,
> Noble respect takes it in might, not merit.
> Where I have come, great clerks have purposed
> To greet me with premeditated welcomes;
> Where I have seen them shiver and look pale,
> Make periods in the midst of sentences,
> Throttle their practis'd accent in their fears,
> And, in conclusion, dumbly have broke off,
> Not paying me a welcome. Trust me, sweet,
> Out of this silence yet I pick'd a welcome
> And in the modesty of fearful duty
> I read as much as from the rattling tongue
> Of saucy and audacious eloquence.
> Love, therefore, and tongue-tied simplicity
> In least speak most to my capacity. (V.i.91–105)

Nor did the propaganda benefits of Elizabeth's visit to an area consist solely in the impact on the individual of the glamour of her personality and presence. Local pride is deep and local memory long (in Lewes, the Pope, recognizably Paul IV, is still burnt in effigy after a mock trial every Guy Fawkes' Night in memory of the Marian Martyrs, and the vividness of the memory in East Anglia of Oliver Cromwell and of the draining of the Fens is notorious). For the Queen to be entertained by a town assured the townspeople of their own importance, and increased their support of the local administration: a necessary factor when taxes were collected by that administration on behalf of the central government, and when the loyalty of a town might be vital were there to be major uprising:

towns often controlled strategic bridges and major routes, and
through them access to London. Similar considerations might be
involved in the Queen's visits to great houses.[89] The days of the
private army had been ended by Henry VII's statute of Livery and
Maintenance, but the local power of the noble families was very
great. Not only the household servants, but the tenants, dependants,
and locals who wished to retain the favour of the land-owner would
jump to his bidding, and the habits of unquestioning following of a
local magnate provided the followers of the Northern Earls in 1569,
substantial portions of the armies of both sides during the Civil War,
and indeed probably last manifested themselves in the Great War,
in those rural communities where the young men joined the Squire's
son in enlisting – a practice vouched for in the pathetic war
memorials in almost every English Parish Church. The strategic
possibilities open to a local landowner are indicated by the incident
in 1660 when Lord Fairfax, not a particularly rich or powerful man,
was able to gather enough followers on his own estate and those of
his friends to seize York.[90] Elizabeth's visits to great houses thus
reinforced the power of the local magnate, enhancing his prestige in
the eyes of his neighbours and dependants, and ensuring that should
they be called upon to follow him on her service, they would do so
more willingly for their belief that their master was high in the
Queen's favour, and might be in a position to prefer his adherents.

These magnates were not, of course, principally military leaders,
and the houses in which they entertained her were already being
constructed to fulfill the Yeatsian ideal of

. . . a house,
Where all's accustomed, ceremonious.

Jonson's formulation of the ideal in *To Penshurst* and *To Sir Robert
Wroth* is well known, and it had already been encapsulated in
Sidney's *Arcadia* in the description of Kalander's house:

'They . . . brought him to the house, about which they might see (with
fit consideration both of the air, the prospect, and the nature of the
ground) all such necessary additions to a great house as might well
show Kalander knew that provision is the foundation of hospitality
and thrift the fuel of magnificence. The house itself was built of fair
and strong stone, not affecting so much any extraordinary kind of
fineness as an honourable representing of a firm stateliness. The lights,
doors and stairs rather directed to the use of the guest than to the eye of
the artificer; and yet as the one chiefly heeded, so the other not
neglected; each place handsome without curiosity and homely

without loathsomeness; not so dainty as not to be trod on, nor yet slubbered up with good fellowship; all more lasting than beautiful but that the consideration of the exceeding lastingness made the eye believe it was exceedingly beautiful. The servants, not so many in number as cleanly in apparel and serviceable in behaviour, testifying even in their countenances that their master took as well care to be served as of them that did serve.[91]

This ideal of decorum, of harmony, of luxury without ostentation, and of social responsibility, is that of *To Penshurst* (Penshurst, Sidney's family home, was probably the model for Kalander's house). Penshurst has passed the test of the great house, and proved itself fit to entertain a king – and proved itself so when the king arrived unexpectedly, without the warnings and elaborate preparations granted on the more formal informal visits of the progresses. Jonson attributes this to Penshurst's being in reality what other great houses pretend to be. Its organic relationship with the country in which it is situated, and of which it forms part, includes its possession of and by real wood-gods and nymphs, the figures who so often populate the grounds of country houses entertaining royalty. Penshurst is not a show but real, unostentatious, perfect. It can entertain a king who comes unannounced because it is always ready to entertain, and its standards are royal. It can even, in the warmth of its welcome, supply the place of a whole area that would normally have turned out to greet its royal visitor. The Sidneys do not have to be there themselves to ensure this – the house is so well-run, almost such a power in its own right, that it can welcome the king in their absence with all due provision and ceremony.[92]

This was the ideal behind the building of the great Elizabethan houses. They were expressions, not only of the power and (often newly-acquired) wealth of the men who built them (Cecil, builder of two of the greatest of such houses, Burleigh and Theobalds, was cynical about such matters), nor of the new standards of domestic comfort, nor even of a concrete expression of the desire inherent in pastoral for an aristocratic refuge among, but not actually a part of, the community of shepherds; but of a desire and willingness to entertain the Queen. Hatton's great work at Holdenby, which bankrupted him, which the Queen never saw, and which he was seldom able to visit, was envisaged by him as a temple of which she was the goddess. Its only *raison d'être* was to entertain her; it would never be complete until she stepped over its threshold.[93] It was on her visits to such houses that the cult of Elizabeth was given its fullest expression.

Since her courtiers saw Elizabeth as a figure out of romance, they did their best to ensure that her life was as romance-like as possible. This, apart from the occasional Tilts, and the Christmas celebrations, was difficult at Court, where Elizabeth was above all the practical politician, running her country with the aid of efficient bureaucrats such as Walsingham and Cecil. But on her numerous progresses the courtiers had the chance to arrange her life for her, and grasped it eagerly. Each Progress became a Quest.

The nature of the progress, with its journeyings from place to place, pauses to hunt, and supposedly unexpected descents on the local gentry for food and lodging,[94] lent itself well to this transformation. And so Elizabeth's journeyings became fraught with adventure. Satyrs[95] and Wild Men[96] lurked behind every tree, ready to address her in Poulter's Measure. Shepherds[97] and Shepherdesses[98] infested the hills, singing pastoral ditties, and demanding that she arbitrate in their disputes.[99] Strangely familiar Unknown Knights fought in clearings through which she must pass,[100] while Ladies swam in the lakes, ready to yield her their sovereignty over the waters.[101] She even occasionally met a hermit, who had always 'been in his youth an inland man'.[102] All these she must answer in suitable fashion, judge, and reward. The Elizabethan courtiers prepared to entertain their Queen in the knowledge that she was both a gifted actress and a skilled improvisor.

The transformations of landscape effected in these entertainments are astonishing in their nature. They are not of the same type as those usually associated with court masquerades of a pastoral world – the Sèvres milk pails at Le Hameau, or the spacious Palladian interiors of Queen Charlotte's thatched and half-timbered country cottage at Kew. In these the royal and noble participants themselves change their natures: Marie Antoinette becomes a milkmaid; Queen Charlotte a gardener's wife. Their whole world is a make-believe one, and exists only for so long as they go to play in it: their villages and ideal cottages are the equivalent of the little girl's Wendy House, in which she may meet Peter Pan for as long as – and only for as long as – she pretends that she is herself Wendy. The world of Elizabeth's progresses was much closer to that of a child who goes down her everyday garden and really meets Peter Pan. The pastoral environments of Marie Antoinette and Queen Charlotte are playrooms, supplied with expensive toys: since the users themselves are in different roles from their actual ones when they use them, there is no pretence that they are real. In the evening the toys must be put away, and the Meissen milkmaids and Chelsea cottagers

cross their parks and become Queens again at Versailles and Kew.
But the Elizabethans are not dealing with play worlds. What they
are doing is transforming the real one. This is Sidney's description of
Arcadia as Musidorus first perceives it:

'There were hills which garnished their proud heights with stately
trees; humble valleys whose base estate seemed comforted with the
refreshing of silver rivers; meadows enamelled with all sorts of
eye-pleasing flowers; thickets, which, being lined with most pleasant
shade, were witnessed so to by the cheerful deposition of many
well-tuned birds; each pasture stored with sheep feeding with sober
security, while the pretty lambs with bleating oratory craved the dams'
comfort; here a shepherd's boy piping as though he should never be
old; there a young shepherdess knitting and withal singing, and it
seemed that her voice comforted her hands to work and her hands kept
time to her voice's music. As for the houses of the country – for many
houses came under their eye – they were all scattered, no two being one
by the other, and yet not so far off as that it barred mutual succour: a
show, as it were, of an accompanable solitariness and of a civil
wildness.'[103]

12. The Entertainment at Bisham, 1592

In 1592, Lady Russell entertained the Queen at Bisham. As she rode
towards the house, she encountered the Russell daughters dressed as
shepherdesses, sitting on a hillside:

At the top of the Hill going to Bissam, the Cornets sounding in the
Woods, a wilde man came forth and uttered this Speech:
  I followed this sounde, as enchanted; neither knowing the reason
why, nor how to be ridde of it: unusuall to these Woods, and (I feare)
to our gods prodigious. *Sylvanus* whom I honour, is runne into a Cave:
Pan, whom I envye, courting of the Shepheardesse: Envie I thee *Pan*?
No, pitty thee, an eie-sore to chast Nymphes; yet still importunate.[104]
Honour thee *Sylvanus*? No, contemne thee: fearefull of Musicke in the
Woods, yet counted the god of the Woods. I, it may bee more stout,
than wise, asked, who passed that way? what he or shee? none durst
answere, or would vouchsafe, but passionate Eccho, who saide
Shee.[105] And Shee it is, and you are Shee, whom in our dreames many
yeares wee Satyres have seene, but waking could never finde any such.
Every one hath tolde his dreame, and described your person; all agree
in one, and set downe your vertues: in this onely did wee differ, that

some saide your Pourtraiture might be drawen, other saide impossible: some thought your vertues might be numbred, most saide they were infinite: Infinite and impossible, of that side was I: and first in humility to salute you most happy I: my untamed thoughts waxe gentle, and I feele in myselfe civility, A thing hated, because not knowen, and unknowen, because I knew not you. Thus Vertue tameth fiercenesse, Beauty, madnesse. Your Majesty on my knees will I followe, bearing this Club, not as a Salvage, but to beate downe those that are.[106]

At the middle of the Hill sate Pan, and two Virgins keeping sheepe, and sowing in their Samplers, where her Majestye stayed and heard this:

Pan. Prety soules and bodies too, faire shephardisse, or sweete Mistresse, you know my suite, love; my vertue, Musicke, my power, a godhead. I cannot tickle the sheepes gutts of a Lute, bydd, bydd, bydd, like the calling of Chickins, but for a Pipe that squeeketh like a Pigg, I am he. How doe you burne time, and drowne beauty, in pricking of clouts, when you should be penning of Sonnets? You are more simple then the sheep you keepe, but not so gentle. I love you both, I know not which best; and you both scorne me, I know not which most. Sure I am, that you are not so young as not to understand love, nor so wise as to withstand it, unlesse you think yourselves greater than gods, whereof I am one. Howe often have I brought you chestnuts for a love token, and desired but acceptance for a favour. Little did you knowe the misterye, that as the huske was thornye and tough, yet the meate sweete, so though my hyde were rough and unkempt, yet my heart was smooth and loving: you are but the Farmers daughters of the Dale, I the god of the flocks that feede upon the hils. Though I cannot force love, I may obedience, or else send your sheepe a wandring, with my fancies. Coynesse must be revenged with curstnesse, but be not agaste, sweet mice,[107] my godhead cometh so fast upon me, that Majestye had almost overrun affection. Can you love? Wil you?

Syb.[108] Alas, poore Pan, looke how he looketh, Sister, fitter to drawe in a Harvest wayne,[109] then talke of love to chaste Virgins, would you have us both?

Pan. I, for oft I have hearde, that two Pigeons may bee caught with one beane.

Isab.[108] And two Woodcocks with one sprindge.

Syb. And many Dotterels with one dance.

Isab. And all fooles with one faire worde.

Nay, this is his meaning; as he hath two shapes, so hath he two harts, the one of a man wherewith his tongue is tipped, dissembling; the other of a beast, wherewith his thoughts are poysoned, lust. Men must have as manie loves, as they have hartstrings,[110] and studie to make an Alphabet of mistresses, from A to Y which maketh them in the end crie, Ay. Against this, experience hath provided us a remedy, to laugh at them when they know not what to saie, and when they speake, not to beleeve them.

Pan. Not for want of matter, but to knowe the meaning, what is wrought in this sampler?

Syb. The follies of the Gods, who became beastes, for their affections.

Pan. What in this?

Isab. The honour of Virgins who became Goddesses, for their chastity.

Pan. But what be these?

Syb. Men's tongues, wrought all with double stitch but not one true.[111]

Pan. What these?

Isab. Roses, Eglentine, harts-ease, wrought with Queenes stitch, and all right.[112]

Pan. I never hard the odds betweene mens tongues and weomens, therefore they may be both double, unlesse you tell mee how they differ.

Syb. Thus, weomens tongues are made of the same flesh that their harts are, and speake as they thinke: Mens harts of the flesh that their tongues, and both dissemble, But prythy *Pan* be packing, thy words are as odious as thy sight, and we attend a sight which is more glorious, than the sunne rising.

Pan. What, does *Jupiter* come this waies?

Syb. No, but one that will make *Jupiter* blush as guilty of his unchaste jugglings, and Juno dismaide as wounded at her Majesty. What our mother hath often tolde us, and fame the whole world, cannot be concealed from thee; if it be, we wil tell thee, which may hereafter make thee surcease thy suite, for feare of her displeasure, and honour virginitye, by wondering at her vertues.

Pan. Say on, sweete soule?

Syb. This way commeth the Queene of this Islande, the wonder of the world, and nature's glory, leading affections in fetters, Virginities slaves: embracing mildnes with Justice, Majesties twinns. In whom Nature hath imprinted beauty, not art paynted it; in whom wit hath bred learning, but not without labour; labour brought forth wisedome, but not without wonder. By her it is (*Pan*) that all our Carttes that thou seest are laden with Corne, when in other countries they are filled with Harneys;[113] that our horses are ledde with a whipp, theirs with a Launce, that our Rivers flow with fish, theirs with bloode: our cattel feede on pastures, they feed on pastures like cattel: One hande she stretcheth to *Fraunce*, to weaken Rebels;[114] the other to *Flaunders*, to strengthen Religion;[115] her heart to both Countries, her vertues to all. This is shee at whom *Envie* hath shot all her arrowes, and now for anger broke her bow; on whom God hath laide all his blessinges, and we for joy clappe our hands, heedlesse treason goeth hedlesse; and close trechery restlesse: Daunger looketh pale to beholde her Majesty; and tyranny blusheth to heare of her mercy. *Jupiter* came into the house of poore *Baucis*, and she vouchsafeth to visite the bare Farmes of her subjects. We upon our knees, wil entreat her to come into the valley, that our houses may be blessed with her presence, whose hartes are filled with quietnes by her governement. To her wee wish as many

yeares, as our fieldes have eares of corne, both infinite: and to her
enemies, as many troubles, as the Wood hath leaves, all intollerable.
But whist, here shee is, run downe *Pan* the hill in all hast, and though
thou breake thy necke to give our mother[116] warning, it is no matter.

Pan. No, give me leave to die with wondring, and trippe you to your
mother. Here I yeelde all the flockes of these fields to your highnes:
greene be the grasse where you treade: calme the water where you
rowe: sweete the aire, where you breathe: long the life that you live,
happy the people that you love: this is all I can wish. During your
abode, no theft shall be in the woods: in the fielde no noise, in the
vallies no spies, my selfe will keepe all safe: that is all I can offer. And
heare I breake my pipe, which *Apollo* could never make me doe; and
follow that sounde which followes you.

At the bottome of the hill, entring into the house Ceres with her
Nymphes in an harvest Cart, meete her Majesty, having a Crowne of
wheat-ears with a Jewell, and after this song, uttered the speech
following.

Swel Ceres now for other Gods are shrinking,
    Pomona pineth,
    Fruitlesse her tree;
    Fair Phoebus shineth
    Onely on mee.
Conceite doth make me smile whilst I am thinking,
    How every one doth read my story,
    How every bough on Ceres lowreth,
    Cause heaven's plenty on me powreth,
    And they in leaves doe onely glory,
    All other Gods of power bereven,
    Ceres only Queene of heaven.
With Robes and flowers let me be dressed,
    Cynthia that shineth,
    Is not so cleare,
    Cynthia declineth,
    When I appeere,
Yet in this Ile she raignes as blessed,
    And every one at her doth woonder,
    And in my ears still fonde fame whispers,
    Cynthia shal be Ceres Mistres,
    But first my Carre shall rive a sunder.[117]
Helpe Phoebus helpe my fall is suddaine,
Cynthia, Cynthia, must be Soveraigne.

Greater than *Ceres*, receives Ceres Crowne, the ornament of my
plenty, the honour of your peace, heere at your highnes feete, I lay
downe my feined deity, which Poets have honoured, truth contemned.
To your Majesty whome the heavens have crowned with happines, the
world with wonder, birth with dignitie, nature with perfection, we doe
all Homage, accounting nothing ours but what comes from you. And

this muche dare we promise for the Lady of the farme, that your presence hath added many daies to her life, by the infinite joies shee conceyves in her heart, who presents your highnesse with this toye[118] and this short praier, poured from her hart, that your daies may increase in happines, your happines have no end till there be no more daies.[119]

Here we see the process of mutual validation of experience which was an integral part of the Jonesian masques already in evidence. By her presence Elizabeth both transforms England into Arcadia and makes it reveal its true nature as Arcadia. The courtly shepherdesses, the entertainment offered her, are not games, like Marie Antoinette's, for Elizabeth is unchanged: her steadfastness guarantees the reality of the characters she meets. The idyllic vision of Sidney turns out to be situated, not in Ancient Greece, but in sixteenth-century England.

Elizabeth's hostess on this visit, Lady Russell, while not apparently in the innermost circle of the court, was well-connected and favoured by the Queen. The sister of Ladies Burleigh and Bacon, and widow of Sir Thomas Hoby, who had died as Elizabeth's first ambassador to France, her main object in life seems to have been to secure advantageous marriages for her children. This entertainment is obviously designed both to honour the Queen, and to bring Lady Russell's daughters (by her second marriage) to her notice. The Russells were rather poor, and it is noticeable that, apart from the pleasingly personal note introduced by the participation of the two daughters, this episode requires little expenditure – there are three speakers apart from the daughters (possibly professionals imported for the occasion), some sort of accompaniment for Ceres's song, and one minor effect (the collapse of Ceres's cart) required besides the present given to Elizabeth, and the costumes of Pan and the Wild Man at least were presumably minimal. Lady Russell managed to combine thrift, family advancement, and graceful compliment to the Queen in a supremely elegant fashion.

13. *The entertainment at Rycote, 1592*

Later in the same progress Elizabeth visited the Norrises at Rycote, and here the personal note is dominant. The Norrises were among her closest and most trustworthy friends; all their sons were in her service as soldiers (one of them had already died in it and four more were to do so), and the Norrises were neither particularly purse-pinched, nor constantly on the look-out for familial advancement:

> The 28. of September her Majesty went from Oxforde to Ricort, where an olde gentleman, sometimes a souldier,[120] delivered this speech.
>
> Vouchsafe dread Soveraigne, after so much smooth speeches of Muses,[121] to heare a rough hewen tale of a souldier, wee use not with wordes, to amplifie our conceites, and to pleade faith by figures, but by deedes, to shew the loyalty of our harts, and to make it good with our lives. I meane not to recount any service, all proceding of duety, but to tell your Majesty, that I am past al service, save only devotion. My horse, mine armour, my shielde, my sworde, the riches of a young souldier, and an olde souldiers reliques, I should here offer to your highnesse; but my foure boies have stollen them from me, vowing themselves to armes, and leaving mee to my prayers, fortune giveth successe, fidelitye courage, chance cannot blemish faith, nor trueth prevent destinye, whatever happen, this is their resolution, and my desire, that their lives maye be imployed wholy in your service, and their deathes, bee their vowes sacrifice.[122] Their deathes, the rumor of which, hath so often affrighted the Crowe[123] my wife, that her hart, hath bene as blacke as her feathers. I know not whether it be affection, or fondnes, but the crowe thinketh her owne birds the fairest,[124] because to her they are dearest. What joies we both conceive, neither can expresse, sufficeth they be, as your vertues, infinite. And although, nothing be more unfit to lodge your Majestye, then a crowes neste,[125] yet shall it be most happy to us, that it is by your highnesse, made a Phoenix neste.[126] *Qui color ater erat, nunc est contrarius atro.*[127] Vouchsafe this trifle (a faire gowne);[128] and with this my heart, the greatest gift I can offer, and the chiefest, that I ought.
>
> On Sunday,[129] her Majesty going to the garden, received with sweete Musicke of sundry sorts, the olde Gentleman meeting her, saide thus:
>
> Pardon dread Soveraigne, the greatnes of my presumption, who having nothing to say, must follow still to wonder, but saft, some newes out of Irelande.
>
> A Letter delivered by an Irish lacque,[130] in which was inclosed a Darte of gold,[131] set with Diamonds, and after the letter read, delivered to her Majestye, with this motto in Irish, 'I flye onely for my soveraigne'.[132]
>
> My duety humbly remembered. It is saide, the winde is unconstant, I am gladde it is, otherwise had I not heard that, which I most wished, and least looked for. The winde blowing stifly in the weste, on the suddaine turned easterly, by which meanes I received letters, that her Majestie woulde bee at Rycort, nothing could happen to mee more happy, unlesse it were my selfe to be there to doe my duety. But I am a stranger in mine owne countrye, and almost unknown to my best frends, onely remembered by her Majestie, whose late favours have

made me more than fortunate. I should account my ten years absence a flatt banishment, were I not honoured in her Majestie's service, which hath bound all my affections, prentises to patience.[133] In all humility, I desire this Dart to be delivered, an Irish weapon, and this wish of an English hearte, that in whose hart faith is not fastened, a Darte may. I can scarce write for joy, and it is likely, this lacque cannot speak for wondring.[134] If he doe not, this is all that I should say, that my life is my dueties bondman, dutie my faiths soveraigne.[135]

The Dart delivered, a skipper[136] comming from Flaunders, delivered another letter, with a key[137] of golde set with Diamonds with, this motto in dutch, 'I onelie open to you'.[138]

My duety remembred, The enemy of late hath made many braveadoes, even to the gates of Ostend, but the succese was onely a florish. My selfe walking on the Ramparts, to over see the Sentenels, descryed a pink,[139] of whom I enquired, where the Court was hee saide hee knew not, but that the 28 of September, her Majesty would be at Rycort. I was over-joyed, and in making haste, to remember my duety, I had almost forgot it, for I was shipping my selfe for England, with this Skipper, but to come without leave, might be to returne without welcome. To signifie that my hart is there, I most humbly entreat, that this Key be presented; the Key of Ostende, and Ostend the Key of Flaunders, the wards are made of true harts, treachery cannot counterfeit the Key, nor treason her selfe picke the locke. None shal turne it, but whom her Majesty commands, none can. For my selfe, I can but wish, all happines to her highnes, and any occasion, that what my toung delivers, my bloud may seale, the end of my service, that in her service, my life may end.[140]

The Key delivered, a french page came with three other letters; the one written to the lady Squemish,[141] which being mistaken by a wrong superscription, was read before her Majestie. In the second was inclosed a sword of golde, set with Diamonds and Rubyes, with this motto in French, 'Drawen onelie in your defence'. In the thirde was inclosed a trunchion set with Diamonds, with this motto in Spanish, 'I do not commaunde but under you'.[142]

A Letter, written by a Souldier to his Mistris the Lady Squemish.

Faire Lady and sweete Mistris, I seldom write, because I write not well, if I speake, you say I chatter, because I speake so fast, and when I am silent, you thinke me carelesse. You say love cannot be in soldiers, I sweare it is, only this the difference, that we prove it by the sword, others, by their Sonets, theirs inke, blacke for colde, ours bloud, redde for heate. Often have you tolde me, that I know not what love is, and often have I tolde you, that this it is, that which makes the head ake, and the heart to; the eies jelous, and the eares to, the liver blacke,[143] and the Splen[144] to, the vaines shrinke[145] and the purse to. Wit is but loves wiredrawer, making of a short passion an endlesse perswasion, yet no more mettall. You object, that I have many Mistresses, I answere, you have ten times as many servants, and if you should picke a quarrel, why should not I bring my Mistresses into the field against your servants? But inconstancy is a soldier's scarre, it is true, but the wound came by constancie, what a patient vertue is staidnes? like a nail in a dore, rusty, because never removed, I cannot be so superstitious as these nice lovers, who make the pax of their mistris hands,[146] tis flat Popery. I would not purchase love in fee-simple,[147] a lease of two years to me were tedious, I meane not, to have my tongue ringed at my Mistris eare like a Jewel, alwaies whispering of love, I am no earewigg, nor can I endure still to gaze on her face, as though my eies were bodkins to sticke in her haire.[148] Let me have my love answered, and you shall finde me faithfull, in which if you make delaies, I cannot be patient, the winde calls me away, and with the winde, awaie shall my affections.[149]

The second Letter.

My duetie to your L[adyship] remembered &c. Being readie to take shipping, I heard that her Majesty would honor Ricort, with her presence, which wrought no small content, but to have made it ful, I wished I might have seene it. In this place is no choise of anie thing, whereby I might signifie my dutifull affection, but that which a Souldier maketh his chiefest choise, a sword, which most humblie I desire to have presented to her highnes. With this protestation pourde from my hart, that in her service, I will spende the bloud of my hart. Eloquence and I, am vowde enemies, loialty, and I, sworne brothers, what my words cannot effect, my sworde shall.[150]

The thirde Letter from the Sea coast.

My duetie humbly resembred, the same time that I received letters that her Majesty would be at Ricort, the winde served for Britaigne; I was over joied with both, yet stoode in a mamering [151] whether I should take the opportunity of the winde, which I long expected or ride poste to do my duetie, which I most desired, necessitye controled affection, that bid me unlesse I could keepe the winde in a bagge,[152] to use the windes when they blew, I obaide yet, wishing that they would turne for a while, to serve my turne, being unfurnished, of al presents I would have this my excuse that cheapside[153] is not in my Shippe, and therefore having nothing to offer but my Trunchion the honour which I received of her Majestie, by whom I am only to be commaunded, and ever else let me be only miserable and ever.[154]

These Letters read, and the presents delivered, the olde man kneeling downe ended thus:

That my sonnes, have remembered their dueties, it is my harts comfort, that your Majestie accepteth them, their harts heaven. If fortune, and fidelitie had bin twinnes, they might have beene as rich, as faithfull, but this is the Jubyle[155] of my life, that their faithes are without spot, and your Majesty I hope, confident, without suspition. Among my joies, there is one griefe, that my daughter, the Mistris of a Moole hil,[156] hath so much forgotten; that most she should remember, duetie. I doubt not her excuse, because shee is a woman, but feare the truth, of it, because it must be to her soveraigne. For my selfe, my crowe, and all our birds, this I promise, that they are all; as faithfull in their feathers, as they were in their shels.

This being done, there was sweete musicke, and two sonnets which ended, her Majesty went in.

On munday morning, as her Majesty was to take horse, a messenger, comming out of Jersey, and bringing a Daysie of golde, set with Rubies, delivered it to her Majestie, with this speech.

At length, though verie late, I am come, from the Ladie of the Moold hill, sent long since, but the passage troublesome, at every miles end, a lover, at every sentence end a lie, I staide to heare, the conclusions,[157] and found nut-browne gyrles to be cheapned. But none to be bought, but the amyable. Thus much for my excuse, now for my Mistris, who hearing, that your Majesty would enter this cabbine, was astonished, with joie, and doubt, joie, for so great honour done to her father. Doubt, by what meanes shee might shew her duety to your Majesty. At the last, sitting upon the top of a moole hill, she espied, a red Daysie, the fairest flower, that barren place[158] doth yeeld, which, with all humilitie she presents to your Majestie, it hath no sweetnes, yet manie vertues, her hart hath no tongue, but infinite affections, In you she saith are all vertues, and towards you all her affections.[159]

Both Lord Norris and his wife were tied to Elizabeth by long acquaintance and family loyalties. His father had been one of the young men executed with Anne Boleyn as her 'lovers'; hers, Lord Williams of Tame, had shown kindness to Elizabeth when, as a state prisoner under her sister, she had visited Rycote (the house came through Lady Norris). They entertained Elizabeth there on at least five occasions, in 1566, 1568, 1570, 1575 and 1592, and were eager for her to come to them: in 1582, Lady Norris was upset because the Earl of Leicester had dissuaded Elizabeth from visiting Rycote as the insalubrious weather had made the roads difficult of passage.[160] The entertainment is highly personal, and even more simple than Bisham in its *mise-en-scène*; besides himself, Lord Norris needed only the musicians, and the four messengers who brought the letters, and one of these may have doubled the carrying of the daughter's letter and that of one of the sons. The gifts from the family are lavish, but also highly personal, referring as they do to the quality of the giver: the enormous number of pins and jewels given to Elizabeth, both on her Progresses and at New-Year, seems to have been not just the result of their being small and suitable, combining portability with compact richness and the possibility of neat mythological or personal allusion. The Elizabethans seem to have favoured the Christmas-tree style of dressing, sticking jewels all over for a glittering effect; the numerous parts into which contemporary costume broke down[161] all required to be pinned or tied together,[162] and Elizabeth herself passed them out as gifts for occasional services, so that her supply was in need of replenishment.[163]

The Rycote entertainment forms no long part of Elizabeth's stay at the house (28th September–11th October, which is quite long for a progress-visit). The speeches take about twelve minutes to read: even allowing for the music and the audience-reaction, the whole cannot have taken more than half, or possibly three-quarters, of an hour, and the welcoming and farewell speeches must have taken less than five minutes each. It is more in the nature of a *divertissement* arranged for a family friend than a lavish spectacular such as those mounted at Kenilworth or Elvetham, or a display of regional loyalty like Cowdray.

14. *The drawbacks of entertaining the Queen*

Whatever the cheapness of the staging of Lord Norris's entertainment, his gifts were more lavish than was considered necessary. A worried prospective host was informed that it would be considered adequate were his wife to present the Queen with a fine ruff or waistcoat:[164] the gift was probably the least of the expenses to which the eager welcomers of the Queen would be put. Whether they stayed to welcome her, like the Norrises, or merely vacated their house in her favour, like the recipients of the advice about the gifts,[165] the expense and disruption involved in entertaining Elizabeth and her train was enormous.[166] The plan made out by Lord Burleigh for the entertainment of the Queen at Theobalds in 1583 gives an indication of the difficulties involved:

Of the Roomes and Lodgyngs in the two Courts at Theobalds, 27 May, 1583.
　　Roomes and Lodgyings in the first Court, beinge the Base Court.
　　　　The South side beneathe.
　　The brewhouse.
　　The backhouse.
　　The laundrie.
　　A chamber for joynores from the
　　steare-foot Eastward.
　　A chamber next to that Westward ⎫ For the
　　from the steare-foot Westward, Chamber. ⎬ Groomes of the Privie
　　an other chamber next thereto ⎭ Chamber
　　Westward.

The same syde above at one steares-head.

One chamber over the backhouse towards the brewhouse.	For the Officers of the sellor and pantrye.
One other chamber next to that Westward.	For the Queene's Cookes.

The same syde above at an other steares-head on the left-hand.

One chamber at the East end of the entrie above the steare.	For Mr. Howard and Mr. Edward Norrice.
One other next to it Westward.	For the Clerk of the Kitchine.
One other next to the steare-head.	For the Squires of the Bodie.

And on the right-hand of the same steare.

One at the Steare-head.	For the Gentlemen Ushers.
One other with a chimney.	For my Lady of Lincolne.[167]

The North syde beneath.

A longe rooffe that served for the Joyners.	For a common hall and a buttery.
A little roome that serveth the Paynter.	For the Groome Porter.
Another lardge longe roome that serveth for a stoarehouse.	One part for the wardrobe, another part for pallets for the Lords servants that lack lodginge.

The same syde above.

Four servants chambers to be distributed by the Usher.	For Mr. Farnham, Mr. Novell, Mr. Bowes, Mr. Bronkard, Mr. Goringe, &c.

Roomes and Lodgings in the Inner Court.

Beneath Southward.

At the entry of the gate.	The Porter's lodge.
In the corner, a chamber with a baye windowe towardes the Base Court, with an inner roome openinge towards the greate garden.	The robes.
Twoe roomes westward.	
One chamber at the East end of the chappell.	
The chappel under the withdrawinge-chamber.	
The greate parlor under the privie chamber, with a wyne cellor under it.	The presence chamber.

On the West syde.

The hall.	The Queen's great chamber.
The pantrye.	
The buttery, with a butterye for beare under the hall.	
A Winter parlor over the	

surveying place, openinge Easte
and West.
   Under the grounde Northwarde.
The kitchin, with bylinge-house
scullery, pastry, and larders.
Another kitchin and larder under
the ground.
The Steward's chamber at the
East end of the court.   } A platehouse.
   The second stage in the Inner   Court.
Over the gate, a gallery painted
with the Armes of the Noblemen
and Gentlemen of England in
Trees.
   Southward.
A chamber, named the Lord
Admirall's chamber, with an inner } The Lord Admirall.
chamber openinge towards the
garden.
Another chamber, named the
Earle of Warwick's chamber, with } The Erle of Warwick.
a pallett-chamber.
Another chamber, named the Lord
Keper's chamber, under the   } The Ladie Stafforde.
Queen's bed-chamber.
Another roome, beinge the closett
over the chapell, and under the
withdrawinge-chamber.
   Upon the same stage, retorninge to the Lord Admirall's chamber,
      there are,
One chamber, with a pallett-
chamber, named the . . . having   } The Ladie Marques.
a steare downeward towards the
East into a garden.
One chamber, with a pallett-
chamber, named the . . . having   } For the Lord Howard.
a steare downewards the East into
a garden.
One chamber in a tower next
under the Erle of Leicester's   } The Lord Hunsdon.
chamber, with two pallett-
chambers.
And one other chamber, called
the Still House chamber.   } The Erle of Leicester's servants.
   The South syde, a third stage.
A Gallery for the Queen's Majestie .

At the South end in a tower one chamber, with two pallett-chambers.	} The Erle of Leicester.
At the East syde of the same gallery, towards the Base Court, in a garrett two roomes.	1. The Gentlewomen of the Privie Chamber. 2. Theire servants.

At the North-west end of the Gallery.

Two chambers, whereof one with a chymney.	The Gentlewomen of the Bedchamber.
A bed-chamber in a turrett.	The Queen's Majestie.
An inner dyneinge-chamber over the clossett.	The Queen's withdrawinge-chamber.
A dyneinge-chamber. A fourth stage.	The Queen's privie chamber.
A chamber in the uppermost part of the South-east turrett.	} Mrs. Blanche.[168]
A chamber in the turrett, over the Queen's bedchamber.	
A chamber, with a pallett-chamber over the privie chamber.	Sir Christopher Hatton, Vice-chamberlaine.
A gallery over the hall, with a closett vawted with stone for evidences.[169]	

The North syde of the said Inner Court.

In the second stage, beginninge at the North end of the painted gallery.

A chamber over the Steward's chamber, with an inner chamber towards the privie garden, both with chymnyes, and one pallett-chamber.	Mr. Grevell, Mr. Rawley, Mr. Gordge, Mr. Cooke, &c.
A second chamber Westward, with a pallett-chamber over the privie kitchin.	} Sir Thomas Henneage.
A third chamber Westward, named the Erle of Rutland's chamber, with a pallett-chamber.	} Mr. Secretarie Walsingham.
A fourth chamber, named the Ladie Veare's chamber, with a pallett-chamber and a labbye.	} The Ladie Cobhame.
For the third stage.	
A gallerie, named the suitors gallerie, with a roome like a square.	} The Lord Treasurer's table.
A chamber at the West end of the gallery.	

A chamber at the West end thereof, with a pallett-chamber.	The Lord Treasurer's Bed-chamber.
At the West end, and terninge Southward towards the hall, two lodgings.	The Lady Burghley.
For the fourth stage. A single chamber in the turret, over the East end of the suitor's gallery. Another single chamber in the tower, at the West end of the gallery.	An evidence-house.[170]

What Burleigh had to cater for was not just Elizabeth and her court, but that Court's servants, the servants' servants, the Queen's private kitchen staff, and the administrative staff that was necessary even when she was away from London on holiday. He must make arrangements for the accommodation elsewhere of his own (large) household, give suitable lodgings to noblemen jealous of their privileges and quick to spot a slight, and, most important, cater to the moods of the Queen so that the favourite of the moment should be within easy reach. It is notable that the Earl of Leicester is given lodgings corresponding to those of the Queen, with her favourite cousin, Hunsdon, close to him, but that the courtiers put nearest the Queen are Hatton, presumably as leading favourite, and the group of young men, Greville, Ralegh, Gorges, Coke, and &c. (this last presumably intended to allow for any new favourite who might arise between the drawing-up of Burleigh's plan and the Queen's arrival at his house). If this was a daunting task for Burleigh, with a huge house, a genius for administration, and *au fait* with the latest rivalries and successes at Court, for a poorer man whose modest house happened to lie conveniently along the route of a progress it must have been a nightmare. Despite contributions by neighbours, and the assurance, for what it was worth, that his expenses for the maintenance of the Court would be reimbursed, the provision of food for the Queen and her suite was a major undertaking,[171] and the host might expect to spend between five hundred and two thousand pounds, depending on the length of the Queen's visit.[172] He would almost certainly have to spend something of the same order on clothes for himself and his household, since it is difficult to imagine anyone having the Queen to stay and not buying themselves a new outfit in which to welcome her. It is hard to translate Elizabethan values into modern ones, but multiplication by a factor of thirty or forty probably gives the right equivalent. The host might expect to have his park denuded of deer, his gardens trampled, and his plate and linen stolen.[173] For a few days all was enchantment, and then Elizabeth and her suite moved on and left their host surveying the wreck of his fairyland.

Nor was the Queen the easiest of guests. She was capable of the most appalling and brutal rudeness, as when she thanked her hostess, Archbishop Parker's wife, with the words, 'Madam I may not call you; mistress I am afraid to call you; yet, as I know not what to call you, I thank you:',[174] her disapproval of the marriage of the clergy extending as far as her own primate. She shared with more modern queens the ability to spot a valuable piece of furniture, and was liable to help herself to it in compliment to her host: at a visit to the Lord Keeper, Puckering, in 1595, 'To grace his lordship the more, she of herself took from him a salt, a spoon, and a fork, of fair agate'.[175] She might throw a tantrum for causes as diverse as the strength of the beer,[176] the tenor of the entertainment,[177] or the religion of the host.[178] Her suite was notorious for its pilfering of plate and linen, and although theoretically such losses would be made good, in practice too often they were not.[179] Small wonder that the suggestion that Elizabeth might visit was as often seen as the work of an enemy as of a friend,[180] and that for every couple like the Norrises, eager to welcome her, there were several whose reaction on hearing of the proposed visit was stark panic and a desperate search for reasons as to why the visit should not be made at this time.[181]

15. The present selection of entertainments

The entertainments here presented are not necessarily literarily the most distinguished of those presented to Elizabeth, but they are, together with those included in the text of the Introduction, among the most representative. There are three substantial omissions, which should perhaps be mentioned, although two of them are dealt with at some length in the Introduction to the Ditchley Entertainment. These are the two entertainments mounted by Leicester at Wanstead in 1578, and Kenilworth in 1575, and Lee's Woodstock Entertainment, again of 1575. *The Lady of May*, the Wanstead entertainment, written by Sir Philip Sidney, is literarily the most distinguished of the Elizabethan entertainments, a charming combination of comedy, sylvan/pastoral debate, and compliment to the Queen. But because it is by Sidney, it has been substantially discussed in books and articles,[182] and has recently been published in a new edition.[183] *The Lady of May* has, however, been treated rather in isolation, and hopefully this book may be of some use in setting it in its *genre* – particularly as what may be Sidney's other incursion into the entertainment form, *The Four Foster Children of Desire*, is included. The Kenilworth Entertainment was famous in its own time – it is the only one of which two different printed accounts survive – and has remained to the present the epitome of the Entertainments mounted for Elizabeth. It may be doubted, however, when it is compared with those printed here, and with the fragmentary but charming Harefield Entertainment which has had regretfully to be omitted for reasons of space, whether it owes its eminence to its literary quality and spectacular effects or to the popularizing power of Sir Walter Scott's *Kenilworth*, in which it forms a major episode (1821, III, 70ff). Certainly the popularity of the castle itself as a venue of tourism must be at least partly ascribed to the fame of the novel in which it stars – its dilapidated condition renders it otherwise much less attractive than other historic buildings in the area. Both accounts of the Kenilworth entertainment are available in comparatively accessible form,[184] so it was decided to omit it from this volume. *The Hermit's Tale at Woodstock*[185] is also easily available, and was omitted for this reason, a summary of it being given in the introduction to the Ditchley entertainment.

The entertainments chosen for this volume are, it is hoped, representative of the spectrum of Elizabethan entertainments. From the small-scale, personal divertissements of the Norrises and Russells, through the expressions of regional loyalty at Cowdray, the lavish Italianate aquaticisms of Elvetham, to the urban political chivalry of *The Four Foster Children of Desire*, and its rural counterpart at Ditchley, they exhibit the diversity of forms used to express her subjects' feelings about the Queen and her relationship to them and to her own position as head of Church and State. Two omissions should perhaps be mentioned. There is no example of the Prologues and Epilogues frequently added for the Court performances of plays,[186] nor is there any example of the Christmas celebrations, in which a visiting comic masque from the Inns of Court might take the place of the ceremonial visit of the Boy Bishop to a medieval Great household.[187]

The evidence for the staging of these entertainments must be largely inductive. Only the engraving of the Elvetham entertainment and the masque-episode on the Unton biographical portrait[188] survive to give any idea of the appearance of such an occasion, and other conclusions must be based on the work done on the Jacobean masque,[189] depictions of Elizabethans in fancy dress, either as part of the chivalric cult of Elizabeth, or for some allegorical purpose of their own,[190] and odd fragments of evidence in book-illustrations[191] and tomb-sculpture.[192] From these it seems evident that the occasions were lavishly costumed, but that they still relied on some decorated topographical feature (even if this was artificially pre-created)[193] or on some moveable set-piece, either of the pageant-cart, or of the pantomime-horse type,[194] to provide a setting. Although the influence of French and Italian water-fêtes may perhaps be detected in the water-pageants at Kenilworth, Norwich and Elvetham, the vessels used on the water are much less sophisticated than the galleys at the *naumachia* in the Pitti Palace in Florence of 1589,[195] or the whale and barges depicted on the Valois tapestries.[196] Nevertheless the Valois tapestries probably give the best impression of the appearance of an Elizabethan entertainment, and we should envisage them as being less mechanically sophisticated, but no less visually rich, than the fêtes of Catherine de' Medici. Just as in the theatre the amount spent on costume was lavish, so it seems likely that this was true of the entertainments; the Rainbow Portrait of Elizabeth at Hatfield shows the splendour that such costumes could attain, and even the masque in the Unton memorial picture is costumed with a richness which contrasts with the more sombre garb of the participants in the banquet.[197] In both cases it is noteworthy that the costumes (apart from the naked torchbearers of the Unton picture) are basically contemporary in style, with mythological trimmings: the Unton masquers (who are, interestingly, wearing red masks[198]) indicate their roles mainly by their headgear: Diana and her maidens wear the loose hair of virginity and elaborate coronets, Mercury has wings on his sixteenth-century hat, and on his back, and presumably (though these are hidden) on his ankles as well; Elizabeth in the Hatfield picture classicizes her emblematically-embroidered contemporary dress with a heavy cloak thrown toga-wise around it. The classicism of the costumes of Buontalenti had evidently not yet reached England, nor was it to do so until the years of Jones's supremacy.[199]

Even if it is difficult to reconstruct the visual aspect of these Elizabethan entertainments, their comparative neglect through the past years of growing interest in the masque seems difficult to explain. This must be at least partly due to the relative inaccessibility of texts of the entertainments, which it is hoped this book will do something to counteract. Not only do these entertainments provide a link between the diversions and mummings of the medieval and early Tudor courts, and the masques of James I and Charles I, so that it can be seen how a native tradition was welded with French and Italian influence to provide the great achievement of Jones and Jonson, but they give further evidence of the Elizabethan obsession with self-dramatization: the desire to make the outward events of the individual life reflect the truth of the individual's social and spiritual state.[200] They make apparent the centrality of the cult of Elizabeth in the thought of the Elizabethan court, and they illuminate the need of all female monarchs, even the most popular and successful, to reconcile their femaleness with their power: they suggest, indeed that the most successful female monarchs may be those who best manipulate this reconciliation.

TEXT

A Note on the Texts

In general I have tried to keep as close as possible to the orthography and punctuation of the originals, but I have silently corrected obvious printer's errors, for example transposition of letters or words, as in 'huose' or 'the and'. The punctuation seems in most cases to relate to oral delivery, and the stops indicate pauses or breaths of varying lengths.

The versions of Cowdray and Elvetham used by Nichols have proved impossible to trace: because his versions are fuller than those now available I have chosen to print from his text, and have noted the variants in the other editions.

The *Four Foster Children* has always been assumed to exist in one version only, but the variations between the version printed by Nichols and that used here (BM C 33 a 38 – referred to as BM 2) are so great as to suggest that there were in fact two editions. The Huntingdon library version seems to be the same as that printed here, but the other BM copy (C 33 a 4) is unavailable at the time of going to press, so it is uncertain whether Nichols was printing from an edition now lost. I hope to be able to comment further on this when the second BM copy becomes available again.

Variants noted do not include simple changes in spelling.

Throughout the notes to all the texts, 'N' = Nichols.

The Four Foster Children of Desire: 1581

Although this is not one of the Accession Day Tilts, it shares much of their imagery, assumptions, and practices. The basic situation posited is that of a medieval romance, with lovers jousting in order to win their lady's favour. The conventional castle and the seige engine which moves to the sound of hidden music and shoots scented powders and waters are taken from the medieval traditions of English Court entertainment, which often included attempts to storm mock-fortresses, defended with scented waters and comfits.[1] The Tilt itself, with its preparatory challenge, emblematic entrances and speeches of the knights (which may perhaps be compared, in their tiny narratives of the incidents which brought the knights to the Tilt, with the Breton *Lai*) and the entry of Sir Henry Lee as an Unknown Knight, is very close to what we know of the conventions of the Accession Day celebrations.

This entertainment is, however, far more than an Accession Day Tilt. It is a spectacular occasion mounted to impress visiting Ambassadors, seeking Elizabeth in marriage for the Duke of Alençon, fourth son of Catherine de' Medici and Henri II, and heir apparent to the French throne. The court from which they came was renowned for its sophisticated pageantry,[2] and besides the display of loyalty and assurance of the security of the leisured classes of England inherent in this entertainment,[3] it was important that the English Court should not seem provincial and old-fashioned in its pageantry. Certainly the costumes, mechanism, and splendour of the display mounted sounds as though it was not unworthy to stand beside those of the Valois tapestries.[4]

The prospective marriage was generally unpopular, most strongly opposed by the party of the Earl of Leicester, who sympathized with those Protestants who were firmly against a Catholic marriage. This opposition had been voiced by Sir Philip Sidney, Leicester's nephew and probable heir, in his *Letter to Queen Elizabeth*.[5] It is usually dated at late 1579, and it is assumed that its publication caused Sidney to retreat from court in disgrace, and write the *Arcadia*:[6] Sidney's latest editors suggest that it may not in fact have alienated him from the Queen,[7] and this entertainment would seem to add force to their argument.

For the message in the tournament is clear. The Four Foster Children realize that they have overreached themselves, that Perfect Beauty is unattainable, that Desire by its nature cannot have what it desires, and, yielding to the Queen, withdraw from the contest. The significance of this would not be lost on the French audience.

Alençon is a foster child of Desire, and he will never attain the Fortress of Perfect Beauty to which he is laying siege, for it is impregnable: as it proved. Negotiations dragged on, and did not officially conclude until Alençon's death in 1584, but it became steadily clearer, even when Alençon arrived to pursue his courtship in person, that the show of the Four Foster Children meant what it said. Sidney's presence in it is not, therefore, incongruous: the spokesman of the party opposed to the marriage had been chosen to demonstrate to the French that his party's arguments had prevailed.

The text of the speeches is interesting, for they may be, at least partly, by Sidney himself. Sidney's editors concede that he may have 'had a hand in devising'[8] the entertainment, but do not print it in their volume of *Miscellaneous Prose*, although Ringler prints the two lyrics sung at the tilt among the possible poems, and is inclined to accept them.[9] The arguments for the acceptability of the poems can be made to apply to the prose speeches, certainly those of the Four Foster Children themselves;[10] they are basically stylistic: the style of the speeches does not particularly resemble that of Greville, either in his poems, or his prose; Sidney was probably engaged on the *Arcadia* at the time of this entertainment, and was therefore certainly in practice at writing romance-matter, and the speeches, with their ornate imagery and repeated parentheses, are Sidnean in feeling. Readers will have to decide for themselves (a comparison with the extended passage from *Arcadia* printed on pages 32–34 may be helpful) how close these similarities are. Certainly Sidney had already written one Entertainment for the Queen: *The Lady of May*, performed at Wanstead in 1578 or 1579, and Ringler accepts as his the *Dialogue betweene two shepherds, utterd in a pastorall shew, at Wilton*.[11] It is true that professional writers were sometimes – perhaps, possibly, usually – employed by those entertaining the Queen (for instance, Gascoigne at Kenilworth in 1575). But such use of a substitute rather argued an inability on the entertainer's part to devise a suitable entertainment than any intrinsic reason why he should not do so: Lee seems to have written or devised both the Woodstock and Ditchley entertainments, and provided much of the material for the Accession Day Tilts,[12] and it would be natural that any group containing Sidney and Greville would seek internally for its writer. One would expect Sidney to write the speeches for the pages of the foster Children, even if the Defendants looked elsewhere for the authors of their effusions. Lee himself seems to have regarded, or presented, Sidney, as something of a presiding genius of these occasions: the Accession Day Tilt in 1586, the year of his death, was evidently dedicated to his memory,[13] and in his own

Arcadia Sidney presents himself as the deviser of his own imagery.[14] It is always difficult with Sidney to sort out the man from the myth: the expectations that were held for him, both intellectual and financial (he was Leicester's heir), his premature death caused by an access of chivalric feeling, his archetypal self-denial *in extremis*, above all his authorship of both *Astrophil and Stella* and the *Arcadia*, would have made him the epitome of Elizabethan chivalry whether or not he had been a good jouster (which he was) and concerned with the courtly Tilts. But it would be natural to assume that he was involved in the devising of at least some of the Tilts in which he took part, and that *The Four Foster Children of Desire* is an insufficiently recognized example of his prose, and as such, should be set beside his other entertainment, *The Lady of May*.[15]

TEXTS

SR. 1581 July 1. 'The tryumphe Shewed before the Quene and the Ffrench Embassadors.' *Robert Walgrave.* (Arber. ii. 396).

ND. 'A briefe declaration of the shews, devices, speeches, and inventions, done & performed before the Queene's Majestie, & the French Ambassadours, at the most valiaunt and worthye Triumph, attempted and executed on the Munday and Tuesday in Whitson weeke last, Anno 1581. – Collected, gathered, penned and published, by Henry Goldwel, Gen.' *Robert Waldegrave.* BM: C.33.a.38 (Referred to in the notes as "BM2"). (The discrepancies between the version printed here, and that given by the usually reliable Nichols suggest that there were two editions of the work; see the Note on the texts).

> A briefe declaration of the shews, devices, speeches, and inventions, done & performed before the Queene's Majestie, & the French Ambassadours, at the most valiant and worthye Triumph, attempted and executed on the Munday and Tuesday in Whitson weeke last, Anno 1581. – Collected, gathered, penned, and published by Henry Goldwel,[1] Gen. Imprinted at London, by Robert Waldegrave, dwelling without Temple-barre, neere unto Sommerset-House.

To the verie worshipfull and his approved patrone,

Master Rowland Brasebridge of great Wickombe, in the countie of Buck. Gen. his humble and faithful avowed: Henrie Goldwell wisheth that welfare which highteth eternall happiness.

Sir, I stande at a stay like the Ladie of Thessalie, and in a mammering maze like Alexanders man, the on making pitious plaintes in beholding the picture of her person, fearing shee shoulde not be fancied, and alwaies lamented when she wrote any letter, doubting it shoulde be disliked: The other wept in winter for extremitie of colde, and sorowed, in summer to remember the returne of Hyems. So rest I assayled with such perplexities, and frozen with like feare, not only doubting to discover these honourable Actions, for feare of the misreporting: but also fearing mine owne unworthinesse and want of skillfull eloquence to set forth so woorthie a matter (as was the last Triumph perfourmed before her Majestie:) Yet I considered with my selfe, better an ill reporter then a dumme speaker, better badly laid open then quite forgotten, and better Porredge then no repast? When Appollo is a sheepe[2] then Pan is chiefe minstrill: when Pallas is absent, then Seres is eloquent: when Tullie is out of town, then Crassus may crake[3] of his cunning. Therefore sith no man writeth at all of these worthies, nor no person publisheth the exploits of these nobles, rather then oblivion should diminish their merits, I have attempted the writing. And so nere as I could I have made a collection both their names, speaches, and chiefest inventions, which as they bee, I present to your presence in name of a newse or noveltie, knowing none more worthie then your self, to whom to present this Pamphlet, both for your knowledge in approved Martial Chivalrie, nor none whom I honour or owe more dutifull loyaltie. As report hath rong forth your deserved worthynes, and flying Fame hath resounded your service, both in greene youth, and these your grave yeres, employed as well in warres as in peace, in quailing the enemie, as in ruling your countrey, in adventuring abroad, in advertising[4] at home, then a conductor,[5] now a director,[6] then valiant as Mars, nowe made a civill Magistrate, then boldly in battell till the last blowe, nowe busied at home in trayning up souldiers, and to be short, then accounted a Captaine, like Achilles for courage, nowe esteemed as Scipio for singuler counsaile. And knowing it would delight you to heare of the towardnesse of our English Nobles, and of the courage of our courtlie crue, sith you were absent at the perfourming of these pleasures, I have at this present for your recreation thus certified these courtly and knightly discourses, to you who in times past have bene, as gallant a Courtier as a valliant souldier: But if you ere this have bene tolde of this Triumph, it may be you heard not the names of the parties; and though you have heard of the number of rumours, yet paradventure you knowe not the effect of their speaches, and though you have had of their several coppies:[7] yet happely you misse of their sundrie inventions and though you be privie to most of these matters, yet hope I you will like nere the worse of my labours, nor make lesse account of this my wel meaning: therefore as one more adventurus then warie, more presumptuous then wittie, more foolehardie then praiseworthy, I submit my selfe to the knees of your courtesie, to like of me and my present, hoping to find that favour at your handes which an Emperour once shewed to his simplest Subject, who more esteemed his poore dish of water, then the gifts of gold of his richest marchants, the one proceeding of love to his power, the other in hope of a greater gain? whose Image if you imitate I pronounce myselfe happie, and the gain that I looke for, is your gracious goodwill? whereby I shall be emboldened to attempt some worke more worthy, to gratifie your goodnes and to make more manifest my dutifull loyaltie, wishing you nowe and ever al things wordly to your vertuous will, & after the time of this transitorie life, your soule may sing *Alleluia* with the number of thelect, and reap that reward which remaineth endlesse.

Yours most willing to be commaunded, & most desirous to discharge his duety. H.G.

A Declaration of the Triumph shewed before the Queenes Majestie, and the French Ambassadours, on Whitson[8] Munday & Tuesday.

To beginne particularly to wright of these attempts, and briefly to runne over eache severall action, the cause of the same is firste to be considered. After the arrival of

the French Ambassadours, and upon their comming to
the English court, The Nobles and Gentlemen of the
same, desirous to shew them al courtesie possible fittest
for such estates, and to sporte them with all courtly
pleasure, agreede among them to prepare a Triumphe,
whiche was very quickly concluded, and being devised in
moste sumptuous order, was by them performed in as
valiant a manner, to their endlesse fame and honour.
The cheefe, or challengers in these attemptes, were these.
The Earle of Arundel,[9] the Lord Windsore[10] Master
Philip Sidney, and Master Fulke Grevill,[11] Who calling
themselves the four Foster Children of Desire, made their
invention of the foresaide Triumphe in this order and
forme following.

The
excellent
invention
of the
Triumph

The Gallory or place at the end of the Tiltyard
adjoining to her Majesties house at Whitehall, whereas
her person should be placed, was called and not without
cause, the Castle or *Fortresse of perfect beautie*, for as much
as her highness should be there included, whereto the
said Foster children layde Tytle and claime as their due
by discent to belong unto them. And uppon deniall or
any repulse from that their desired patrimonie, they
vowed to vanquishe & conquer by force who so shoulde
seeme to withstand it. For the accomplishing whereof
they sent their challenge or first defiance to the Queens
majestie: which was uttred by a boy on Sunday, the
sixteenth of April last, as her Majesty came from the
Chappel, who being apparelled in red and white, as a
Martial massenger of Desires fostered Children, without
making any precise reverence at all, uttered these
speeches of defiaunce, from his masters to her Majestie,
the effect whereof ensueth.

The first
defie or
challenge

O Lady, that doth intitle the titles you possesse with
the honour of your worthinesse, rather crowning the
great crowne you holde, with the fame to have so
excellinge an owner, then you receivinge to your selfe any
encrease, keeping that outward ornament? Vouchsafe
with patient attention to heare the wordes which I by
commandement am here to deliver unto you, wherein if
your eares (used to the thankes giving of your people
and the due prayses of the earth) shall feele a stately
disdayne to heare once the sounde of a defie? yet dare I
warrant my selfe so farre upon the reply deceiving show

of rare beauty, as that malice can not fall from so fayre a minde upon the sely[12] messenger, whose mouth is a servant to others direction: Know ye therefore al onely Princesse, that hereby (for far of they are never) there lyes encamped the foure long haples, now hopeful fostered children of Desire: who having bin a great while nourished up with that infective milke, and to to much care of their fiery fosterer, (though full oft that dry nurse dispaier indevered to waine[13] them from it) being nowe as strong in that nurture, as they are weake in Fortune, incouraged with the valiaunt counsaile of never fainting Desire, and by the same assured, that by right of inheritaunce even from ever, the Fortresse of Beautie doth belong to her Fostered Children, Lastly, finding it blazed by all tongues, ingraved in all hearts, and proved by all eies that this fortresse built by nature is seated in this Realme: These foure I say and say againe, thus nourished, thus animated thus entituled, and thus enformed, doe will you by me, even in the name of Justice, that you will no longer exclude vertuous Desire from perfect Beautie? Whereto if you yelde, (O yelde for so all reason requireth) then have I no more to say, but rejoice that my sayings hath obteined so rightfull, and yet so blissefull a request. But if (alasse but let not that be needful) Beautie be accompanied with disdainfull pride, and pride waighted on by refusing crueltie. Then must I denounce unto you (Woe is me, answere before it be denounced) that they determine by request to accomplish their claim, And because they will better testifie to the worlde, they have bene brought up under the wings of honourable Desire, this honourable fore warning they sende you. That upon the xxiiii day of this month of April they will besiege that fatal Fortresse, vowing not to spare (if this obstinacie continue) the swoorde of faithfulnesse, and the fire of affection? Nowe if so it fall out, the worthie knights of your Court (moved with passion in them selves) disdaine of my senders boldnesse, or partiall liking (whiche I moste doubt[14]) to the majestie of your eyes, will either bid them battell before they approch, or suffering them to approch, will after labor to levye[15] the siege, They protest to meet them in what sort they will chuse, wishing onely it may bee perfourmed before your own eies, whome they know as even in judgement, as daintie in chusing, where if so they list. First at the Tilte in so many courses, as your self shall please to appoint. And then if any wil call them to the course of the field with Launce and sword, they hope to give such true proofes of their valler, as at least shal make their desires more noble vowing on the other side, that if before the night part the fray, they do not overcome all them that come in against them, they wil yeeld themselves slaves unto you for ever?[16] This therefore O Queene (greater in that you are Queen of your selfe, then in passing the whole compasse of the earth) have I delivered my charge, not as a challenge to your knightes? against whome, (but in so just a cause) they acknowledge themselves unable to match the meanest, But as a plaine proclaimation of Warre, unlesse the Fortresse of Beautie, that hath woon so many to lose themselves, be speedily surrendered: And now it shal be seene what knights you have, whom Beautie may draw to resist a rightful title, And I for my pore part moved by that I see in you (thogh I serve your enemies) will daily pray that all men may see you, & then you shal not feare any arms of adversaries: Or if enimies you must have, that either they may have the mindes of them that send me, or their fortunes in that they have long desired.[17]

Urgent causes why the challenge was defered

At which day abovesaid for certain urgent occasions, the saide Challenge and Triumph by her Majesties commandement, was deferred till the first day of May. At which day for like causes it was further deferred til the next Munday following, beeing the eighth day of May: And so till Whitson Munday, when they first began to perfourme it.

The order of rowling trench with most excellent inventions

The said day being come, the foure Foster children had made preparation to besiege the Fortresse of Beawtie. And thereto had provided a frame of wood which was covered with Canvas, & painted outwardly in such excellent order, as if it had bene very naturall earth or moulde, and caried the name of a Rowling trench, which went on wheeles, which way soever the persons within did drive it.[18] Upon the top whereof was placed two Cannons of wood, so passing well coullered, as they seemed to be in deed two fayre fielde pieces of ordinances, and by them was placed two men for Gunners clothed in Crymson Sarcenet, with their baskets of erth for defence of their bodies by them. And also there stood on the top of the trench, an Ensigne bearer, in the same sute with the gunners, displaying his ensigne, and within the saide trench was cunningly conveyed, divers kinde of most excellent musicke against the castle of Beauty. These things thus al in a readinesse, the Challengers approched, & came from the Stable toward the Tyltyard, one after another in brave and excellent order. And the manner of their several entrings was as followeth.

The Earle of Arundels entrie the firste day

First, the Earle of Arundell entred the Tylteyarde, all in Gylt and engraven Armour, with Caparisons and furniture richly and bravely embrodered, having attendaunt on him, Two gentlemen ushers, iiii Pages riding on foure spare horses, and twentie of his Gentlemen. Al which aforesayde were apparrayled in shorte Clokes and venetian hose of Crymson velvet, layd with gold lace, doublets of yellow Satten, hattes of Crymson velvet with gold bands and yellow fethers, and yellow silke stocks. Then had hee sixe trumpetters that sounded before him. And xxxi yeomen that waited after him apparailed in Cassock coats, and venetian hose of Crimson velvet, layde on with red silke and golde lace, Dublets of yellow taffatie, Hats of crimson Taffatie, with yellowe feathers, and yellowe worsted stockings.

The Lorde Windsors entrie the first day

After him proceeded the Lord Windsore, in gilte and engraven Armour, with caparisons and furniture, richely embroydered with golde, having attendant on him foure Pages riding on foure spare horses, and foure and twentie gentlemen, All apparailed in short cloaks of scarlet, lined through with orange tawnie taffatie, & laide about with silver lace, Doublets of orange tawny Satten, venetian hose of orange tawny velvet, blacke velvet caps, with silver bandes and white feathers, and silvered rapiers & daggers, with scabberds of blacke velvet. Foure trumpetters, and two footemen in cassocke coats and venetian hose of orange tawnie velvet, and blacke velvet caps with silver bands & white fethers, foure groomes of his stable leading of his foure horses, in cassocke coats and venetian hose of orange tawnie taffatie, and orange tawnie feltes[19] with silver bands, and white fethers. Then had he three score yeomen in coates of Orenge tawnie clothe, with the Unicorne[20] of silver plate on their sleeves, and orange tawnie feltes with silver bands and white feathers.

Then proceeded M. Philip Sidney, in very sumptuous maner,[21] with armor part blewe,[22] & the rest gilt & engraven, with foure spare horses, having caparisons and furniture veri riche & costly, as some of cloth of gold embroidred with pearle, and some embrodred with gold and silver feathers, very richly & cunningly wrought, he had foure pages that rode on his four spare horses, who had cassock coats & venetian hose al of cloth of silver, layd with gold lace, & hats of the same with golde bands, and white fethers, and eache one a paire of white buskins.[23] Then had he a thirtie gentlemen & yeomen, & foure trumpetters, who were all in cassocke coats and venetian hose of yellow velvet, laid with silver lace, yellowe velvet caps with silver bands and white fethers, and every one a paire of white buskins. And they had uppon their coates, a scrowle or bande of silver, which came scarfe wise over the shoulder, and so downe under the arme, with this poesie, or sentence written upon it, both before and behinde, Sic nos non nobis.[24]

Then came M. Fulke Grevill, in gilt armour, with riche and fayre caparisons and furniture, having foure spare horsses with foure Pages riding upon them, and foure Trumpeters sounding before him, and a Twentie men gentlemen and yeomen attending upon him, who with the Pages & Trumpeters were all apparelled in loose Jerkins of Tawnie taffatie, cut and lined with yellowe sarsenet, & laied with golde lace, and cut downe the arme and set with loopes and buttons of golde, Veneta[24] in hose of the same lined as aforesaid, laied with golde lace downe the side with loopes and buttons of golde, with each a paire of yellow worsted stockings. And hatts of Tawnie Taffatie with golde bands and yellow Fethers. Having thus all entred the Tilteyard, they proceeded on with the rowling trenche before them, which staied against the Queene,[25] and they passed by, as though they would behold the Fortresse of Beauty, And so went about the Tilt,[26] At last the boie that uttered the first defiaunce pronounced these speeches to her Majestie.

If the message latelie delivered unto you had bene beleeved and followed. (O Queene) in whom the whole

The
second
defie or
chalenge
storie of vertue is written with the language of Beautie. Nothing should this violence have needed in your inviolate presence, your eyes which til now have bene onely wont to discerne the bowed knees of kneeling heartes, and inwardly tourned, found alwaies the heavenly peace of a sweete mind, Shoulde not nowe have their faire beames reflected with the showe of Armoure, shoulde not nowe be driven to see the furie of Desire, nor the fyery force of fury: But since so it is (alasse that so it is) that in the defence of obstinate refusal ther never groweth victory but by compassion? They are come, what neede I say more, you see them, ready in hart as you knowe, and able with handes as they hope, not only to assailing but to prevailing. Perchance you dispise the smalnesse of number, I say unto you, the force of Desire goes not by fulnesse of company. Nay rather Vew with what unresistable determination themselves approch, And howe not onely the heavens send their invisible

Meaning
the
musicke
within the
mount
Instrument to ayde them. But also the very earth the dullest of al the Elements which with naturall heaveinesse still strives to the sleepie Center, yet for advancing this enterprise is contented actively as you shal see to move it self upon it selfe, to rise up in height, That it may the better command the high & high minded

Wherewith
the mount
moved
and rose
up in
height
Fortresse? Many wordes when deedes are in field are tedious both unto the speaker and hearer, you see their forces but know not their fortunes, if you be resolved, it boots not, and threats dread not, I have discharged my charge, which was even when all thinges were ready for the assaulte, then to offer partlie[27] a thinge not so much unused as gratious in besiegers, you shal nowe be sommoned to yeld, which if it be rejected, then looke for the affectionate Allarme to bee followed with desirous Assaulte: The time approcheth for their approches: But no time shall stay me from wishing, that how soever this succeede, the worlde may long time enjoy hir cheefest ornament, which deckes it with her selfe, and herselfe with the love of goodnesse.

Which speach being ended, the Rowlling trench or Mounte of earth was mooved as nere the Queenes Majestie as might be, which being setled, the musike playd very pleasauntly, and one of the Boyes being then accompanied with Cornets, summoned the Fortresse with this (delectable)[28] song:

> Yeelde yeelde, O yeelde, you that this Forte do holde,
>   which seated is, in spotlesse honors fielde,
> Desires great force, no forces can withhold:
>   then to Desiers desire, O yeelde, O yeelde.
>
> Yeelde yeelde O yeelde, trust not on beauties pride,
>   fayrenesse though fayer, is but a feeble shielde,
> When strong Desire, which vertues love doth guide,
>   claymes but to gaine his due, O yeelde O yeelde
>
> Yeelde yeelde O yeelde, who first this Fort did make,
>   Did it for just Desires, true children builde,
> Such was his minde, if you another take:
>   defence herein doth wrong, O yeelde O yeelde,
>
> Yeelde yeelde O yeelde, now is it time to yeelde,
>   Before thassault beginne, O yeelde O yeelde.

When that was ended, another Boye turning him
selfe to the Foster children and their retinue, sung
this Allarme (with pleasant voice and seemlie
countenance):[29]

> Allarme allarme, here will no yeelding be,
>   such marble eares, no cunning wordes can charme,
> Courage therefore, and let the statelie see,
>   That naught withstandes Desire, Allarme allarme.
>
> Allarme allarme, let not their beauties move
>   remorse in you to doe this Fortresse harme,
> for since warre is the ground of vertues love,
>   no force, though force be used, Allarme allarme.
>
> Allarme allarme, companions nowe beginne,
>   about this[30] never conquered walles to swarme,
> More prayse to us we never looke to winne,
>   much may that was not yet, Allarme allarme.
>
> Allarme allarme, when once the flight is warme,
>   then shall you see them yelde. Allarme allarme.

The shooting of, of the two Canons, the one with sweet water and the

Which ended, the two Canons were shott off, the one
with sweet powder, and the other with sweete water, very
odoriferous and pleasaunt, and the noyse of the shooting
was very excellent consent of mellodie within the
Mounte: And after that, was store of prettie scaling

other with sweet poulder

ladders, and the footemen threwe Flowers and such fancies against the walles, with all such devices as might seeme fit shot for Desire, All which did continue till time the Defendaunts came in.

The manner of the defendants coming in

Then came in the defendaunts in most sumptuous manner, with every one his servants, Pages, and trumpeters, (having some more, some lesse) in such order as I have here under placed them, with every one his sundrie invention, which for that some of them be mistical and not knowne to manie,[31] I omit therefore for brevities sake to speake of anie, yet such speeches as weare spoken or presented for them to her Majestie, so manie as were, or at the least as I could come by,[32] I have here in their order placed them, whereby their inventions for whome they were spoken, and therein plainlie declared. Therefore I refer you to the reeding of them hereafter, But thus the defendaunts, entred the tilte yarde, one after an other as followeth.

The defendant names that run at Tilte

First M. Henry Grey, Sir Thomas Parat, M. Anthonie Cooke, M. Thomas Ratcliffe, Master Henrie Knowles, M. William Knowles, M. Robert Knowles, M. Frauncis Knowles, M. Raffe Bowes, M. Thomas Kelway, M. George Goring, M. William Tresham, M. Robert Alexander, M. Edwarde Dennie, M. Hercules Meautus, M. Edward Moore, M. Richard Skipwith, M. Richard Ward, M. Edward Digbie, M. Henry Nowell, M. Henry Brunkerd. And afterwards in the middest of the running, came in Sir Henrie Lea, as unknowne, and when he had broke his six staves, went out in like manner againe.

So passing on one after another, when Sir Thomas Parat and M. Cooke[33] came to the end of the Tilt, over aginst the Queens Majestie, one of their pages arraied like an Angel, utterd these speeches unto her.

The speeche of Sir Thomas Parrat and mastere Cooke, to the Queene

Dispayre, no not dispaire (moste high and happie Princesse) could so congeale the frozen knighte[34] in the ayer but that Desire, (ah sweete Desire) enforced him to behold the Sun on the earth, whereon as he was gasing with twinckling eye[35] (for who can behold such beames steadfastly), he begun to dissolve into droppes, melting with such delighte, that hee seemed to preferre the lingering of a certaine death, before the lasting of an uncertaine life, suche is the nature of engraven loyaltie, that it chuseth rather to have the body dissolved then the minde disliked, Thus consuming with content, (a sweete sicknesse is conceite) and pining with more than speakable passions, he suddenly beheld that Sunne to be besieged which he so devoutlie served, wherewith boiling in no lesse disdaine, then surprised with immoderate pensivenesse, he uttered these wordes: O Jove, if thou mean to resolve nature into contraries, why doe I live to see it, if into nothing, why doe I live at all, if the foote scale the head, there is no rest if Desire overshoote duetie, there is no reason, and where either of these are, there can be no rule. And so setting more sighes then maie be numbred by syphers, this present time, (ah greefe) this present time, that honest and fayre harted frozen Knighte died, (What said I) even that which againe with grief I must say died, whose ghost making speedy passage into the Elisian fieldes (for what more

swifte then a soule) in the middest of the infernall multitude, with screeches, cryes, and clamers, made both Heaven and hell to redouble this Eccho: O times, O men, O corruption of manners, the Sunne is besieged, the Sunne (O mischiefe) the Sunne is besieged which strange and unacquainted tearmes, caused not onelie murmuring amongst the Ghosts beneathe, but a musing amongst the Gods above, who as well to represse the tumultes which might have risen among the shadowes, as to revenge the pride which began to growe on the earth, sente downe an Angell with this commaundemente, Goe

discende, and cause Adam and Eve to appeare on the earth in that sort as they were in Paradise, that the world may know them and wonder at them, for seeing out of their loines have issued those preposterous lymmes,[36] I know none more fit to correct them. Certes none more willing: They will attempte any thing for thy sake and service of that earthly, and yet (O straunge consceite) most heavenly Sunne, For as they were before driven from their Desire, because they desired to knowe the best, so now shall they be driven to their Desire whiche they covet to honour most, This shall be their rewarde, they shall come neere and yet shall not searche, and bee they farre of, it shall warme,[37] A cloud may sometimes barre their sight, but nothing shall deprive them the saveguard,[38] yet commaunde them to be humble in affection, thoughe fervente, leaste they seeme to disdayne

that pride in others, whiche they desire themselves. The
Sunne in the higheste, delighteth in the shaddowe which is
shortest, and nourisheth the tree whose roote groweth
deepest, not whose toppe springeth loftiest. This com-
mission and counsell ended all thinges were in a moment
accomplished with such seleritie (for to the Gods time is
tied) that they were sped as soone as they were spoken,
And now, most renouned and devine Sunne, Adam and
Eve being present, vouchsafe to heare somwhat in their
behalfs pronounced. Sir Knights, if in besieging the
sunne ye understood what you had undertaken, ye would
not destroye a common blessing for a private benefite:

He
speaketh
to the
Challen-
gers in
the
behalfe of
the two
knights
Adam
and Eve

Will you subdue the sunne, who shall rest in the shadow
where the weary take breath, the disquiet rest, and all
comforte, wil ye bereave all men of those glistering and
gladsome beames, what shall then prosper in the shining,
but you will climbe it by the rayes: O rare exhalations,
brothers you may bee to Desire, but sonnes ye are to ill
hap, whiche thinkes you can not sincke deepe enoughe
into the sea, unlesse you take your fal from the sunne,[39]
Desist you knights, desist, sithe it is impossible to resist,
content your selves with the sunnes indifferent succor,[40]
suffer the Jeniper shrub to growe by the loftie Oake, and
claime no prerogative where the sun grauntes no
priviledge, for being of the same mettall that others are,
the sunne will worke the like effects, as she doth in
others, The Giants wold have ben gods, if they could
have scaled the heavens[41] & you no lesse then starres,
could you conquer the same But as their throwing hil
upon hil did manifest their pride, but nothing further
their pretense; So your laying challenge upon claim, and
conquest upon challenge, may wel prove a wil, but no
worthinesse, A desire to reach, but no possibility to
recover, In which your soaring attemptes if you chance
to fal, the only comfort you have is to crie with Phaeton,
'Magnis excidimus ausis';[42] But if no perswasions may
moove your minds, Know ye proud Knights, there are
that have hearts as big as mountaines, and as far above
you in proewesse, as ye are above all in presumption, yet
not so vaine (whiche ye terme valiant) to assault the
sunne, and why, because it is impregnible, wee content
to enjoy the light, ye to ecclipse it, we to rest under the
feete, ye to run over the head, we to yeeld to that which

nothing can conquer, you to conquer that which maketh all men Captives. But weare it possible, that head could devise, courage attempt, or hand execute any thing that might shew the depth of our unspotted Loialty, soone should be seene (and for your selves to soone) that your enterprises should bee of as small account then, as now they are of lightlihood, so deepe an impression is ingraven in our thoughts, for the majestie of that sunne which now pearcing our eyes hath fully subdued our hearts, that we are prest in her defence to offer the whole world defiance. In proofe whereof I am charged to throwe down his[43] Gauntlet, which who so dareth take up, shall feele both the heate of their just conceived quarrell, and the reproch of their owne deserved folly, not by riding in breaking a fewe staves to ende the strife, but at Tournie, or what else so ever they can devise or dare adventure for to win the benefite of Beautie, Thus moste renowned and devine Beautie, whose beames shine like the Sun, have Adam and Eve adventured to defend the Sunne, the same I call Beautie the lighte of the worlde, the marvel of men, the mirour of nature, on which their encounter, if those favourable gleams may fall, they wil not onely thinke to have done goode herein, but to be restored againe to Paradice, the one meaneth to repose his trust in a woman, who like Eve cannot be beguiled,[44] the other to rest on a Saint, which by a Serpent will not be tempted, Thus being placed in the Garden of your Graces, O of all thinges moste gratious where vertues growe as thicke as leaves did in Paradise. They will take heede to taste of the forbidden fruite, contented to beholde, not coveting to take holde, And for that it hath bin long argued, and no arguing can end? whether the first offence came by the crudelitie[45] of Adam, or the simplicitie of Eve, the one defending his faulte by sounde arguments, the other excusing hers by sharp answers, they most humbly sue for this, that either by Six courses betwene them the quarrell may bee ended, or by your highnes peremptory sentence determined, for they both being in the world are desirous that one might beare the blame of both, And what herein your excellencie shall set downe, there is none shall gainesay, For whensoever the question shall be moved, No other reason shall be allowed then this: *Elizabetha dixit*.

This Speech being thus ended, Sir Thomas Parat and M. Cooke proceded backward on the other side of the Tilte, And when M. Ratcliffe came likewise against the Queene,[46] one of his Pages pronounced these speeches in his Masters behalf to her Majestie.

M.
Ratcliffes
speech
to the
Queene

So manie were the misfortunes, (most renoumed and beawtifull Princesse) of the desolate Knight my master, as neither the shortnes of the time will suffer me to repeat, nor the greatnes of the misterie to remember? But let this suffise that some there were and so manifold, that Geometrie whereon the body of man hangeth could not beare being intollerable, nor the minde which consisteth in Arithmeticke, number being infinite. Thus alwayes crossed by fortune, whose crossing is no blessing, he determined to separate him selfe as farre from societie, as his actions were from successe, who wandering through manie desertes, yet finding as he thought no place desolate, happened at the last to come to a Cliffe adjoining to the maine Sea, covered all with mosse whereon he was walking, much delighted with the solitarie seate, but not well liking the cold scituation,[47] he suddenly sunke into a hollow vaulte, surprised at the first with feare, but seeing it at the last a place of succour, he accounted his former miseries meetlie appeased by this present fortune. In this Denne he used for his bed mosse, for his candle mosse, for his ceeling mosse, and unlesse now and then a few coales,[48] mosse for his meate. A dry food God wot and a fresh, but so moistened with wette teares, and so salt, that hard was it to conjecture, whether it were better to feede or to fast. Here he gave himselfe to continuall meditation, seperating his mind from his body, his thought from his hart, yea devorcing him self from himselfe, in so much that with his strange diet & new conceites, he became so enchaunted, that neither the remembrance of others, nor a thought touching himselfe coulde enter into his minde: An alteration seldome heard of, that the place whereas he was shrowded in, should make him to forget who he is?[49] Living thus a long time for that no limme should seem short,[50] rising according to his maner to walke in the mosse in the grisping[51] of the day, hee espied upon the shore certaine men either cast away by shipwrake, or cast overborde by Pyrattes, unto whome he went and perceiving by their plaints one which lay dead amongst them to be their master, enquired whence they were, but they not willing to repeate their misfortunes, opened the bosome of the gentleman, and pulled out a crowle[52] containing a claime, a challenge, nay a conquest of Beawtie. At the sight whereof, suddenly (quoth he) Beawtie, and therewithall appalled paused, entring by litle and litle out of his present Melancholies into his former misfortunes, who as one awaked out of a long dreame, beganne thus to debate. O Beawtie where thy Fortresse is founded I know, but what these brethren should mean I maruaile for as I am assured that to winne thee none coulde be so fortunate, so did I thinke that to claime thee none could be so fonde, when as thou O devine Beawtie art of every one to be desired, but never to be conquered of Desire. But as the Eagle beholding the sunne, coveteth to builde hir nest in the same, and so dimmeth her sight.[53] So they vewing the brightnesse of Beawtie are incensed to conquere it by Desire. And what then? because she is invincible, shall I be indifferent? No, I will forsake this caytifly Cottage, and will take Armes to defend that Beawties Castle. Nothing shall remooue me from mine attempt, which being perfourmed, nothing can moove me, yea but shee hath servantes alreadie a number, I but unlesse I be there, not the whole number, but many were[54] famous but none more faithfull, yet alas, if thou go, thou shalt ever be infortunate, better alwaies infortunat, then one[55] disloyal, which words being ended, he demanded whether they woulde in like case adventure with one of no lesse courage then their master, but certainly of greter affection: Whose service he having upon small entreatie obteined, for that belyke they were desirous to see the event for the which they had suffered such adventures, he departed to his cave, hewing a shield out of the hard cliffe enriched onely with soft mosse:[56] A double signe of his desire, thinking that nothing could manifest Beawtie so well as Pithagoras wallnut, a tender ryne and a hard shell. And nowe most excellent and devine Beawtie, devine it must needes be that worketh so heavenly, sith he is called from his solitarie Cave to your sumptuous Court, from bondage to liberty, from a living death to a never dying life, and all for the sake and service of Beawtie: vouchsafe his shielde, which is the

Here the boy delivered M. Radclifs shild to the Queene

ensigne of your fame to be the instrument of his fortune. And for prostrating himselfe to your feete, he is here readie preste to adventure any adventures for your gracious favour.

Here entreth the iiii sons of S. Francis Knowles

Which speeche beeing ended, he retyred back as the rest. And after him came the foure Sonnes of Sir Frauncis Knowles,[57] on after another, according to their age, and all in like armour, who comming to the end of the Tilt, stayed till these speeches were uttered by one of their Pages, who being apparailled like unto Mercurie, pronounced these speeches in the Knights behalves to her Majestie.

The speech of the foure sonnes of Sir Francis Knowles, pronounced by their page being apparelled like unto Mercurie

Report hath bruted all abroad, that desperate Desire with a wonderfull armie of affections hath laid his siege against the invincible Fortresse of Peerelesse Beawtie, and that the chiefest champions of this most famous enterprise, are foure of fancies fellowes, Fosterbrothers to Desire, and drie nurst by dispaire, valiant Knights, and honourable personages, whose hautie hearts deserve renowne at least, for venturing to win the golden fleece without Medeas helpe.[58] The Gyaunts long agoe did scale the cloudes men say, in hope to winne the fort of Jupiter.[59] The wanton youth, whose waxed wings did frie with soaring up aloft,[60] had scapt unscorcht if he had kept a meaner gale[61] below. So falles it out in this attempt, Desire vaunts to conquer Beawties Forte by force, wherin the goddesse keepes continually watch and warde, so that Desire may dispaire to win one ynche of her against her will. Her stately seate is set so high, as that no levell can be laid against her walles, and sooner may men undertake to hit a starre with a stone, then to beate hir brave bulwarkes by batterie. No undermining may prevaile, for that hir forte is founded upon so firme a Rocke, as will not stirre for either fraude or force: And is there any hope to winne by famine such a forte as yeeldes continuall foode to all her foes, and though they feede not fat therewith, yet must they either feede thereon or fast, for Beawtie is the only baite whereon Desire bites, and love the chiefe restoritie that ladie Beawtie likes, so that she can no more be left without meat, then men can live without mindes: Of all affections that are, Desire is the most worthie to woe,[62] but least deserves to win Beawtie, for in winning his sainct, he loseth him selfe, no soner hath desire what he desireth, but that he dieth presently: so that when Beawtie yeeldeth once to desire, then can she never vaunt to be desired againe: Wherefore of force this principle must stand, it is convenient for Desire ever to wish, necessarie &[63] that he alwaies want. O rare & most renowned Beawtie, O goddes to be honored of all, not to be equalled of any, become not nowe a prisoner, your Fortresse is invincible, no doubt Desire will content him selfe with a favourable parley, & waight for grace by loyaltie not chalenge it by lawnce, although he make nere so brave, the worlde doth knowe, that Ladie Beawtie needes no rescue to rayse this siege, for that she sits above al reach, her heavenly looks above when she so listes can dazell all mens eyes. But though she liste not use those meanes, yet it is meete that all her servantes come and shewe themselves devout to doo hir wil: perchance hir pleasure is to see the fortes[64] tried of these iiii Foster friendes. O happie, tenne times happy they whose happe shal be with favour of her Deitie, to take in hand this brave attempt: In hope whereof these iiii legitimate sonnes of Despaire, brethren to hard mishappe, suckled with sighes, and swathed up in sorow, weaned in wo, & drie nurst by Desire,[65] long time fostered with favourable countenance, & fedde with sweet fancies, but now of late (alas) wholy given over to griefe & is[66] disgraced by disdain, are come with readie hearts and hands, to proove against these other 4. that Desire doth not deserve one winke of good favour from Ladie Beawties smiling eyes, for threatning to winne her forte by force? They dout not the victorie if only they may find some litle shew from their Saint in favour of their enterprise. If Mercurie have saide amisse, blame those bright beames which have bereft him of his wit, if well, vouchsafe one becke[67] to bid him packe away.

　　These speeches beeing ended, both they & the rest marched about the Tylt, and so going backe to the nether end thereof prepared themselves to run, every one in his tourne, each Defendant six courses againste the former challengers, Who performed their partes so valiantly on both sides, that their prowesse hath demerited perpetuall memory, and worthilye woone honoure both to them selves and their native countrie, As Fame hath the same reported.

The boy
that
uttered
the
defiance,
in this
speeche
tooke his
goodnighte
of the
Queene

When this dayes sporte was thus accomplished the boy
that uttered the defiances, in these fewe speeches tooke
his goodnight of the Queene.

In the tryall of this debatefull question (O your selfe)
then with [68] what can be said more,[69] you see that seeing
begins to faile. Might the ordinary truce maker though
no truce be treated, (if at least your presence make it not
lightsome to wrappe all in her blacke and mourning
weedes) perchaunce mourning that since night first, was
noblest Desire, have been subject to undeserved
tormentes:[70] And therefore these knights by th'
aucthoritie of darknesse verie undesirously are compelled
to departe from whence they came. (never part yet ere
they goe[71]). Thus much they command me in their
names to confesse. That such excellencie they find in
your knights and in comparison of them, such unablenes
in their selves. That if Desire did not banish dispaire as a
traytor out of his kingdome, it woulde have already
undermined their best grounded determination: but no
inward nor outwarde wounde, no weakenesse, no
wearinesse, can daunt Desire, nor take away the naturall
effects that followe it. Therefore having left them no
other courage then Desire, no other strength then Desire,
no other beginning or ending cause but Desire. They will
continue this harde and hardie enterprise to morrowe, in
the meane time they can find no place in their heartes
that doeth not wish you as sweet rest, as Psiche was
conveyed unto by the gentle Zephirus,[72] and if it be
possible by the same gueste visited.[73] They wishe that
when your liddes looke up, their Juelles they may
preserve them,[74] to see tomorrow a better day then this,
& yet not[75] so singuler successe,[76] as you may long,
freely, & joyfully enjoy your selfe, to the delight of
lookers, and woonder of markers: this said, the Knightes
in order as they came departed.[77]

Et fessos solvunt artus, mollissima quaeque
Gustant, and dulci membra quiete fovent.[78]

The seconde dayes Sport.

The next dayes showe was done in this order. The four
foster children of Desire entered in a brave Charriot

Here
entereth
a most
excelling,
and brave
chariot,
with rare
curious
and costly
work with
the foure
challen-
gers in it,
which
chariot
was
curiously
shadowed
with fine
Lawne

The
First
speech on
the second
day

(very finely and curiously decked) as men forwearied &
half overcome, The charriot was made in suche sort as
upon the top the 4 knights sate, with a beautiful Lady,
representing Desire about[79] them, Whereunto their eyes
were turned, in token what they desired.[80] In the bulke of
the Charriot was conveied roome for a full consort of
Musicke, who plaied still very doleful musicke as the
Charriot moved, the charriot was drawne by four horses
according to the foure knightes, which horses were
apparelled in White and carnation silke, beeing the
colloure of Desire, and as it passed by the upper end of
the Tylt, a Harrault of Armes was sent before to utter
these speeches in the knights behalfe to hir Majestie.

No confidence in themselves, O most unmached
Princesse, before whome envy dieth, wanting all nerenes
of comparison to susteine it, And admiration is expressed,[81] finding the scope of it void of conceavable limits,
Nor any slight regarding the force of your valliant
knights, hath encouraged the Foster children of Desire to
make this day an inheritour of yesterdayes action: But
the wing of Memorie alasse the sworne enimie to the
wofull mans quietnesse, being constantly helde by the
hande of perfection, And never ceassing to blow the cole
of some kindled Desire, hath broughte their inward fyer
to blaze forth this flame unquenchable by any meanes:
till by death the whole fewel be consumed, and therefore
not able to maister it, they are violently borne whether
desire drawes. Although they must confes (alasse) that
yesterdayes brave onset should come to such a
confession: That they are not greatly companied with
hope, the common supplier to Desires army. So as nowe
from summoning this Castel to yeld, they are fallen lowly
to beseech you to vouchsafe your eyes out of that
Impregnable Fortresse, to beholde what will fal out
betwixt them and your famous knights: wherein though
they bee so overpressed with the others vallure that
already they could unnethe[82] have bene able to come
hither, if the charriot of Desire had not carried them, yet
will they make this whole assemblie witnesses so farre of
their wil, That sooner their souls shall leave their bodies
then Desire shall leave[83] soules: In that onelye standes
their strength that gave them their first courage, and
must be their last comfort. For what resistance is there

where not onely they are met with forren enemies, such as stately disdain, which looks from so high a Tower to pore Desire. That though (in it selfe) it bee greate yet in hir eies (so seated) it seemes smal, or such on the other side as unfortunat dispair,[84] which makes the countrie so barren where they lay their siege, that it woulde take away all the foode of fancie: But even civill warre yesterdaye grew betwixt them and others, who beares the same badge of Desire: that they do so, as thus bestead they are brought to this fayer passe, to desire no more, but that this death or overthrowe, may be seene by those eyes who are onely unhappy, in that they can neither finde fellowe, nor see them selves.

Which speech being done, the defendants came in, in such order as they came in the day before, therefore I shal not need to make a new repetition of the same, sith al hath bene touched already. Then wente they to the Tourney, where they did very Nobly, as the shivering of the swordes might very well testifie, And after that to the barriers,[85] where they lashed it out lustely, and fought couragiously, as if the Greeks and Trojans had dealt their deadly dole, no partie was spared, nor estate excepted, but eache knight indued to win the golden fleece, that expected eyther fame or the favoure of his maistresse,[86] which sporte continued all the same daye, And towardes the evening the sport being ended, ther was a boy sent up to the queen being clothed in Ash colored[87] garments in token of humble submission, who having an Olive branch in his hande, and falling down prostrate on his face, and then kneeled up, concluded this noble exercise with these wordes to her Majestie:

Most renowned Princesse of Princesse, in whom can nothing obtein victorie, but Vertue, The Foster children of Desire (but heires onely to misfortune) send me to deliver in such wordes as sorrowe can afforde their most humble hearted submission, they acknowledge this Fortresse to be reserved for the eye of the whole worlde, farre lifted up, from the compasse of their destinie, They acknowledge the blindenes of their error, in that they did not know desire (how strong so ever it be) within it self to be stronger without it selfe then it pleased the desired, they acknowledge they have degenerated from their Fosterer in making violence accompany Desire, They

Tourneyes, and Barriers couragiously tried

The last speeche to the Queene

acknowledge that Desire received his beginning and nourishment of this Fortresse, and therefore to committe ungratefulnesse in bearing Armes (though desirous Armes) against it: They acknowledge Noble Desire shoulde have desired nothing so much, as the flourishing of that Fortresse, which was to be esteemed according to it selfes liking: They acknowledge the least determination of vertue (which stands for guard of this Fortresse) to be to strong for the strongest Desire, And therefore they do acknowledge them selves overcome, as to be slaves to this Fortresse[88] for ever, which Tylt[89] they will beare in their foreheades, as their other name is engraven in their hearts: For witnesse thereof they present this Olive branch to your presence, in token of your Triumphant peace, And of their peaceable servitude.

Whereby they present themselves as bondmen by those bondes, which the losse of life can onely loose: Only from out of that which was theirs they crave thus much, to give some token to those knights which may be judged to have doone best in each kind of weapon, or who by his devise hath come in best sort in this desirous strife, this being don they being now slaves (in whom much duetie requires) for fear of offence, dare say no further, but wish from the bottom of their captived[90] hearts, That while this Realme is thus fortified and beautified: Desire may be your chiefest adversarie.

Which speech being ended, her Majestie gave them al praise and great thankse, which they esteemed so well and thought themselves rewarded according to their own wishing, And so they departed each one in order, according to the first coming in.[91]

The Aucthor's conclusion to the Reader.

Thus have I (good Reader) according to my simple skill set forth this singuler pastime that thou maiest, being farre of? peradventure knowe more, then they that were present and eye beholders of the same, which so neere as I coulde either gather or get, I have for thy pleasure here placed it, If any thing be wanting which is not here mentioned, or ought awry and not right reported, let this suffice, that my wil was good to have gotten all, and most unwilling to do ought amisse, yet such as it is, if though well accept it I shall thinke my paines wel emploied for thy pleasure, and gratified enough with that good will: Therefore wishing thee to thinke no worse of my work, then I thought the labor litle in working, craving but *Bona Verba*[92] for my well meaning, I give the friendly Farewell.

Thine to command in all courteous manner. HENRI GOLDWEL.

Cowdray 1591

While on a grander scale than the modest intimacies of Bisham and Rycote, the Cowdray entertainment falls far short of the lavish spectacles at Kenilworth and Elvetham. The cast is small: Porter, Nymph, Pilgrim, Peace and Wild Man, Angler and Netter, and as no more than three of these appear on any one day, they could have been played by three actors (possibly two men and a boy for Peace and the Nymph). Besides this, there was music, probably the 'music of the house', and the effects of the two wooden porters, the tree hung with shields, and the miraculous draught of fishes: all fairly easy to arrange and requiring no special construction. The most expensive was probably the painted escutcheons.[1] The only gift recorded is the Porter's golden key.

There is a strong personal note in the welcome of Elizabeth: the weeping greeting of Lady Montague, the visit to the Montagues' own lodging, the knighting of son and son-in-law, but the overall impression of this entertainment is that it is not so much a family affair as a county one. What is affirmed repeatedly is the loyalty of Sussex as a whole, rather than the Montagues in particular, to Elizabeth. The tree hung with shields is an image of the hearts of oak of Sussex dedicated to her, and also a reference, presumably, to the maritime situation of the county (this may be the earliest reference to English ships as hearts of oak), which is reiterated in the draught of fishes presented to her. The theme of area loyalty reappears in the dance on Thursday, in which Lord Montague and his wife join, among the country people. Against this is set the theme of instability and misleading appearance, treachery and graft, which Pilgrim, Wild Man, Angler and Netter claim invest the world outside Cowdray and Sussex. This Sussex patriotism is not, however, without its unspoken *piquancies*. Lord Montague was a Catholic, and Cowdray a centre of Catholicism. The repeated assurances of loyalty were all the more necessary, and Elizabeth's reply to the Porter that she does not doubt him is addressed more to his real employer than to his fictional self. The presentation of Lord Montague, despite his Catholicism, as the centre of the ultra-loyal men of Sussex would contribute to this emphasis on his personal loyalty and assure the Queen of his position of strength in the area, while the Queen's obvious favour shown to Montague would reassure his neighbours about the strength of his position with regard to the Queen, which his Catholicism might have caused them to doubt.

Cowdray is firmly of the chivalric cult of Elizabeth, and casts her as the knight-errant, who follows the code of chivalry. In her encounter with the Pilgrim and the Wild Man she is appealed to, by a chance encountrant, as a protector of the helpless and weak (a Pilgrim carried no weapons, was traditionally old, if not a female in disguise, and should have been respected as a religious). She is compelled by the knightly code which she follows to accompany him and deal with his assailant – when she is, of course, rewarded with an elaborate compliment. The encounter is supposedly fortuitous, and probably inconvenient for the Queen – the Pilgrim's protestations about the nearness of the oak sound a little too eager to be completely sincere, and Elizabeth was recreating herself in admiring the gardens of Cowdray at the time of the encounter. The Pilgrim and the Wild Man were both stock romance-figures, the Wild Man often, as for instance in *Ywain and Gawain*, being the guardian of mysteries, as well as a traditional supporter of achievements of arms,[2] which makes his role as guardian of the heraldic tree more appropriate, and the tree hung with shields indicates that the gentlemen of the shire have chosen a chivalric mode to display their loyalty; they hang their shields on the tree to challenge anyone who denies Elizabeth's supremacy to fight with them.[3]

The episode with the Angler and Netter represents an interesting sub-group of the pastoral, the Piscatory. The best-known example in English is Walton's *The Compleat Angler*, but it was quite extensively written in English in the sixteenth century.[4] It shared with the pastoral both a classical background and Christian implications (the promise of Christ to make his followers 'fishers of men' ensured that the priest might be seen as fisherman as well as shepherd) and the life of the fisherman, working in co-operation with his fellows, or in peaceful solitude, exploiting an abundance of natural resources, his only adversaries the natural forces of wind and sea, was as amenable as that of the shepherd to an idyllic presentation.

Bond assigns the piece to Lyly;[5] this must remain conjectural.

TEXTS

Two descriptions of the Entertainment were printed:
1. 1591. The Speeches and Honorable Entertainment giuen to the Queenes Majestie in Progresse, at Cowdrey in Sussex, by the right Honourable the Lord Montacute: *Thomas Scarlet, sold by William Wright.* [B.M. *c.* 33.d.11].

2. 1591. The Honorable Entertainment . . . *Thomas Scarlet, sold by William Wright.*

The text printed here is composite. 1. Contains only sketchy descriptions of the Queen's actions, and of her reactions to the diversions provided, while 2. omits the songs. I have printed the text of 2., with the insertion of the songs, and other discrepancies in the texts indicated in footnotes. The differences in the texts may be accounted for by 1. being prepared for publication before the Entertainment had taken place, perhaps to be handed out as a programme at the event itself,[6] while 2. was printed after the entertainment had occured, amplified with Elizabeth's reactions.

The Honorable Entertainment given to her Majestie, in Progresse, at Cowdray in Sussex, by the Right Honorable the[1] Lord Montecute, anno 1591, August 15.[2]

The Queene, having dyned at Farnham,[3] came with a great traine to the Right Honorable the Lord Montacutes, vpon saterdaie being the 15[4] daie of August about eight of the clocke at night. Where upon sight of her Majestie, loud musicke sounded, which at her enteraunce on the bridge suddenly ceased. Then was a speech delivered by a personage in armour, standing between two Porters, carved out of wood, he resembling the third:[5] holding his club in one hand, and a key of golde in the other, as followeth.

SATERDAY, AUGUST 15.[6]

The Porters speech.

'The walles of Thebes were raised by Musicke:[7] by musick these are kept from falling. It was a prophesie since the first stone was layde, that these walles should shake, and the roofe totter, till the wisest, the fairest and the most fortunate of all creatures, should by her first steppe make the foundation staid: and by the glaunce of her eyes make the Turret steddie. I have beene here a porter manie yeeres, many Ladies have entred passing amiable, many verie wise, none so happie. These my fellow Porters thinking there could be none so noble,[8] fell on sleepe, and so incurde the seconde curse of the prophesie, which is, never againe to awake: Marke how they looke more like postes then Porters, reteining onlie their shapes, but deprived of their sences. I thought rather to cut off my eie liddes, then to winke till I saw the ende. And now it is: for the musick is at an end, this house immoveable, your vertue immortall. O miracle of time, Natures glorie, Fortunes Empresse, the worlds wonder! Soft, this is the Poets part, and not the Porters. I have nothing to present but the crest of mine office, this keie: Enter, possesse all, to whom the heavens have vouchsafed all. As for the owner of this house, mine honorable Lord, his tongue is the keie of his heart: and his heart the locke of his soule. Therefore what he speakes you may constantlie beleeve: which is, that in duetie and service to your Majestie he would be second to none: in praieng for your happinesse, equall to anie.[9]

'Tuus, O Regina, quod optas Explorare favor: huic iussa capescere fas est.' "[10]

Wherewithall her Highnes tooke the keye, and said, she would sweare for him, there was none more faithfull: then being alighted, she embraced the Ladie Montecute, and the Ladie Dormir her daughter.[11] The Mistresse of the house (as it were weeping in her bosome) said, 'O happie time, O joyfull daie!'

That night her Majestie tooke her rest; and so in like manner the next day, which was Sunday, being most Royallie feasted. The proportion of breakefast was three oxen, and one hundred and fourtie geese.[12]

MUNDAIE.

On Munday at eight of the clock in the morning, her Highnes took horse with all her Traine, and rode into the Parke: where was a delicate Bowre prepared, under the which were her Highnesse musicians placed,[13] and a crossebowe by a Nymph, with a sweet song, delivered to her hands, to shoote at the deere, about some thirtie in number, put into a paddock, of which number she killed three or four, and the Countesse of Kildare one.[14]

A Dittie.

Behold her lockes like wiers of beaten gold,
  her eies like starres that twinkle in the skie,
Her heauenly face not framd of earthly molde,
  Her voice that sounds Apollos melodie,
The miracle of time, the worlds storie,
Fortunes Queen, Loues treasure, Natures glory.

No flattering hope she likes, blind Fortunes bait
  nor shadowes of delight, fond fansies glasse,
Nor charmes that do inchant, false artes deceit,
  nor fading ioyes, which time makes swiftly pas
But chast desires which beateth all these downe;
A Goddesse looke is worth a Monarchs crowne.

Goddesse and Monarch of (t)his happie Ile,
   vouchsafe this bow which is an huntresse part:
Your eies are arrows though they seeme to smile
   which neuer glanst but gald the stateliest hart,
Strike one, strike all, for none at all can flie,
They gaze you in the face although they die.[15]

Then rode hir Grace to Cowdrey to dinner, and about sixe of the
clocke in the evening from a Turret sawe sixteene Buckes (all having
fayre lawe) pulled downe with Greyhoundes,[16] in a laund.[17] All the
huntinge ordered by Maister Henrie Browne, the Lorde Montague's
thirde sonne, Raunger of Windsore forest.[18]

TEWSDAIE.

On Tewsdaie hir Majestie went to dinner to the Priory,[19] where my
Lorde himselfe kept house, and there was shee and her Lordes most
bountifully feasted.
   After dinner[20] she came to viewe my Lorde's walkes, where shee
was mette by a Pilgrime, clad in a coat of russet velvet, fashioned to
his calling; his hatte being of the same, with skallop-shelles of cloth
of silver,[21] who delivered hir a speach in this sort following:[22]

Pilgrime.

'Fairest of all creatures vouchsaf to heare the prayer of a Pilgrime,
which shall be short, and the petition which is but reasonable. God
graunt the worlde maie ende with your life, and your life more
happie then anie in the world: that is my praier. I have travelled
manie Countries, and in all Countries desire antiquities.[23] In this
Iland (but a spanne in respect of the world) and in this Shire (but a
finger in regard of your Realme) I have heard great cause of wonder,
some of complaint. Harde by, and so neere as your Majestie shall
almost passe by, I sawe an Oke, whose statelines nayled mine eyes
to the branches, and the ornamentes beguiled my thoughtes with
astonishment. I thought it free, being in the fielde,[24] but I found it
not so. For at the verie entrie I mette I know not with what
rough-hewed Ruffian, whose armes were carved out of knotty box,
for I could receive nothing of him but boxes,[25] so hastie was he to
strike, he had no leysure to speake. I thought there were more waies
to the wood then one, and finding another passage, I found also a
Ladie verie faire, but passing frowarde,[26] whose wordes set mee in a
greater heate then the blowes. I asked her name, she said it was

Peace. I wondred that Peace could never holde her peace. I cannot
perswade myselfe since that time, but that there is a waspes nest in
mine eares. I returned discontent. But if it will please your
Highnesse to view it, that rude Champion at your faire feete will laie
downe his foule head: and at your becke that Ladie will make her
mouth her tongues mue.[27] Happelie your Majestie shall finde some
content: I more antiquities.'

Then did the Pilgrime conduct her Highnes to an Oke not farre
off, whereon her Majesties armes, and all the armes of the
Noblemen, and Gentlemen of that Shire, were hanged in
Escutcheons most beutifull, and a wilde man cladde in Ivie, at the
sight of her Highnesse spake as followeth.

The Wilde Mans speech at the tree.

'Mightie Princesse, whose happines is attended by the heavens, and
whose government is wondered at upon the earth: vouchsafe to
heare why this passage is kept, and this Oke honoured. The whole
world is drawen in a mappe: the heavens in a Globe: and this Shire
shrunke in a Tree: and what[28] your Majestie hath often heard of
with some comfort, you may now beholde with full content. This
Oke, from whose bodie so many armes doe spread: and out of whose
armes so many fingers spring: resembles in parte your strength and
happinesse. Strength, in the number and the honour: happinesse, in
the trueth and consent. All heartes of Oke,[29] then which nothing
surer: nothing sounder. All woven in one roote, then which nothing
more constant, more naturall. The wall of this Shire is the sea,
strong, but rampired[30] with true hearts, invincible: where every
private mans eie is a Beacon to discover: everie noble mans power a
Bulwarke to defende. Here they are all differing somewhat in
degrees, not in duetie: the greatnes of the branches, not the
greenesse. Your majesty they account the Oke, the tree of Jupiter,
whose root is so deeplie fastened, that treacherie, though she
undermine to the centre, cannot finde the windings, and whose
toppe is so highlie reared, that envie, though she shoote on
copheigth,[31] cannot reach her, under whose armes they have both
shade and shelter. Well wot they that your enemies lightnings are
but flashes, and their thunder which fills the whole world with a
noise of conquest, shall ende with a soft shower of Retreate. Be then
as confident in your steppes, as Caesar was in his Fortune. His
proceedings but of conceit: yours of vertue. Abroad courage hath
made you feared, at home honoured clemencie. Clemencie which the
owner of this Grove hath tasted:[32] in such sort, that his thoughts are
become his hearts laberinth, suprized with joie and loialtie. Joy

without measure, loyaltie without end, living in no other ayer, than that which breathes your Majestie's safetie.

For himselfe, and all these honourable Lords, and Gentlemen, whose shieldes your Majestie doth here beholde, I can say this, that as the veines are dispersed through all the bodie, yet, when the heart feeleth any extreame passion, sende all their bloud to the heart for comfort: so they being in divers places, when your Majestie shall but stande in feare of any daunger, which bring their bodies, their purses, their soules, to your Highnesse, being their heart, their head, and their Soveraigne. This passage is kept straight, and the Pilgrime I feare hath complained:[33] but such a disguised worlde it is, that one can scarce know a Pilgrime from a Priest, a Tailer from a Gentleman, nor a man from a woman. Everie man[34] seeming to be that which they are not, onely doe practise what they should not. The Heavens guide you, your Majestie governes us: though our peace bee envied by them,[35] yet we hope it shall be eternall. – Elizabetha Deus nobis haec otia fecit.[36]

The Dittie.

There is a bird that builds her neast with spice,
    and built, the Sun to ashes doth her burne,
Out of whose sinders doth another rise.[37]
    & she by scorching beames to dust doth turne:
Thus life a death, and death a life doth proue,
The rarest thing on earth except my loue.

My loue that makes his neast with high desires,
    and is by beauties blaze to ashes brought,
Out of the which do breake out greater fires,
    they quenched by disdain consume to nought,
And out of nought my cleerest loue doth rise,
True loue is often slaine but neuer dies.

True loue which springs, though Fortune on it tread
    as camomel by pressing down doth grow
Or as the Palme that higher reares his head,
    when men great burthens on the branches throw
Loue fansies birth, Fidelitie the wombe,
the Nurse Delight, Ingratitude the tombe.[38]

Then uppon the winding of a Cornet was a most excellent crie of hounds, and three buckes kilde by the bucke hounds, and so went all backe to Cowdrey to supper.[39]

WEDNESDAIE.

On wednesdaie the Lordes and Ladies dined in the walkes, feasted most sumptuously at a table foure and twentie yards long.[40]

In the beginning,[41] her Majestie comming to take the pleasure of the walkes, was delighted with most delicate musicke, and brought to a goodlie Fish-pond, where was an Angler, that taking no notice of hir Majestie, spake as followeth.

The Anglers Speech.

Next rowing in a Westerne barge[42] well fare Angling, I have bin here this two houres and cannot catch an oyster. It may be for lacke of a bait, and that were hard in this nibling world, where everie man laies bait[43] for another. In the Citie merchants bait ther tongues with a lie and an oath, and so make simple men swallow deceitfull wares: and fishing for commoditie is growen so farre, that men are become fishes, for Landelords put such sweete baits on rackt rents,[44] that as good it were to be a perch in a pikes belly, as a Tenant in theyr farmes. All our trade is growen to trecherie, for now fish are caught with medicins:[45] which are as unwholsom as love procured by witchcraft unfortunate. We Anglers make our lines of divers colours, according to the kindes of waters: so men do their loves, aiming at the complexion of the faces. Thus Marchandize, Love, and Lordships sucke venom out of vertue. I thinke I shal fish all daie and catch a frog, the cause is neither in the line, the hooke, nor the bait, but some thing there is over beautifull which stayeth the verie Minow (of all fish the most eager) from biting. For this we Anglers observe, that the shadow of a man turneth backe the fish. What will then the sight of a Goddesse? Tis best angling in a lowring daie, for here the sunne so glisters, that the fish see my hooke through my bait. But soft here be the Netters, these be they that cannot content them with a dish of fish for their supper, but will drawe a whole pond for a[46] market.

This saide, he espied a Fisherman drawing his nettes towarde where hir Majestie was. And calling alowde to him,

Ho Sirra (quoth the Angler) What shall I give thee for thy draught, If there be never a whale in it take it for a Noble quoth the Netter.

Ang. Be there any maydes there

Net. Maydes foole, they be sea fish.[47]

Ang. Why?

Net. Venus was borne of the Sea, and 'tis reason she should have maydes to attend hir.[48]

Then turned he to the Queene, and after a small pawse, spake as followeth

Madame, it is an olde saying, There is no fishing to the sea, nor service to the King: but it holdes when the sea is calme and the king vertuous. Your vertue maketh Envie blush and stand amazed[49] at your happines. I come not to tell the art of fishing, nor the natures of fish, nor their daintines, but with a poor Fisher mans wish, that all the hollowe hearts to your Majestie were in my net, and if there bee more then it will holde, I woulde they were in the sea till I went thether a fishing. There be some so muddie minded, that they cannot live in a cleere river but a standing poole, as camells will not drinke till they have troubled the water with their feet: so can they never stanch their thirst, till they have disturbd the state with their trecheries. Soft, these are no fancies for fisher men. Yes true hearts are as good as full purses, the one the sinewes of warre, the other the armes. A dish of fish is an unworthy present for a prince to accept: there be some carpes amongst them, no carpers of state,[50] if there be, I would they might be handled lyke carpes, their tongues pulled out. Some pearches there are I am sure and if anie pearch higher than in dutie they ought, I would they might sodenly picke over the pearch[51] for me. What so ever there is, if it be good it is all yours, most vertuous[52] Ladie, that are best worthie of all.[53]

That ended,

This Song of the Fisherman.

The fish that seekes for food in siluer streame
   is unawares beguiled with the hooke,
And tender hearts when lest of love they dreame,
   do swallow beauties bait, a lovely looke.
The fish that shuns to bite, in net doth hit,
The heart that scapes the eie is caught by wit.

The thing cald Loue, poore Fisher men do feele
   riche pearles are found in hard and homely shels
Our habits base, but hearts as true as steele,
   sad lookes, deep sighs, flat faith are all our spels,
And when to us our loves seeme faire to bee,
We court them thus, Love me and Ile love thee.

And if they saie our loue is fondly made,
   we never leave till on their hearts we lite,
Anglers have patience by their proper trade,
   and are content to tarrie till they bite,
Of all the fish that in the waters move,
We count them lumps that will not bite at love.[54]

Then was the net drawen.

The Netter having presented all the fishe of the ponde, and laying it at hir feete, departed.

That evening she hunted.

THURSDAY.

On Thursday she dined in the privie walkes in the garden, and the Lordes and Ladies at a table of fortie-eight yardes long. In the evening the countrie people presented themselves to hir Majestie in a pleasant dance,[55] with taber and pipe: and the Lorde Montague and his Lady among them, to the great pleasure of all the beholders, and gentle applause of hir Majestie.

FRYDAY.

On Friday she departed towards Chichester.

Going through the arbour to take horse, stoode six gentlemen, whom hir Majestie knighted; the Lorde Admirall laying the sworde on their shoulders.

The names of the sixe Knights them made were these; viz.

Sir George Browne, my Lordes second sonne.

Sir Robert Dormer, his sonne in lawe.

Sir Henry Goaring.

Sir Henry Glemham.

Sir John Carrell.

Sir Nicholas Parker.

So departed hir Majestie to the dining-place, whether the Lord Montague and his sonnes, and the Sheriffe of the Shire, attended with a goodly companie of gentlemen, brought her Highnes.

The escutchions on the Oke remaine, and there shall hange till they can hang together one peece by another. – Valete.

Elvetham 1591

This, together with Kenilworth, and possibly Harefield, which
survives only in fragmentary form,[1] is the most spectacular and
costly of the entertainments offered to Elizabeth on her progresses.
The host, the earl of Hertford, was a family connection of the Queen,
being the nephew of her father's third wife, and having contracted a
disastrously tactless marriage to her cousin Katherine Grey. But the
entertainment has none of the personal qualities of those offered by
the Norrises, or by Lord Burleigh on her visits to Theobalds,[2] which
is hardly surprising in view of the suspicion in which Elizabeth held
Hertford.[3] What it does provide is a striking example of the
readiness and intention of Elizabeth's subjects to build their houses
for the purpose of entertaining her. As the description relates, the
Earl heard a rumour, or was (more probably) warned that Elizabeth
intended to drop in on him unexpectedly, not at one of his major
residences, but at the tiny Elvetham. He immediately set to work to
create a wood-and-canvas palace, together with a large crescent-
shaped artificial lake (it must have been about one hundred yards
across at its widest point) on which he staged a water-pageant which
may well have found its inspiration in those currently fashionable in
Italy.[4]

The quality of the text of this entertainment is probably higher
than that of any other, and the songs are as delightful as the Queen
evidently found them. Bond again ascribes the piece to Lyly, but this
must again remain conjecture. It is notable that it is entirely verse,
in contrast to the other entertainments for which Lyly is the
suggested author.[5] Whoever wrote the piece, it seems likely that the
overall conception of the sea-battle and fireworks, together with
their political references, was the Earl's, and that the author
produced the speeches to order.

An important factor in the success and delightfulness of this
entertainment was the music which attended every action from the
Hours and Graces (these are traditionally the handmaids of Venus,
so that it is as Venus that Elizabeth is led to her lodgings on her
arrival) preceding Elizabeth strewing flowers in her path, to the
musicians in a bower who lamented her departure and prayed for
her return. The deliberate calculation of the aural effects, including
the positioning of the echo in the music on the lake to give the effect
of distance, indicates the care and thought that went into its
presentation.

The celebrations offered to the Queen are represented as
organically related to the countryside.[6] The gods who welcome her

are the gods of water and the forest; the fairy Queen is located under the ground;[7] the songs are about shepherds and shepherdesses, the natural human denizens of the countryside; at the end, the music which begs her to return is hidden inside a bush, so that it seems that the countryside itself is lamenting her departure. The Hours and Graces are goddessess closely associated with this natural world. The only exception to this is the Poet who greets Elizabeth on her arrival and elegizes her departure, and his purpose is to give authenticity to the whole entertainment. The fact that he is a true poet, the Soothsayer, the *vates*, inspired by heaven, and not a feigning maker, the fictionalizer, is stressed in the narrative, and indicated by his costume. Once again, the world is transformed for and by Elizabeth; her presence verifies myths, and the presence of the mythological creatures makes her supernatural.

It is interesting, after the Cowdray entertainment, which took place only a month previously, to note how Renaissance in feeling (if that is a permissible phrase) this entertainment is. It is not only the sustained lyricism of this episode, with its sense of Elvetham as a place removed out of the diurnal world, whereas Cowdray was firmly located in an idealized Sussex. Nor is it simply that Elvetham uses more modern ideas than Cowdray, for the piscatory, which the episode with the Angler and Netter at Cowdray represents, was just becoming fashionable and would only reach its full flowering in the next century with the work of Phineas Fletcher and Isaac Walton. Cowdray is more firmly of the chivalric cult of Elizabeth, and casts her as a knight-errant, who follows the code of chivalry. At Elvetham, Elizabeth performs miracles by her mere presence, as she steadied the trembling building at Cowdray, giving the ship life, and transforming the threatening monster to a snail. The only deed she is called on to perform is the naming of the ship,[8] and this involves no disruption on her part.

The fourth day of the Elvetham entertainment contains one reference to the romance-world, with the *aventure*-like encounter with the Fairy Queen, which so delighted Elizabeth. This portion of the entertainment may well have been suggested by the publication of the first three books of *The Faerie Queene* in 1590,[9] but it has a link with a common *motif* of the romances: the meeting of a knight with the Queen of Faery – the True Thomas theme. It is a feature of these encounters that the Queen always comes to express her love to one of her favourites: here Elizabeth is cast as the favourite of the Faerie Queene, and as such takes over the role of many romance-knights. But she is also presented as above the Queen of the Faeries, and in some sense the goddess whom Aureola adores – her name is invoked every night by the Faery Queen, and a goddess invoked at night must evoke Diana, the moon, with whom Elizabeth was so often identified. Again she is Astreaea, the virgin who brings peace and the golden age.

Elvetham includes interesting anticipations of later developments of the masque. Sylvanus and his followers partake more of the nature of an ante-masque than of equal disputants in a matter, such as are Therion and the foresters in *The Lady of May*, for example,[10] and the structure of the Second Day's entertainment, with the defeat of Sylvanus preceding the arrival of Neaera in her pinnace is that of the later Jonsonian/Jonesian masque (e.g. the suppression of the Satyrs before the arrival of Oberon, or the driving out of the perversions of love before the arrival of the king in *Love's Triumph though Callipolis*).[11] A comparison of Elvetham with the early Woodstock entertainment[12] shows how far advanced it is in sophistication of presentation. Where *The Hermit's Tale* is a prose narrative with dramatic interludes, based on the mysterious irruption into a feast followed by a lengthy explanation which is so frequent a feature of romances, in Elvetham we have a masque which is closely related to contemporary French and Italian entertainments[13] and which is without parallel in England until the full flowering of the form in the succeeding reigns.

What sets Elvetham apart is partly the exquisite realization of the idealized amosphere of Elizabethan mythology – the leading of Elizabeth to the house by the Graces is like an animation of Botticelli's *Primavera* or of Calidore's vision in Book VI of *The Faerie Queene*[14] – and partly the careful modulations of the type of entertainment provided. Restricted by his tiny park, Lord Seymour was unable, unlike Lord Montague, to fall back on hunting to entertain his guest. Variety and novelty had to be provided by the entertainment itself. From the Latin speech of the Poet (an implied – and deserved – compliment to Elizabeth's learning) to the lyricism of the songs under the window (which are themselves various, the pastoral being succeeded by the fantasy) to the spectacle of the fireworks and the procession of the Tritons and the boats across the water – again, in themselves contrasts – to the knockabout of the water-battle, there is no repetition, no tedium. The changes are beautifully modulated, particularly in the water-battle, where the lyricism is restored after the comedy in Neaera's oration.

TEXTS

The first description of the entertainment appeared within a week of Elizabeth's departure. There are three separate editions:

S.R. 1591, Oct. 1. 'The honorable entertainment gyven to the quenes maiestie in progresse at Elvetham in Hampshire by the right honorable the Erle of Hertford.' *John Wolf* (Arber, ii, 596).

1. & 2. 1591. The Honorable Entertainement gieuen to the Queenes Maiestie in Progresse, at Eluetham in Hampshire, by the right Honorable the Earle of Hertford. *John Wolfe.* 2 issues (1,) without, (2.) with woodcut of the pond. (Bond, 1902, considers these two different editions; Chambers, 1923, to be two issues of the same edition.) Cambridge U. Lib. Bb*. 11. 50' (E).

3. 1591 . . . Newly corrected and amended. This has a different woodcut.

3. is followed here, with footnote indications of different readings in 1.

The Honorable Entertainement gieven to the Queene's Majestie in Progresse, at Elvetham in Hampshire, by the Right Hon'ble the Earle of Hertford, 1591.

The Proëme

Before I declare the just time or manner of her Majestie's arrivall and Entertainment at Elvetham, it is needful (for the readers better understanding of everie part and processe in my discourse) that I set downe as well the conveniencie of the place, as also the suffising, by art and labour, of what the place in itselfe could not affoord on the sodaine, for receipt of so great a Majestie, and so honourable a traine.

Elvetham House being scituate in a parke but of two miles in compasse or thereabouts, and of no great receipt,[1] as beeing none of the Earle's chiefe mansion houses; yet for the desire he had to shew his unfained love, and loyall duetie to her most gratious Highnesse, purposing to visite him in this her late Progresse, whereof he had to understand by the ordinarie gesse, as also by his honorable good frendes at Court neare to her Majestie; his honor with all expedition set artificers a work, to the number of three hundred, many daies before her Majestie's arrivall, to inlarge his house with newe roomes and offices. Whereof I omit to speake how manie were destined to the offices of the Quene's Houshold, and will onlie make mention of other such buildings as were raised on the sodaine, fourteene score[2] off from the house on a hill side, within the said parke, for entertainement of Nobles, Gentlemen, and others whatsoever.

First there was made a roome of estate for the Nobles, and at the end thereof a withdrawing place for her Majestie. The outsides of the walles were all covered with boughs, and clusters of ripe hasell nuttes,[3] the insides with arras, the roofe of the place with works of ivy leaves, the floore with sweet herbes and greene rushes.

Neare adjoining unto this, were many offices new builded, as namely, Spicerie, Larderie, Chaundrie,[4] Wine-seller, Ewery,[5] and Panterie: all which were tyled.

Not farre off was erected a large hall, for the entertainement of Knights, Ladies, and Gentlemen of chiefe account.

There was also a severall place for her Majestie's footemen, and their friends.

Then was there a long bowre for her Majestie's guard. – An other for other servants[6] of her Majestie's house.[7] – An other for my Lord's Steward, to keep his table in. – An another for his Gentlemen that waited.

Most of these foresaid roomes were furnished with tables, and the tables carried twenty-three yards in length.

Moreover on the same hill, there was raised a great common buttery. – A Pitcher-house. – A large Pastery, with five ovens new built, some of them foureteene foote deepe. – A great Kitchin, with a very long range, for the waste, to serve all commers.[8] – A Boiling-house, for the great boiler. – A roome for the Scullery. – An other roome for the Cooke's lodgings.

Some of these were covered with canvas, and other some with bordes.[9]

Betweene the Earl's[10] house and the foresayd hill, where these roomes were raised, there had been made in the bottom, by handy labour, a goodly Pond, cut to the perfect figure of a half moon.[11] In this Pond were three notable grounds, where hence to present her Majestie with sports and pastimes. The first was a Ship Ile, of a hundred foot in length, and four-score[12] foote broad, bearing three trees orderly set for three masts. The second was a Fort twenty foot square every way, and overgrown with willows. The third and last was a Snayl Mount, rising to foure circles of greene privie[13] hedges, the whole in height twentie foot, and fortie foote broad at the bottom. These three places were equally distant from the sides of the ponde, and everie one, by a just measured proportion, distant from the[14] other. In the said water were divers boates prepared for musicke: but especially there was a pinnace, ful furnisht with masts, yards, sailes, anchors, cables, and all other ordinarie tackling, and with iron peeces;[15] and lastly with flagges, streamers, and pendants, to the number of twelve, all painted with divers colours, and sundry devises.

Here follows a description of the Great Pond in Elvetham, and of the properties which it contained, at such time as her Majestie was there presented with faire shewes and pastimes:

A. Her majestie's presence-seate, and traine.

B. Nereus, and his followers.

C. The pinnace of Neaera, and her musicke.

D. The Ship Ile.

E. A boate with musicke, attending on the pinnace of Neaera.

F. The Fort Mount.

G. The Snaile Mount.

H. The Roome of Estate.

I. Her Majestie's Court.

K. Her Majestie's wardrop.

L. The place whence Silvanus and his companie issued.[16]

To what use these particulars served, it shall evidently appeare by that which followeth. And therefore I am to request the gentle reader, that when any of these places are briefly specified in the sequele of this discourse, it will please him to have reference to this fore-description: that, in avoiding reiterations,[17] I may not seeme to them obscure, whom I studie to please with my plainnesse. For proeme these may suffise: nowe to the matter itselfe: that it may be *ultimum in executione* (to use the old phrase) *quod primum fuit in intentione*,[18] as is usuall to good carpenters; who intending to build a house, yet first lay their foundation, and square many a post, and fasten manie a rafter, before the house be set up: what they first purposed is last done. And thus much for excuse of a long foundation to a short building.

THE FIRST DAIES ENTERTAINEMENT

On the twentie[19] day of September, being Mundaie, the Earle[20] of Hertford joyfullie expecting her Majesties comming to Elvetham, to supper, as her Highnesse had promised: the same morning, about nine of the clock,[21] when everie other needful place or point of service was established and set in order for so great an entertainment, called for, and drewe all his serveants into the chiefe thicket of the parke:[22] where in fewe wordes[23] he put them in minde what quietnes, and what diligence, or other duetie, they were to use at that present: that their service might first work her Majestie's content, and thereby his honor; and lastly, their own credit; with the[24] increase of his love

and favour towards them. This done, after dinner, with his traine
well mounted, to the number of two hundred and upwardes, and
most of them wearing chaines of golde about their neckes,[25] he rode
toward Odiham, and leaving his traine and companie orderlie
placed, to attende her Majestie's comming out of Odiham Parke,
three miles distant from Elvetham: himselfe wayting on her Majestie
from Odiham House.

As the Earl[26] in this first action shewed himself dutiful, so her
Majesty was to him and his most gracious; as also in the sequel,
between five and sixe of the clock, when her Highnes, being most
honorably attended, entred into Elvetham Parke, and was more
than halfe way between the Park-gate and the house, a poet saluted
her with a Latine Oration, in heroicall verse: I mean *veridicus vates*,[27]
a sooth-saying poet, nothing inferior for truth, and little for delivery
of his mind, to an ordinarie Orator. This poet was clad in greene, to
signify the joy of his thoughts at her entrance; a laurel garland on his
head, to expresse that Apollo was patrone of his studies; an olive
branch in his hand, to declare what continuall peace and plentie he
did both wish and aboade[28] her Majestie:[29] and lastly booted, to
betoken that hee was *vates cothurnatus*,[30] and not a loose or lowe
creeping prophet, as poets are interpreted by some idle or envious
ignorants.

This poet's Boy offered him a cushion at his first kneeling to her
Majestie; but he refused it, saying as followeth:

> The poet to his Boy offering him a cushion.
> Non iam pulvillis opus est, sed corde sereno:
> Nam plusquam solitis istic advolvimur aris.
> The Poet's Speach to her Majestie.
> Nuper ad Aönium flexo dum poplite fontem
> Indulsi placido, Phoebi sub pectine, somno,
> Veridicos inter vates, quos Entheus ardor
> Possidet, et virtus nullis offusa lituris,
> Talia securo cantabant carmina Musae.
> Aspicis insueto tingentem lumine coelum
> Anglorum nostro maiorem nomine Nympham
> Os, humerosque Deae similem, dum tuta Semeri
> Tecta petit, qualis dilecta Philaemonis olim
> Cannae[31] Coelicolûm subiit magalia Rector?
> Olli tu blandas humili dic ore salutes;
> Nos dabimus numeros, numeros dabit ipsus Apollo.
> Sed metues tantae summas attingere laudes:
> Nam specie solem, superos virtutibus aequans,

Maiestate locum, sacrisque timoribus implet.
Doctior est nobis, et nobis praesidet una:
Ditior est Ponto, Pontum quoque temperat una:
Pulchrior est nymphis, et nymphis imperat una:
Dignior est divis, et divos allicit una.
  En supplex adsum, Musarum numine ductus,
Et meritis (Augusta) tuis, ô dulcis Elisa,
Fronte serenata modicum dignare poetam,
Né mea vernantem deponant tempora laurum,
Et miser in cantu moriar. Se námque Semeri
Obsequiosa meis condit persona sub umbris:
Qui fert ore preces, oculo foecundat olivam;
Officium precibus, pacem designat oliva;
Affectum docet officiis, et pace quietem;
Mentes affectu mulcebit, membra quiete.
Hi mores, haec vera tui persona Semeri,
Cui laetum sine te nihil, illaetabile tecum
Est nihil. En rident ad vestros omnia vultus
Suaviter, immensum donec fulgoribus orbem
Elisabetha novis imples: nox invidet una:
Astra sed invidiae tollunt mala signa tenebras.
  Caetera, qua possunt, sacrae gratantur Elisae
Laetitia, promptosque ferunt in gaudia vultus.
Limulus insultat per pictos hoedus agellos
Passibus obtortis; et torvum bucula taurum
Blanda petit; tremulus turgescit frondibus arbos,
Graminibus pratum, generosa pampinus uva:
Et tenui latices in arena dulce susurrant,
Insuetumque melos: Te, te, dulcissima princeps,
Terra, polus, fluvii, plantae, pecudesque salutant:
Dumque tuam cupide mirantur singula formam,
Infixis haerent oculis, nequeuntque tuendo
Expleri; solitis sed nunc liberrima curis,
In placidos abeunt animos: non semina vermes,
Non cervi metuunt cassem,[32] non herba calorem,
Non viscum volueres, non fruges grandinis ictum.
O istos (Augusta) dies, o profer in annos;
Et lustrum ex annis, è lustris saecula surgant;
E saeclis aevum, nullo numerabile motu:
Ut nostros dudum quotquot risere dolores,
Gaudia iam numerent, intabescantque videndo.
  En, iter obiecto qua clauserat obice livor,
Virtutis famulae charites, castrique superni

Custodes horae, blandissima numina, iunctim
Iam tollunt remoras, ut arenam floribus ornent.
   Ergo age, supplicibus succede penatibus hospes,
Et nutu moderare tuo: tibi singula parent,
Et nisi parerent tibi singula, tota perirent.
   Dicite Io Paean, et Io ter dicite Paean,
Spargite flore vias, et mollem cantibus auram.

Because all our Countrymen are not Latinists, I thinke it not
amisse to set this downe in English, that all may bee indifferently
partakers of the Poet's meaning.[33]

   The Poet's speech to his Boy offering him a cushion.
Now let us use no cushions, but faire hearts:
For now we kneel to more than usuall Saints.[34]
   The Poet's Speech to her Majestie.
   While, at the fountaine of the sacred hill,
Under Apollo's lute I sweetly slept,[35]
Mongst prophets full possest with holy fury,
And with true vertue, void of all disdaine:
The Muses sung, and waked me with these wordes:
   Seest thou that English Nimph, in face and shape
Resembling some great Goddesse, and whose beames
Doe sprinkle Heaven with unacquainted light,
While shee doth visite Semers[36] fraudlesse house,[37]
As Jupiter did honour with his presence
The poore thatcht cottage, where Philaemon dwelt?
See thou salute her with an humble voice;
Phoebus and we will let thee lack no verses.
But dare not once aspire to touch her praise,
Who, like the Sunne for shew, to Gods for vertue,
Fills all with Majesty, and holy feare.
More learned then ourselves, shee ruleth us:
More rich than Seas, shee doth commaund the Seas:
More fair then Nimphs, she governs all the Nimphs:
More worthy then the Gods, she wins the Gods.
   Behold (Augusta) thy poore suppliant
Is here, at their desire, but thy desert.
O sweet Elisa, grace me with a looke,
Or from my browes this laurell wreath will fall,
And I, unhappy, die amidst my song.
Under my person Semer hides himselfe,
His mouth yeelds prayers, his eie the olive branch;

His praiers betoken duety, th'olive peace;
His duety argues love, his peace faire rest;
His love will smooth youre minde, faire rest your body.
This is your Semers heart and quality:
To whom all thing are joyes, while thou art present,
To whom nothing is pleasing, in thine absence.
Behold, on thee how each thing sweetly smiles,
To see thy brightnes glad our hemispheare:
Night only envies: whome faire stars doe crosse:
All other creatures strive to shewe their joyes.
The crooked-winding kid trips ore the lawnes;
The milkewhite heafer wantons with the bull;
The trees shew pleasure with their quivering leaves,
The meddow with new grasse, the vine with grapes,
The running brookes with sweet and silver sound.[38]
Thee, thee (sweet Princes), heav'n, and earth, and fluds,
And plants, and beasts, salute with one accord:
And while they gaze on thy perfections,
Their eyes desire is never satisfied.
Thy presence frees each thing, that liv'd in doubt:
No seedes now feare the biting of the woorme;
Nor deere the toyles; nor grasse the parching heat;
Nor birds the snare; nor corne the storme of haile.[39]
O Empresse, O draw foorth these dayes to yeares,
Yeeres to an age, ages to eternitie;
That such as lately joyd to see our sorrowes,
May sorrow now, to see our perfect joyes.
　　Behold where all the Graces, vertues maydes,
And lightfoote Howrs, the guardians of Heav'n's gate,
With joyned forces doe remove those blocks,
Which Envie layd in Majestie's highway.
　　Come, therefore, come under our humble roofe,
And with a becke commaund what it containes:
For all is thine; each part obeys thy will;
Did not each part obey, the wholl should perish.
　　Sing songs, faire Nymphs, sing sweet triumphal songs,
Fill ways with flowrs, and th'ayr with harmony.

While the Poet was pronouncing this Oration, six Virgins were behind him, busily remooving blockes out of her Majestie's way; which blocks were supposed to bee layde there by the person of Envie, whose condition is to envie at every good thing, but especially to malice the proceedings of Vertue, and the glory of true Majestie.

Three of these Virgins represented the three Graces, and the other three the Howres, which by the Poets are fained to be the Guardians of Heaven's gates.[40] They were all attired in gowns of taffata sarcenet of divers colours, with flowrie garlands on their heads, and baskets full of sweet hearbs and flowers upon their armes. When the Poet's Speach was happily ended, and in a scroule delivered to her Majestie (for such was her gratious acceptance, that she deined to receive it with her owne hande);[41] then these six Virgins, after performance of their humble reverence to her Highnesse, walked on before her towards the house, strewing the way with flowers, and singing a sweete song of six parts, to this dittie which followeth.[42]

The Song sung by the Graces and the Houres at her Majesties first arrivall.

With fragrant flowers we strew the way,
And make this our chiefe holliday:
For though this clime were blest of yore,
Yet was it never proud before.
　　O beauteous Quene of second Troy,[43]
　　Accept of our unfained joy.

Now th'ayre is sweeter than sweet balme,
And Satyrs daunce about the palme:[44]
Now earth, with verdure newly dight,
Gives perfect signe of her delight.
　　O beauteous Quene of second Troy,
　　Accept of our unfained joy.

Now birds record new harmonie,
And trees doe whistle melodie:
Now everie thing that nature breeds,
Doth clad itself in pleasant weeds,
　　O beauteous Quene of second Troy,
　　Accept of our unfained joy.[45]

This song ended with her Majestie's entrance into the house: and her Majesty alighted from horsebacke at the Hall-dore, the Countesse of Hertford,[46] accompanied with divers honourable Ladies and Gentlewomen, moste humbly on hir knees welcomed hir Highnesse to that place: who most graciously imbracing hir, tooke hir up, and kissed hir, using manie comfortable and princely Speeches, as wel to hir, as to the Earl of Hertford standing hard by, to the great rejoysing of manie beholders. And after hir Majestie's entrance,[47] where shee had not rested her a quarter of an houre, but from the Snail Mount and the Ship Ile in the pond (both being neare under the prospect of her gallerie windowe) where was a long volley of chambers and two brasse peeces[48] discharged. After this, supper was served in, first to her Majestie, and then to the Nobles and others. Were it not that I would not seem to flatter the honorable minded Earle; or, but that I feare to displease him, who rather desired to expresse his loyall dutie in his liberall bountie, then to heare of it againe, I could heere willingly particulate the store of his cheare and provision, as likewise the carefull and kind diligence of his servantes, expressed in their quiet service to her Majestie and the Nobility, and by their loving entertainment to all other, frends or strangers. But I leave the bountie of the one, and the industrie of the others, to the just report of such as beheld or tasted the plentifull abundance of that time and place.

After supper was ended, her Majestie graciously admitted unto her presence a notable consort of six Musitions, which the Earl[49] of Hertford had provided to entertaine her Majestie withall,[50] at her will and pleasure, and when it should seeme good to her Highnesse. Their musicke so highly pleased her, that in grace and favour thereof, she gave a newe name unto one of their Pavans, made long since by Master Thomas Morley, then organist of Paule's Church.[51]

These are the chiefe pointes which I noted in the first daies entertainment. Now therefore it followeth, that I proceed to the second.

THE SECOND DAIES ENTERTAINMENT

On the next day following, being Tuesday, and Saint Mathewes festivall, there was in the morning presented to her Majesty a faire and rich gift from the Countesse of Hertforde, which greatly pleased and contented hir Highnesse.[52] The forenoone was so wet and stormie, that nothing of pleasure could bee presented her Majestie. Yet it helde up a little before dinner time, and all the day after: where otherwise faire sports would have beene buried in foule weather.

This day her Majestie dined, with her Nobles about her, in the roome of estate new builded on the hil side, above the ponds head. There sate below her many Lords, Ladies, and Knights. The manner of service, and abundance of dainties, I omit upon just consideration; as also the ordinance discharged in the beginning of dinner, a variety of consorted music at dinner time.[53]

Presently after dinner, the Earl[54] of Hertford caused a large canapie of estate to bee set at the ponds head, for her Majestie to sit under, and to view some sportes prepared in the water. The canapie was of greene satten, lined with greene taffeta sarcenet; everie seame covered with a broad silver lace; valenced[55] about, and fringed with greene silke and silver, more then a handbredth in depth; supported with four silver pillers moveable; and dekt above head with four white plumes, spangled with silver.[56] This canapie being upheld by foure worthie Knightes (Sir Henrie Greie, Sir Walter Hungerford, Sir James Maruin, and Lord George Caro);[57] and tapestry spread all about the pondes head, her Majestie, about foure of the clocke, came and sate under it, to expect the issue of some devise, being advertised[58] that there was some such thing towards.

At the further end of the ponde, there was a bower, close built to the brinke thereof; out of which there went a pompous array of sea-persons, which waded brest-high or swam till they approached neare the seat of her Majestie. Nereus, the Prophet of the Sea, attired in redde silke, and having a cornerd-cappe on his curlde heade, did swimme before the rest, as their pastor and guide. After him came five Tritons brest-high in the water, all with grislie[59] heades, and beardes of divers colours and fashions, and all five cheerefully sounding their trumpets. After them went two other Gods of the Sea, Neptune and Oceanus, Phorcus and Glaucus,[60] leading betweene them that pinnace whereof I spake in the beginning of this treatise.

In the pinnace were three Virgins, which, with their cornets,[61] played Scottish gigs, made three parts in one. There was also in the saide pinnace an other Nymph of the Sea, named Neaera, the old supposed love of Sylvanus, a God of the Woodes. Neare to her were placed three excellent voices, to sing to one lute, and in two other boats hard by, other lutes and voices, to answer by manner of eccho.[62] After the pinnace, and two other boats which were drawne after it by other Sea-gods, the rest of the traine followed brest-high in the water, all attired in ouglie marine suites, and everie one armed with a huge woodden squirt in his hand: to what end it shall appear hereafter. In their marching towards the pond, all along the middle of the current, the Tritons sounded one halfe of the way; and then they ceasing, the cornets plaid their Scottish gigs. The melody was sweet, and the shew stately.

By the way, it is needful to touch here many thinges abruptly, for the better understanding of that which followeth.

First, that in the pinnace are two jewels to be presented to her Majestie: the one by Nereus, the other by Neaera.

Secondly, that the Fort in the Pond is round environed with armed men.

Thirdly, that the Snayl Mount nowe resembleth a monster, having hornes full of wild-fire, continually burning.

And lastly, that the god Silvanus lieth with his traine not farre off in the woodes, and will shortly salute her Majestie, and present her with a holly scutchion, wherein Apollo had long since written her praises.

All this remembred and considered, I now returne to the Sea-gods; who having, under the conduct of Nereus, brought the pinnace neare before her Majesty, Nereus made his Oration, as followeth; but before he began, hee made a privie signe unto one of his traine, which was gotten up into the Shippe Ile, directly before her Majestie; and hee presently did cast himselfe downe, dooing a summer-sawt[63] from the Ile into the water, and then swam to his companie.

The Oration of Nereus to her Majesty.[64]
Faire Cinthia the wide Ocean's Empresse,
I watry Nereus hovered on the coast,
To greete your Majesty with this my traine
Of dauncing Tritons, and shrill singing Nimphs.
But all in vaine: Elisa was not there;
For which our Neptune grievd, and blamd the star,
Whose thwarting influence dasht our longing hope.
Therefore impatient, that this worthles earth
Should beare your Highnes weight, and we Sea-gods,
(Whose jealous waves have swallowd up your foes,
And to your Realme are walles impregnable),[65]
With such large favour seldome time are grac't:
I from the deepes have drawen this winding flud,
Whose crescent forme figures the rich increase
Of all that sweet Elisa holdeth deare.[66]
And with me came gould breasted India,[67]
Who, daunted at your sight, leapt to the shoare,
And sprinkling endlesse treasure on this Ile,
Left me this jewell to present your Grace,[68]
For hym, that under you doth hold this place.[69]
See where her ship remaines, whose silke-woven takling
Is turnde to twigs, and threefold mast to trees,
Receiving life from verdure of your lookes;
(For what cannot your gracious looks effect?)
Yon ugly monster creeping from the South[70]

To spoyle these blessed fields of Albion,
By selfe same beams is chang'd into a snaile,[71]
Whose bullrush hornes are not of force to hurt.
As this snaile is, so be thine enemies!
And never yet did Nereus wishe in vaine.
That Fort did Neptune raise, for your defence;
And in this barke, which gods hale neare the shore,
White-footed Thetis[72] sends her musicke maydes,
To please Elisaes eares with harmony.
Hear them, fair Quene: and when their musick ends,
My Triton shall awake the Sylvane gods,
To doe their hommage to your Majesty.

This Oration being delivered, and withall the present whereof he spake, which was hidden in a purse of greene rushes, cunningly woaven together: immediately the three voices in the pinnace sung a song to the lute, with excellent divisions, and the end of every verse was replied by lutes and voices in the other boate somewhat afarre off, as if they had beene ecchoes.

The Song presented by Nereus on the water, sung dialogue-wise, everie fourth verse answered with two Echoes.

Dem.   How haps it now when prime[73] is done,
         Another spring-time is begun?
Resp. Our happie soile is overrunne,
         With beautie of a second sunne.
                Eccho A second sunne.

Dem.   What heavenlie lampe, with holie light,
         Doeth so increase our climes delight?
Resp. A lampe whose beams are ever bright,
         And never feares approching Night.
                Eccho. Approching Night.

Dem.   Why sing we not eternall praise,
         To that faire shine of lasting daies?
Resp. He shames himselfe that once assaies
         To fould such wonder in sweete laies.
                Eccho. In sweet laies.

Dem.   O yet devoid of envious blame,
         Thou maist unfold hir sacred name.
Resp. 'Tis dread Eliza, that faire name
         Who filles the golden trump of Fame.
                Eccho. Trump of Fame.

Dem.   O never may so sweete a Quene,
    See dismall daies or deadly teene.[74]
Resp.   Graunt Heavens hir daies may stil be greene,
    For like to hir was never seene.
        Eccho. Was never seene.[75]

This song being ended, Nereus commaunded the five Tritons to sound. Then came Sylvanus with his attendants, from the wood: himselfe attired, from the middle downewards to the knee, in kiddes skinnes with the haire on; his legges, bodie, and face, naked, but died over with saffron, and his head hooded with a goates skin, and two little hornes over his forehead, bearing in his right hand an olive tree, and in his left a scutchion, whereof I spake somewhat before. His followers were all covered with ivy-leaves, and bare in their hands bowes made like darts.[76] At their approche[77] neare her Majesty, Sylvanus spake as followeth, and delivered up his scutchion, ingraven with goulden characters, Nereus and all[78] his traine still continuing near her Highnesse.

    The Oration of Sylvanus.
Sylvanus comes from out the leavy groaves,
To honor her whom all the world adores,
Faire Cinthia, whom no sooner Nature fram'd,
And deckt with Fortunes and with Vertues dower,
But straight admiring what her skill had wrought,
She broake the mould; that never sunne might see
The like to Albion's Quene for excellence.
Twas not the Tritons ayr-enforcing shell,[79]
As they perhaps would proudly make theyr vaunt,
But those faire beames that shoote from Majesty,
Which drew our eyes to wonder at thy worth.
That worth breeds wonder; wonder holy feare;
And holy feare unfayned reverence.
Amongst the wanton dayes of goulden age,
Apollo playing in our pleasant shades,
And printing oracles in every leafe,
Let fall this sacred scutchion from his brest;
Wherein is writ, 'Detur dignissimae.'[80]
O therefore hold what Heaven hath made thy right,
I but in duety yeeld desert her due.
Nereus. But see, Sylvanus, where thy Love doth sit.
Sylvanus. My sweet Neaera, was her eare so neare?
    O set my hearts delight upon this banke,

That, in compassion of old sufferance,
Shee may relent in sight of Beauties Quene.
Nereus. On this condition shall shee come on shoare,
That with thy hand thou plight a solemne vow,
Not to prophane her undefiled state.[81]
Sylvanus. Here, take my hand, and therewithall I vowe.
Nereus. That water will extinguish wanton fire.

Nereus, in pronouncing this last line, did plucke Sylvanus over
head and eares into the water, where all the sea-gods, laughing, did
insult over him. In the meane while her Majesty perused the verses
written in the scutchion, which were these:
Aöniis prior, et Divis es pulchrior alti
AEquoris, ac Nymphis es prior Idaliis.
Idaliis prior es Nymphis, ac aequoris alti.
Pulchrior et Divis, ac prior Aöniis.[82]
Over these verses was this poesy written:
Detur dignissimae.

After that the sea-gods had sufficiently duckt Sylvanus, they
suffered him to creep to[83] land, where he no sooner set footing, but
crying 'Revenge, Revenge,' he and his begunne a skirmish with
those of the water; the one side throwing their darts, and the other
using their squirtes, and the Tritons sounding a pointe of warre. At
the last, Nereus parted the fray with a line or two, grounded on the
excellence of her Majestyes presence, as being alwaies friend to
Peace, and ennemy to Warre. Then Sylvanus, being so ugly, and
running toward the bower at the end of the Pound, affrighted a
number of the countrey people, that they ran from him for feare, and
thereby moved great laughter.[84] His followers retired to the woods;
and Neaera his faire Love, in the pinnace, presenting her Majestie a
sea-jewell, bearing the forme of a fanne, spake unto her as followeth:

The Oration of faire Neaera.
When Neptune late bestowed on me this barke,
And sent by me this present to your Grace:
Thus Nereus sung, who never sings but truth.
Thine eyes (Neaera) shall in time behold
A sea-borne Quene, worthy to governe Kings:
On her depends the fortune of thy boate,
If shee but name it with a blisfull word,
And view it with her life-inspiring beames.
Her beames yeeld gentle influence, like fayre starres;
Her silver soundinge word is prophesie.

Speake, sacred Sibyl, give some prosperous name,
That it may dare attempt a golden fleece,[85]
Or dive for pearles, and lay them in thy lap.
For winde and waves, and all the worlde besides,
Will make her way, whom thou shalt doome to blisse,
For what is Sibyl's speech but oracle?

Here her Majesty named the pinnace, The Bonadventure; and
Neaera went on with her speech, as followeth:

Now Neaeraes barke is fortunate,[86]
And in thy service shall imploy her saile,
And often make returne to thy availe.
O live in endlesse joy, with glorious fame,
Sound trumpets, sounde, in honor of her name.

Then did Nereus retire backe to his bower, with all his traine
following him, in selfe same order as they came forth before, the
Tritons sounding their trumpets one halfe of the way, and the
cornets playing the other halfe.

And here ended the second daies pastime, to the so great liking of
her Majestie, that her gracious approbation thereof, was to the
actors more than a double reward; and yet withall, her Highnes
bestowed a largesse uppon them the next daie after, before shee
departed.

THE THIRDE DAIES ENTERTAINMENT

On Wednesday morning, about nine of the clock, as her Majesty
opened a casement of her Gallerie window, there were three
excellent Musicians, who, being disguised in auncient countrey
attire,[87] did greet her with a pleasant song of Coridon and Phyllida,
made in three parts of purpose. The song, as well for the worth of the
dittie, as for the aptnes of the note thereto applied, it pleased her
Highnesse, after it had been once sung, to commaund it againe, and
highly to grace it with her chearefull acceptance and commendation.

The Three Men's Song, sung the third morning, under hir
Majesties Gallerie window.[88]
In the merrie moneth of May,
In a morne, by breake of day,
Forth I walked by the wood side,
Where as May was in his pride.

There I spied, all alone,
Phyllida and Corydon.
Much adoe there was, God wot,
He would love, and she would not.
She said, never man was true:
He said, none was false to you.
He said, he had loved her long:
She said, love should have no wrong.
Coridon would kisse her then:
She said, maides must kisse no men,
Till they did for good and all.
Then she made the shepheard call
All the heavens to witnesse truth,
Never lov'd a truer youth.
Thus with many a pretie oath,
Yea and nay, and faith and troth,
Such as silly shepheardes use,
When they will not love abuse;
Love, which had beene long deluded,
Was with kisses sweet concluded:
And Phyllida, with garlands gay,
Was made the Lady of the May.[89]

The same day after dinner, about three of the clocke, ten of the Earle[90] of Hertford's servants, all Somersetshire[91] men, in a square greene court, before her Majesties windowe, did hang up lines, squaring out the forme of a tennis-court, and making a crosse line in the middle. In this square they (beeing stript out of their dublets) played, five to five, with the hand-ball, at bord and cord (as they tearme it) to so great liking of her Highnes, that she graciously deyned to beholde their pastime more then an houre and a halfe.[92]

After supper there were two delights presented unto her Majestie: curious fireworks, and a sumptuous banket. The first from the three Ilands in the Pond: the second in a lowe Gallerie in her Majesties Privie-garden. But I will first briefly speake of the fire-works.

First, there was a peale of a hundred chambers discharged from the Snail Mount; in counter whereof, a like peale was discharged from the Ship Ile, and some great ordinance withal. Then was there a castle of fire-works of all sorts, which played in the Fort. Answerable to that, there was in the Snail Mount, a globe of all manner of fire-works, as big as a barrel. When these were spent on either side, there were many running rockets uppon lines, which past between the Snail Mount and the castle in the Fort. On either side were many fire-wheeles, pikes of pleasure, and balls of wilde fire,[93] which burned in the water.

During the time of these fire-workes in the water, there was a banket[94] served, all in glasse and silver, into the lowe Gallerie in the garden, from a hill side foureteene score off, by two hundred of my Lord of Hertforde's gentlemen, everie one carrying so many dishes, that the whole number amounted to a thousand: and there were to light them in their way a hundred torch-bearers.[95]

THE FOURTH DAIES ENTERTAINMENT

On Thursday morning, her Majestie was no sooner readie, and at her Gallerie window looking into the Garden, but there began three Cornets to play certaine fantastike dances, at the measure whereof the Fayery Quene came into the garden, dauncing with her maides about her. Shee brought with her a garland, made in fourme of an imperiall crowne; within the sight of her Majestie shee fixed upon (sic) a silvered[96] staffe, and sticking the staffe into the ground, spake as followeth:

The Speech of the Fairy Quene to her Majestie.
I that abide in places under-ground,
Aureola, the Quene of Fairy land,
That every night in rings of painted flowers
Turne round, and carrell out Elisaes name:
Hearing, that Nereus and the Sylvane gods
Have lately welcomde your Imperiall Grace,
Oapend the earth with this enchanting wand,
To doe my duety to your Majestie,
And humbly to salute you with this chaplet,
Given me by Auberon, the Fairy King.
Bright shining Phoebe, that in humaine shape,
Hid'st Heaven's perfection, vouchsafe t'accept it:
And I Aureola, belov'd in heaven,
(For amorous starres fall nightly in my lap)[97]
Will cause that Heavens enlarge thy goulden dayes,
And cut them short, that envy at thy praise.

After this speech, the Fairy Quene and her maides daunced about the Garden, singing a Song of Sixe parts, with the musicke of an exquisite consort; wherein was the lute, bandora, base-violl, citterne, treble-violl, and flute. And this was the Fairies Song:

Elisa is the fairest Quene,
That ever trod upon this greene.
Elisaes eyes are blessed starres,
Inducing peace, subduing warres.
Elisaes hand is christal bright,
Her wordes are balme, her lookes are light.
Elisaes brest is that faire hill,
Where Vertue dwels, and sacred skill,
O blessed bee each day and houre,
Where sweet Elisa builds her bowre.[98]

This spectacle and musicke so delighted Her Majesty, that shee commaunded to heare it sung and danced three times over, and called for divers Lords and Ladies to behold it:[99] and then dismist the Actors with thankes, and with a gracious larges, which of her exceeding goodnesse she bestowed uppon them.

Within an howre after her Majesty departed, with her Nobles, from Elvetham. It was a most extreame rain, and yet it pleased hir Majesty to behold and hear the whole action.[100] On the one side of her way, as shee past through the parke, there was placed, sitting on the Pond side, Nereus and all the sea-gods, in their former attire: on her left hand Sylvanus and all his[101] company: in the way before her, the three Graces, and the three Howres: all of them on everie side wringing their hands, and shewing signe of sorrow for her departure, he being attired as at the first, saving that his cloak was now black,[102] and his garland mixed with ugh branches, to signifie sorrow.[103] While she beheld this dum shew, the poet made her a short oration, as followeth:

The Poet's Speech at her Majestie's departure.
O see, sweet Cynthia, how the watry gods,
Which joyd of late to view thy glorious beames,
At this retire doe waile and wring their hands,
Distilling from their eyes salt showrs of teares,
To bring in Winter with their wet lament:
For how can Sommer stay, when Sunne departs?[104]
See where Sylvanus sits, and sadly mournes,
To thinke that Autumn, with his withered wings,
Will bring in tempest, when thy beames are hence:
For how can Sommer stay, when Sunne departs?
See where those Graces, and those Howrs of Heav'n,
Which at thy comming sung triumphall songs,
And smoothd the way, and strewed it with sweet flowrs,

Now, if they durst, would stop it with greene bowes,
Least by thine absence the yeeres pride decay:
For how can Sommer stay, when Sunne departs?
Leaves fal, grasse dies, beasts of the wood hang head,
Birds cease to sing, and everie creature wailes,
To see the season alter with this change:
For how can Sommer stay, when Sunne departs?
O, either stay, or soone returne againe,
For Sommers parting is the countries paine.

Then Nereus, approching from the ende of the Pond, to hir Majesties coach, on his knees thanked hir Highnesse for hir late largesse, saying as followeth:

Thankes, gracious Goddesse, for thy bounteous largesse,
Whose worth, although it yeelds us sweet content,
Yet thy depart gives us a greater sorrow.[105]

After this, as her Majestie passed through the parke gate, there was a consort of musicians hidden in a bower; to whose playing this dittie of 'Come againe' was sung, with excellent division, by two that were cunning.

The Song sung at the gate, when hir Majestie departed. (As this Song was sung, hir Majestie, notwithstanding the great raine, staied hir coach, and pulled off hir mask,[106] giving great thanks.)

Come againe, faire Nature's treasure,
Whose lookes yeeld joyes exceeding measure.

Come againe, worlds starre-bright eye,
Whose presence bewtifies the skie.

Come againe, worlds chiefe delight,
Whose absence makes eternall Night.

Come againe, sweete lively Sunne,
When thou art gone our joyes are done.

O come againe, faire Nature's treasure,
Whose lookes yeeld joyes exceeding measure.

O come againe, heavens chiefe delight,
Thine absence makes eternall night.

O come againe, worlds star-bright eye,
Whose presence doth adorne the skie.

O come againe, sweet beauties Sunne:
When thou art gone, our joyes are done.[107]

Her Majestie was so highly pleased with this and the rest, that she openly said to the Earle of Hertford,[108] that the beginning, processe, and end of this his entertainment, was so honorable, she would not forget the same.[109]

And manie[110] most happie yeares may her gratious Majestie continue, to favour and foster him, and all others which do truly love and honor her.

Ditchley 1592

To understand fully this elaborate entertainment, the culmination of Sir Henry Lee's years of formulation of Elizabeth's cult through a series of tilts and entertainments, it is necessary to look in some detail at two visits which Elizabeth paid on the Progress of 1575. The first of these was to the Earl of Leicester at Kenilworth. The theme of the entertainment was Arthur, and Arthur-come-again as Elizabeth; the object was to persuade Elizabeth to marry Leicester. From the first, the emphasis was on the splendour of Arthur's days, and how Elizabeth and Leicester might make them live again. On her approach to the castle Elizabeth was greeted by the Lady of the Lake, a figure from romance,[1] and later in her stay she was to be instrumental in rescuing this same lady from the persecution of Sir Bruse sans Foy, who was to hold the Lady of the Lake in subjection until a better virgin than she should arrive at Kenilworth. The awkward question of why the Lady had not been freed on either of Elizabeth's two previous visits to the place was not raised. In this episode Elizabeth has performed an adventure – the rescue of a Lady from oppression – in the tradition of her ancestor, Arthur.

In case Elizabeth, or anyone else, failed to perceive the Arthurian references and implications of the Kenilworth entertainment, they were clearly pointed out in an encounter which Elizabeth had on the Sunday of her stay. Riding in the wooded park she met, appropriately enough, a Sylvan Man, who proceeded to wonder at the events taking place in his haunts, the causes of his bewilderment being ingeniously explained by a convenient Echo:[2]

'And what meant those great men, which on the walls were seen?[3]
They were some Gyants certainly, no men so bigge have been.
    Have been.
Have been? why then they served King Arthur, man of might;
And ever since this castle kept for Arthur's heyres by right.
    Right.'[4]

'Arthur's heyres' are of course Leicester's family in their position as guardians of Arthur's castle, and Elizabeth as his descendant, the ruler of his kingdom. The whole entertainment is designed to show that Arthur's heirs, Elizabeth of his kingdom, and Leicester of his castle, should bring back the Arthurian golden age by the harmony of their marriage.

After the pointed moral of this entertainment it is a relief (as it probably was for Elizabeth) to turn to the entertainment which Sir Henry Lee offered her at Woodstock later in the same progress. Here the object was to celebrate, flatter and amuse Elizabeth; and also to provide some sort of answer to the persuasion of Leicester's entertainments.[5] Again the visit was put in the context of a chivalric romance. During Elizabeth's visit Lee staged three days of major entertainment for her. They were centered on the tale of Contarenus and Gaudina, and Elizabeth found herself taking part in a chivalric romance. But she was no longer as she had been at Kenilworth, the Errant Damsel. Rather she was a *dea ex machina* whose presence resolved all difficulties and brought harmony and order to the tangled affairs of the romance-knights and ladies.

The first day's entertainment consisted of the tale of Hemetes the Hermit. It appears that two knights, Loricus (Lee) and Contarenus, came in and began to fight before the Queen. A lady was also present (at this stage all the characters were of unknown identity and their irruption a complete surprise). Hemetes came in and stopped the fight, saying that the prophecy was now fulfilled, and then proceeded to explain these strange events to the Queen. Gaudina (Gandina in some versions), daughter of Occanon, Duke of Cambaya, fell in love with Contarenus, a knight 'of estate meane, but of value very greate'. Occanon employed an enchantress (at a cost of twenty thousand crowns) to cause Contarenus 'to be caught upp and carryed in the ayre from the coaste of Cambaya to the very bounds of the Occean sea'. The enchantress told the justifiably astonished Contarenus that 'within seven years he should have for his reward the height of his desire. But first he should fighte with the hardyest Knighte, and see the worthiest Ladie, in the whole world'. In the interim he must take under his care a blind hermit 'who shold recover his sighte and he his satisfaction both at one tyme'. Meanwhile Gaudina, unhappy over the dissappearance of Contarenus, heard of her father's trick. She left the court to go in search of her lover, and eventually arrived 'at the grot of Sibylla'. There she met a knight called Loricus, who 'loved a Ladie that was machless in such manner as was strange; for, after much devyse and dyllygens to attayn to that favour that she wold be pleased, he mighte but love her without lokinge for reward'. Loricus has left his country, betaking himself 'to travell and to armes, desiering with most endevour but to deserve that reputacion as this greate and noble mistress wold but thinke hym worthy to be hers thoughe she would never be none of his'. Sibylla told Gaudina and Loricus 'that as they were now coupled by fortune, they should never part fellowshipe till they had found owt a place wheare men were moste stronge, and women most fayre, the country moste fertyll, the people most wealthy, the government most just, and the Princes most wourthy: so should the Ladie see that would content her, so should the Knighte here that would comforte him'. The Hermit himself was once a 'Knighte knowne and accepted of with the best in the world', who loved a Lady with a Protean facility in shape-changing when touched. She eventually changed into a tigress, whereupon Hemetes let her go, and embarked upon a pilgrimage to the temple of Venus at Paphos, hoping to hear of her. As he entered the temple, he was suddenly struck blind for his presumption in attempting to serve both Love and Learning. Mercury carried him to Delphos,[6] where the oracle told him that the remedy for his blindness was 'The best beside the beawtyfullest'. The priest of Apollo explained to him that it is fear which has lost his mistress: he will 'be able to decypher the destyny of every one in love; and better to advise them than the best of hear dearlings', but he will remain blind 'tyll at one tyme and in one place, in a country of most peas, two of the most valyaunt Knights shall fighte, two of the most constant lovers shall meete, and the most vertuous lady in the world shall be there to looke on'. At that time Hemetes will see 'a Ladie in whome enhabiteth the most vertue, learnyng and beawtie, that ever was in creature' and the restoration of his sight will prove that he is in her presence. And now the oracles had all been fulfilled – Contarenus and Loricus had fought, Loricus[7] and Gaudina had met, and Hemetes received his sight. All of which had happened by virtue of Elizabeth's presence. The Hermit then led the Queen to his hermitage, where a banquet was prepared.[8]

The intended, and complicated, compliment to Elizabeth is of course clear, but there are some interesting features. Loricus, unlike Leicester, knows that he cannot attain the Lady whom he loves – he can only hope at the most for some sign of favour from her. There is no claim that they are in any sense equals, as was implied at Kenilworth in the claim that Elizabeth and Leicester are the co-heirs of Arthur. Hemetes loses his lady through fear, and fear has no place in love, but it is not suggested that had he not feared he would not have lost his lady – rather the implication is that he was mistaken in attempting to love *par amours* a lady towards whom fear is the appropriate emotion. And it is made clear that Hemetes himself, not being single-minded in his pursuit of love, is not acceptable as a lover. Elizabeth herself is involved in the action in only a passive way, although she is the catalyst which sets all to rights. She does not participate as she did at Kenilworth by answering the Lady of the Lake.[9] But several of the characters in *The Hermit's Tale* have clear references to her – the mistresses of Loricus and Hemetes, and as will be seen, Gaudina.

During the banquet which followed *The Hermit's Tale* 'to the sound
of music from a hollow room beneath the house' Elizabeth 'was
visited by the Queen of the Fayry',[10] who greeted her and paid her
compliments. The second day's entertainment, on September 20,
consisted of a playlet in which the story of Gaudina and Contarenus
was resumed:

> 'Occanon, who has traced Gaudina by inquiry of Sibylla, comes to
> seek her at the court. With the aid of the Fairy Queen, here named
> Eambia, he persuades his daughter and Contarenus to resign each
> other, in order that Gaudina may return home with him, and for the
> sake of the country make a match more befitting her degree.'[11]

The contrast with Kenilworth is again striking. Leicester had
argued constantly for a marrige which would have been both
unsuitable and unpopular (an unperformed masque[12] argued the
superiority of Juno, goddess of marriage, to Diana, goddess of
virginity, in their claims for Elizabeth's allegiance). Elizabeth had in
fact been greatly displeased by the tenor of the entertainment, and
was with difficulty persuaded not to terminate her visit earlier than
intended: Yates's claim that Kenilworth pleased less than
Woodstock because it was old-fashioned[13] will not stand; Kenilworth was visually more varied, and contained an up-to-date
Italianate water-spectacle, whereas Woodstock was essentially a mini-
romance, based on the premise of the interrupted feast, in which the
strange events which disrupt the meal of a chivalric leader are
explained to him and then brought to a conclusion by his
mediation.[14] Lee's entertainment argued the priority of duty to one's
kingdom over personal inclination, and that the proper relationship
of Elizabeth's knights to her was one of unquestioning adoration
which accepted the fact that there would be no return, and no
reward, save perhaps that of having their service recognized. It is an
almost open contradiction of the Kenilworth theme. It is possible
that Lee, knowing the tenor of the entertainment to be put on by
Leicester (Gascoigne, translator of *The Hermit's Tale*, was the deviser
of the Kenilworth entertainment) decided to make his present
(although much more tactfully) the opposition case. Certainly his
theme of duty to one's kingdom and the importance of 'self-esteem
founded on just and right' proved more acceptable to Elizabeth than
the oblique proposals of an over-mighty subject.

At Ditchley, Lee returns to the story of Loricus with which he had
diverted Elizabeth at Woodstock seventeen years earlier. Once more

the entertainment takes the form of a romance, but this time Elizabeth is the Lady-Errant, the righter of wrongs and dispeller of enchantment. The inspiration for the romance-*motifs*, too, seems to have changed, and although there are still elements from the Arthurian tradition, notably the knight-turned-hermit, the influence of Spenser's *Faerie Queene* may be traced in the incidents of the Knights and Ladies in the trees, and in the sleeping knight in the bower, which must recall the enchanted Verdant in the Bower of Bliss.[15] The source of the *motifs* in the Ditchley Entertainment may indicate something about its nature: while it does not, like Woodstock, refer to a specific issue (the right relationship of Elizabeth's servants to her, and, more generally, the place of personal considerations in the marriages of those in power), it is concerned with the freeing of knights and ladies from a moral failing, rather than from a physical or supernatural danger: like a Spenserian heroine Elizabeth, by her constancy, rescues those trapped by the inconstancy of their own natures. And like an episode in *The Faerie Queene*, different aspects of inconstancy and constancy are explored. Elizabeth shows constancy, i.e. fortitude, in her refusal to be daunted by the warnings of the guardian of the grove and her passage through it, but it is her constancy, i.e. unchangingness, which enables her to make that passage in safety and to free the sleeping knight. The arboriform knights have displayed constancy, i.e. faithfulness in love, as does the speaker for constancy in the formal debate. The forms of inconstancy are equally varied. Inconstancy in the dialogue with Constancy is unfaithfulness and changeability in love, but the Inconstancy which has claimed the ladies imprisoned in the leaves seems to be an instability of purpose and lack of steadfastness which has led to their inability to correctly interpret the enchanted pictures, and thus to their transformation to leaves, the epitome of inconstancy, always in motion, subject to every wind, doomed to fall at the onslaught of winter. The Old Knight's inconstancy has been in his unfaithfulness to the Fairy Queen, as custodian of the enchanted pictures, in becoming the 'stranger ladies thrall': his sin is 'neglect of dutie'.

Elizabeth's epitomization of constancy was a major theme of her cult. It is encapsulated in her motto, 'Semper eadem', in the device of the crowned pillar, which figures both in the tilts and in this entertainment, and is implied in the linking of Elizabeth's reign with the golden, prelapsarian age: the Fall of Man brought mutability. Dekker sums up the almost hysterical celebration of Elizabeth's abiding sameness that is typical of the celebrations of the later part of her reign:

'I weepe for joy to see so many heads
Of prudent Ladies, clothed in the liverie
Of silver-handed age, for serving you,
Whilst in your eyes youthes glory doth renue:
I weepe for joy to see the Sunne looke old,
To see the Moone mad at her often change,
To see the Starres onely by night to shine,
Whilst you are still bright, still one, still divine;
I weepe for joy to see the world decay,
Yet see *Eliza* flourishing like May.'[16]

It is the attitude which was to culminate in the posthumous

'She was, she is, (what can there more be said?)
In earth the first, in heaven the second Maid'.[17]

The last day's entertainment at Ditchley, with its continuation of
the story of Loricus begun at Woodstock, raises Elizabeth's status
from that of co-equal to the Fairy Queen, perhaps a Fairy Queen
herself, to that of a goddess. The healing of Loricus is wrought by
the Queen herself, the 'sole vertue of her sacred presence', which has
improved the weather and made the ground fruitful, having cured
him. The healing of the incurably sick is the highest deed that may
be performed by the knight. It marks him out as the 'best knight in
the world'. Sir Urry in *Le Morte D'Arthur* could only be healed when
the 'beste knyght of the world had serched his woundis'[18] and
Lancelot proves himself this by healing him. The culmination of the
long series of miracles performed by Galahad is the healing of the
Maimed King.[19] These miracles put the knight on a level with the
saints. But in both the cases cited from Malory, the knight performs
the miracle by touching the afflicted person. Elizabeth can cure by
her very presence.

It is the zenith of her adventures. She has already, in her enterprise
in the Enchanted Grove, proved herself a bold Lady-Errant, and she
now proves herself 'the beste knyght of the world'. And Loricus's
words to the Chaplain concerning the originator of his recovery,
'whosoever blesseth her, blesseth God in her' recall 'the Father is in
me, and I in him.'[20]

Elizabeth does sometimes seem to be, as well as the Virgin Mary,
Christ himself. This is not as blasphemous as it seems: Christ is
sometimes portrayed as a Knight[21] and it is logical that, their
similarity of function being so emphasized, the knight should
become a type of Christ. There is a suggestion in Galahad's many
miracles and purity of life that he is a Christ-figure. For Elizabeth to

be presented as Christ is merely to stress the perfection of her knighthood.

TEXTS

The entertainment, presumably devised by Lee, may have been written either wholly or in part by Dr. Richard Edes, a royal chaplain.[22] It survives in three MSS, which are fully described by Chambers (1936, App. D, p. 268), and by Leech, 1935. They are (or were)

1. The Hamper MS, a volume of collections made by Henry Ferrers of Baddesley Clinton in Warwickshire, owned and printed by William Hamper in 1820 as *Masques: Performed before Queen Elizabeth*, in 1821 in *Kenilworth Illustrated*, and by Nichols in the 1823 edition of *Progresses of Queen Elizabeth* III, pp. 193 ff. This MS, like so much used by Nichols, is now apparently lost. It contained (VII), (VIII), (IX), (X), (XI), (XII), (XIII), and (XIV) (numbering Chambers's).

2. The Petyt MS in the Inns of Court, another collection, has (ii) and (ix). (Inner Temple Petyt MS 538/43).

3. The Ditchley MS has (I), (II), (III), (IV), (V), (VI), (VII), (VIII), (IX), (X), and parts of (XI). It is imperfect, very scruffy, and comprises of a collection of items related to Elizabethan entertainments, of which the 1592 entertainment material forms items 14 to 24, in a sixteenth-century hand (not Lee's). It seems to have been at Ditchley until Lord Dillon presented it to the British Museum.

In addition the dialogue between Constancy and Inconstancy was printed in *The Phoenix Next* (1593). I have followed Chambers's text of the Ditchley Entertainment but have noted the major variations in *The Phoenix Nest*, and have occasionally preferred the reading of the Ditchley MS (Add. 41499a; Victorian transcription 41499B).

Ditchley, 1592

i. The knight that had charge of the grove.[1]

> Ladye or queene or both: for both may be
> your state, your trayne your person shewes you so
> presse not too far, unlesse you wishe to see
> the dolefull case of them that live in woe
>   & pittie wer it such a one as you
>   shold se the sight wold make your hart to rew.

> This grove (the charge whereof to me belonges
> who stand to give all passengers deniall)
> yealdes nothinge els but syghes & mornfull songes
> of hopeless people by ther haples tryall
>   for everie one in matters that are hidden
>   will seeke the more, the more they are forbidden.

> Yet if you build upon your owne perfection
> as what perfections may not in you rest
> doo as you list follow not my direction
> who feare the worst & praye not for the best
>   or tarry here or if you needes will enter
>   myne be the warning & yours be the venter.[2]

ii. The Second Knights Complaynt:[3]

> What troops are theise which ill advised presse
> in to this more then most unhappie plase
> the very seat of malcontentednes,
> ladyes with loves & lovers with disgrace
>   here shall you see: I shame to name the sightes
>   light harted ladies, heavy harted knightes:

> Light harted ladies, but the fault ther owne,
> by the too much presuminge of ther witts,
> knights heavy harted, but yet overthrowne
> by lovinge those that only love by fitts.
>   both malecontent, they for ther foolishe doinge,
>   & we with them, for our more folishe wooinge.

> But this it is to creditt weomen kynde
> who have ther harts as rowlinge as ther eies
> whose thoughts are fancies, wordes & othes but wynde
> love as a dew wich in the morninge dries
>   with long suit gotten & with endless cost
>   yet by & by with lesse than nothinge lost.

Despayr is all our hope, distrust our staye,
contempt our favore, our reward dysdayne
our answer doubt, our comfort but delaye
our very end but to beginn agayne
    in sorowes circle we runne ever round
    most constantly to most unconstant bound.

Yet in this night of our accursed state
we doe but for that morninge star attend
wich is apoynted by the secret fate
to bringe this hard enchauntment to an end
    wherein tho all that came did take the foyle[4]
    I hope some one in tyme maye it assoyle.

Meane while this grove must be our restinge place
we knights are trees whome roots of faith doe bynd
our ladies [leaves] who sometyme give us grace,
but fall awaie with everie blast of wynd,
    our Springe, our Autumne by ther loue is made
    as they affecte we florish & we fade.[5]

            finis

iii. The [maid]ens[7] song.[6]
    Unconstancie and presumptious yocke
    layd by mishap on ladyes neckes
    whie dost thou all the world prouocke
    to [misiudge][7] & condemne our sexe
        Alas the fault is not in us
        if [it][7] agaynst our wills be thus.

Unconstancie pore woemens shame
witnes theise wants we fynd by the[8]
whereof (tho women beare the blame)
yet men in ded cannot be free,
    Alas thou plaguest not only us
    for men themselves ar punisht thus.

Nor maye ther errors make us cleare:
nor will we joye at others fall
nor do [we][7] question any hear
nor can they Justly touch us all
    Alas ther is but one of us
    A woman & she is not thus.[9]

            finis

iv. The third Knights Songe.[10]

When first I entred this enchaunted wood
to suffer for unconstant weomens sin
I hoped some goodes might have done me good
& locked[11] for end when cares[12] did first beginn
   for tho I fynd myne nowne wer much to blame
   I deamed all others wold not prove the same.

But heare behold the worth of weomens kynd
and for our constant love theise goodly fees,
In this dark grove light weomen are unshrinde
& captive bound as many knights as trees;
   that wishing death hath made with on[13] consent
   this ground ther grove,[14] this grove ther monument.

But leave I now ther follyes to disclose
tho non maye better speack thereof then I
for while this wood or ground [whereon][7] it growes
Shall named be, ther names shall never die
   nor wold I wish to live or bereath on[15] daye
   but that I breath ther follies to displaye.

finis

v. The Knight that had the Charge of the Grove.[16]

This is the farthest gate (most excellent ladie) of that unfortunate grove wherunto your owne only virtue wayted on by the continewal wonder of constant followers[17] hath safely conducted you; yf the darknes of this place[18] or the deadness of theise passiones have breed dyspleasure in you, the openes of a freshe ayer, & the freeddome such od humours, will bringe a better delight; what other contentment my pore service, & humble attendance can procure, you may assuredly presume of, & this I dare promise you (wich is somewhat worth in a straunge Countrye) that so longe as I lead you you shall not lose your waye: Heare abouts not long agoe (most vertuous ladye) did I heare a dolorous knight bewayle his hard hap in a pittiful accent, ther[19] beinge growne (as it should seeme) to some hight of expostulations with himselfe, and hearing the vere[20] to make answer to his wordes, brack forth into the curious demandes of love & quick interragatories of the Nature of lovers, wich passage betwixt him and thechoo, because it then lyked me, I committed to memorie, & will now make report thereof unto your Majestie: and after the riminge of a long examiter he spake thus in a short verse:

Eccho refer misero quid sit amare: E: mare.
si mare, qui fluctus? E. luctus. quid nauita? E: vita:
    quid flumen? E: lumen: dic mihi crimen? E: himen.
qui terrores? E: errores. quis ne erro precor? E: cor.
    cor si erit que tum spes in amore? E: mori[21]

and so dyscontentedly depart.

vi. The page.[22]

Blessed be you swet ladie from above
on earth above all [other][7] ladies blessed
in whom my hart reades arguments of love
conceavinge joyes wich cannot be exprest,
the hope of comfort for this knight distrest
    this knight distressed, & in wofull taking
    whose thoughts although his bodie sleeps ar wakinge

Lo here the matter of his overthrow
thos charmed pictures on the wall depending[23]
what was his error yet I maye not knowe
but suer it was the fayrie quenes offending
& well I trust it shortly shall have endinge
    for never was ther man that prince displeased
    who might not by a prince agayne be eased[24]

Drawe nere & take a vew of everie table
in them no doubte some secreats are concealed
wich if you will (for who denies you able)
Cannot but by your wisdom be revealed,
So hapely my Mr may be healed.
    And you so highly of the godes regarded
    Shall for your speciall vertue be rewarded.

                    finis

vii. [The olde Knightes Tale.][25]

Now drowsie sleepe, death's image, ease's prolonger,
Throw that hast kept my sences windowes closed,
Dislodge these heauie humors, stay no longer,
For light itself thie darkesom bandes have losed,
And of mine eies to better use disposed:
    To better use, for what can better be
    Then substance in the steede of shades to see.

O mortall substance of immortall glorie!
To whom all creatures ells are shaddowes demed;
Vouchsafe an eare unto the woeful storie
Of him who, whatso eare before he semed,
Is nowe as you esteme to be estemed:
    And sence himself is of himself reporter
    To tell your praise, will make his part the shorter.

Not far from hence, nor verie long agoe,
The fayrie Queene the fayrest Queene saluted[26]
That ever lyved (& ever may shee soe);
With sportes and plaies, whose fame is largelie bruted,[28]
The place and persons were so fitlie shuted:[29]
    For who a Prince can better entertaine
    Than can a Prince, or els a princes vayne?

Of all the pleasures there, among the rest,
(The rest were Justes and feates of Armed Knightes),
Within her bower she biddes her to a feast,
Which with enchaunted pictures trim she dightes,
And on them woordes of highe intention writes:
    For he that mightie states hath feasted, knowes
    Besides theire meate, they must be fedd with shewes.

Manie there were that coulde no more but vewe them,
Manie that over curious nearer pried,
Manie would construe needes that never knewe them,
Som laught, som lyked, som questioned, some enuied,
One asked them too who should not be denied:
    But she that thwarted, where she durst not strugle,
    To make her partie good was fayne to Juggle.[30]

Forthwith the Tables were conveied hither,
Such power she had by her infernall Arte;
And I enjoyned to keepe them altogether,
With speciall charge on them to set my harte,
Ever to tarrie, never to departe:
    Not bowing downe my face upon the grounde.
    Beholding still the Piller that was crounde.[31]

I whom in elder tyme she dearelie loved,
Deare is that love which nothing can disgrace,
I that had ofte before her favor proved,
But knewe not howe such favoure to embrace,
I, I am put in trust to warde this place:
    So kinde is love, that being once conceavid,
    It trustes againe, although it were deceaved.

Servant, quoth shee, looke upward and beware
Thou lend not anie Ladie once an eye;
For divers Ladies hither will repaire,
Presuming that they can my charmes untie,
Whose misse shall bring them to inconstancie:[32]
 And happie art thou if thou have such heede,
 As in anothers harme thine owne to reede.

But loe unhappie I was overtaken,
By fortune forst, a stranger ladies thrall,
Whom when I sawe, all former care forsaken,
To finde her out I lost my self and all,
Through which neglect of dutie 'gan my fall:[33]
 It is the propertie of wrong consenting
 To ad unto the punishment lamenting.

With this the just revengefull Fayrie Queene,
As one that had conceaved anger deepe,
And therefore ment to execute her teene,
Resolvde to caste mee in a deadlie sleepe,
No other mulcte[34] cold lyke decorum keepe:
 For Justice sayth, that where the eie offended,
 Upon the eye the lawe should be extended.

Thus have I longe abode, without compassion,
The rygor which that wrathefull Judge required;
Till now a straung and suddaine alteration
Declares the date of my distres expired:
O peareles Prince! O presence most desired!
 By whose sole resolution this ys found,
 That none but Princes, Princes mindes expounde.

In lue whereof, though far beneath your merrit,
Accept this woorthles meede that longes thereto,[35]
It is your owne, and onlie you may weare it,
The fayrie queene gives everie one his due,
For she that punisht me rewardeth you;
 As for us heare, who nothing have to paie,
 It is ynough for poore men if they pray.
             Coelumq' solumq' beavit.[36]

vii. The song at the ladies thangkgevinge.[37]

To that Grace that sett us free,
Ladies let us thankfull be;
All enchaunted cares are ceast,
Knightes restored, we releast;
Eccho change thie mournefull song,
Greefes to Groves and Caves belong;

Of our new deliverie,
Eccho, Eccho, certifie.

Farwell all in woods that dwell,
Farwell satyres, nymphes farewell;
Adew desires, fancies die,
Farwell all inconstancie,
Nowe thrice welcome to this place,
Heavenlie Goddesse! prince of grace!
She hath freed us carefull wightes,
Captiue Ladies, Captiue Knightes.

To that Grace that set us free,
Ladies let us thankfull bee.

finis

ix. The ladies Thancsgevinge for ther delyvery from inconstancie.[38]

Most excellent: shall I saie Ladye, or Goddes? whom I should envie to be but a Ladie, and can not denie to have the power of a Goddesse; vouchsafe to accept the humble thankfulnes of vs lately[39] distressed Ladies, the pride of whose witts was justlie punished with the unconstancie of ouer willes, wherebie we were carried to delight, as in nothing more than to love, so in nothing more than to chaunge lovers; which punishment, though it were onlie due to our desertes, yet did it light most heauily upon those Knightes, who, following us with the heate of theire affection, had neither grace to gett us, nor power to leave us. Now since, by that mortall power of your more than humane wisdome, the enchaunted tables are read, & both they & we released, let us be punished with more than unconstancie if we fayle eyther to love Constancie, or to eternize your memorie.

Li.[40] Not to be thankfull to so greate a person, for so greate a benefite, mighte argue as little judgement as ill nature; and therefore, though it be my turne to speake after you, I will strive in thankfulnes to goe before you, but rather for my lybertie, because I may be as I lyste, than for anie minde I have to be more constant than I was.

Co. If you have no minde to be constant, what ys the benefite of your deliverie?

Li. As I sayd before, my libertey, which I esteeme as deare as my selfe, for, though I esteme unconstancie as my selfe, & had as live not be as not be inconstant, yet I must hate that which I love best, when I am once inforced unto yt; and, by your leave, as dayntie as you make of [that matter],[41] you would hate even your owne selfe yf you were but wedded unto your selfe.

Co. Selfe love ys not that love that we talke of, but rather the kinde knitting of twoe hartes in one, of which sorte yf you had a faithfull lover what should you lose by being constant[42] unto him?

Li. More than you shall gett by being so.

Co. I seeke nothing but him to whom I am constant.

Li. And even him you shall lose by being constant.

Co. Wha reason have you for that?

Li. No other reason than that which is drawen from the comon places of Love, which are for the most parte Reason upon Reason.

Co. You may better call them Reason without Reason, if they conclude that faith & love the more they are the lesse they fynde.

Li. Will you beleve your owne experience?

Co. Far beyonde reason.

Li. Have you not then founde among your lovers that they woulde flie you when you did most followe them, & follow you when you did most fly them?

Co. I graunt I have founde it true in some, but nowe I speake of a constant Lover in deede.

Li. You may better speake of him, than finde him, but the onlie way to have him is to be unconstant.

Co. How so?

Li. I have heard Philosophers saye that *Acquisitio termino cessat motus.*[43] There is no motion, and you know Love is a motion, but it ceaseth, or rather dieth when it hath gotten his end. Now love hath no edge when it is assured: and the hope of having is dull.[44]

Co. It was against nature for her, which is but one, to love more than one; and if it be a fault to beare a double harte, what is it to devide the harte among manie?

Li. I aske no other judge than Nature, especiallie in this matter of Love, than the whiche there is nothing more naturall; and, as farr as I can see, Nature is delighted in nothing so muche as in varietie. And it were harde that sence she hath appoynted varietie of

coullers for[45] the eye, varietie of soundes for the eare, varietie of
meates for the mouth, and varietie of evrie other thinge for everie
other sence, she should binde the harte, to the which all the rest do
service, to the love of one; rather than the eye to one couller, the eare
to one sounde, or the mouth to one kinde of meate.

Co. Neyther doth she denie the harte varietie of choyce, she onely
requireth Constancie when it hath chosen.
Li. What yf we comitt an error in our choyse?
Co. It is no error to chuse where wee like.
Li. But if our lyking varrie we may not be better advised?
Co. When you have once chosen, you must tourne your eyes inwarde
to looke onlie on him that you have placed in your harte.
Li. Whie then I perceave you have not yet chosen, for your eyes
looke outward; but, as long as your eyes stande in your heade as they
doe, I doubt not but to finde you inconstant.
Co. I doe not denie but I loke upon other men, besides him that I
love best, but they are all as dead pictures unto me, for anie power
they have to touch mine harte.
Li. If they were as you account them, but dead pictures, they were
lyke to make another Pigmalion[46] of you, rather than you would be
bounde to the love of one. But what if that one do prove inconstant?
Co. I had rather the fault should be his than mine?
Li. It is a coulde comforte to saie the fault is his, when the losse ys
youres. But how can you avoyde the fault that may helpe it, & will
not?
Co. I see no way to helpe it, but by breach of faithe, which I holde
dearer than my lyffe.
Li. What is the band of thy faith?
Co. My worde.
Li. Your worde ys winde, & no sooner spoken than gonne.
Co. Yet doth it binde to see what is spoken donne.
Li. You can do lyttle yf you cannot maister your worde.
Co. I should do lesse yf my worde did not maister me.
Li. It maisters you indeede, for it makes you a slave.
Co. To none but one whome I chuse to serve.
Li. It is basenes to serve though it be but one.
Co. More base to disemble with more than one.
Li. When I love all alyke I dissemble with none.
Co. But if I love manie will anie love me?
Li. No doubt they will, & so much the more by howe much the more
they are that stryve for you.
Co. But the harte that is everie where, is in deede no where.

Li. If you speake of a manes harte I graunte it so be trew: but the harte of a woman is lyke a soule in a bodie: Tota in toto, et tota in quilibet parte.[47] So that, although you had as manie lovers as you have fingers and toes, you might be one among them all, and yet wholy everie ones. But, sence I perceive you are so perversely devoted to the còuld synceritie of ymaginarie constancie, I leave you to be as you maye, minding myselfe to be as I liste.

Neverthelesse to your Matie by whom I was sett at libertie, in token of my thankfullnes, I offer this simple woorke of mine owne handes, which you may weare as you please; but I made them to be worne, after mine owne minde, loose.[48]

Co. And I, who by your coming am not only sett at libertie, but made partaker also of Constancie, do present you with as unwoorthie[49] a wark of mine owne handes; which yett I hope you will better accept, because it may serve to binde the loosenes of this inconstant Dames token.[50]

Li. To binde the loosenes & that of an inconstant Dame! Say no more than you know, for you cannot knowe so much as I feele. Well may we betray ourselves betweene ourselves, and thinke we have never sayde enough, vntill we have said all. But now a greater power than eyther your or my reason woorketh in me, & draweth me from the circle of my fancies to the centre of true Love; there representing vnto me what contentment it is to love but one, & howe the heart is satisfied with no number, when once it loveth more than one. I am not, I cannot be, as I was; the leave that I take of myselfe is to leave myself, & to chaunge, or rather to be chaunged, to that state which admitteth no change, by the secrett power of her who though she were content to lett us be carried almost owt of breth by the winde of Inconstancie, dothe nowe with her scilence put me to scilence; & with the gloriouse beame of her countenaunce, which disperceth the flying cloudes of vaine conceites, enforceth me to wishe others, & to be myselfe, as shee is – Semper eadem.[51]

Finis.

The Song at ther departure.

Happie houre, happie daie,
That Eliza came this waie!
    Great in honor, great in place,
    Greater yet in geving grace,
    Greate in wisdome, great in minde,
    But in bothe above her kinde,
    Greate in vertue, greate in name,
    Yet in power beyond her fame.

Happie houre, happie daie,
That Eliza came this waie!
    She, with more than graces grace,
    Hath made proude this humble place,
    She, with more than wisdomes head,
    Hath enchaunted tables read,
    She, with more than vertues mighte,
    Hath restorid us to right.

Happie houre, happie daie,
That Eliza came this waie!
    Heavie harted Knightes are eased,
    And light harted Ladies pleased,
    Constant nowe they vowe to be,
    Hating all inconstancie,
    Constant Piller, constant Crowne,
    Is the aged Knightes renowne.

Happie houre, happie daie,
That Eliza came this waie!

    Thus much this first day.

The second daies woorke where the chaplayne maketh this relation.[52]

Da mihi quicquid habes, animumqu' fidemq' manumq'
Hac tria si mihi des, das mihi quicquid habes.[53]

Elizae laudes, et vox et lingua loquntur.[54]

The chaplaynes Narration.

1592 September 21th.

Most excellent Princes! Princes of excellencie! whom God framed in heaven to grace his woorkmanshippe on earth, and whose gratiouse abiding with us belowe is privileged by the singular grace of God above! Vouchsafe, I beseeche you, from the matcheles heighte of your Royall graces, to loke downe on the humble dwelling of a reverent owlde Knight, now a newe religiouse Hermite; who, as heretofore he professed the obedience of his youthe, by constant service of the worldes best Creature, so at this present presentethe the devotion of his yeares, by continuall serving of the worldes onlie Cretor. In the one, kind judgment was the usher, & beleefe the follower of his sounde love: in the other, meditation is the forerunner, & zeale the usher, of this streite lyfe. This solitary man, Loricus,[55] for such is his condicion & so is he called, one whose harde adventures were once discovered, and better fortune fore-shewed, by a good father of his owne coate, not farr from this Coppies,[56] rann the restles race of desire, to seeke content in the state of perfections; comaunding his thoughtes & deedes to tender theire dutie & make solemne sacrifices to the Idoll of his harte, in as manie partes as his minde had passions, yet all to one ende, because all from one grounde, to wit the consent of his affections. Sometymes he consorted with couragious Gentelmen, manifesting inward joyes by outwarde justes, the yearlie tribute of his dearest Love. Sometimes he summoned the witnesse of depest conceiptes, Himmes & Songes & Emblemes, dedicating them to the honor of his heavenlye Mistres. Sometymes by lyking drawen to looking, he lost himselfe in the bottomles vewe of unparragonized vertues, eche good ymagination overtaking other with a better, and the best yelding a degree above the best, when they all were deemed too weake for her woorth which overweyeth all worthinesse.

Thus spent he the florishe of his gladdest dayes, craving no rewarde ells, but that he might love, nor no reputation beside but that he might be knowne to Love;[57] till the two enimies of Prosperitie, Envie and Age, (the one greving at him, & the other growing on him,) cutt him off from following the Cowrte, not from goyng forwarde in his course. Thence, willingly unwilling, he retired his tyred lymes into a corner of quiet repose, in this Countrie, where he lyved private in coelestiall contemplation manie winters together, and, as he once told me, seriouslie kept a verie courte in his owne bosome, making presence of her in his soule, who was absent from his sight. Amongst manie other exercises (whereof fervent desire ys not scant) he founde it noe small furtheraunce of divine speculation, to walke thorow by-pathes & uncoth passages, under the coole shadowes of greene trees.

And one daie above the rest, as he ranged abrode, having forgotten himself in a long sweet ravishment, his feete wandring astray, when his mind went right, he hit by chaunce on a homelie Cell of mine which had helde a little space, to my greate solace, & taking mee on a soddaine at my ordinarie Orisons; – By your leave, verteouse Sir, quoth he, where lyes the highe-waie [I pray you].[58] Marry here, gentell Knight (sayde I) looking on my booke with mine eyes, & poyntyng up to heaven with my finger; it is the verie Kinge's hie-waye. [You saye true][58] in deede (quoth he) the verie Queene's hie-waye,[59] which my harte inquired after though my

tongue asked for another. And so, as it is the use with fellowe
humors when they fortunately meete, we light bothe upon one
argument, the universall fame of that miraculouse government,
which by truthe & peace, the harbengers of heaven, directeth us the
verie way to eternall blessedness. Much good discourse had we
more, of the vanitie of the world, the uncertainetie of frendes, the
unconstancie of fortune; but the upshoot of all was this, that he
would become an Heremite, I should be his Chaplaine, & both
joyntlie joyne in prayers for one Prince, & the prayses of one God.
To which purpose, because this plott pleased him, hee here
forthwith erected a poore Loddging or twoe, for me, himselfe, & a
page, that wayteth on him, naming it when he had donne the
Crowne Oratory; and therefore advaunsed his devise on the
entrance after the Romaine fashion in a Piller of perpetuall
remembraunce. But, alas! whilst he seekes to raise one buylding, hee
sees the rewins of another; & whilst he shapes a monument for his
minde, he feeles the miserie of his bodie, whose roofe was roughe
with the mosse of greene haires, whose sides were crased[60] with the
tempestes of sicknes, whose foundacion shooke under him with the
waight of an unwildye carcase: and when he perceaved his olde
house in a manner past reparacions, considering his owne
unablenes, he recomended the care thereof to the conningest
Architect of [the] Worlde,[61] who onlie was able to pull it downe unto
the earth, & raise it anewe, in better glorie than it stoode before.
Then began I to call him to his former preceptes, & his latter
practizes, shewing him in fewe woordes (for he conceaved much) that
nowe was the time of tryall. A good sayler was better seene in a
storme than in a calme. It was no straunge thing to lyve; for slaves
lyve and beastes lyve too. Nature had provided him comforte, who
made that most common which shee had made most greevouse; to
the ende the equallnes might aleye the egernes of death. To which he
mildelie replied that my motions fytlie touched him, he was as
desirouse to encounter with Death, as to heare of Death, for
Fortitude still abode his bedfellowe. Extremitie thought it could not
be overcom yet it might be overborne, since his minde had secured
him by fearing nothing, and overiched him by desiring nothing. Hee
had longe lyved in the Sea, and ment now to die in the Haven.
Haven (saide I). Yea! the Haven (quoth he); lett me be carried into
the Haven. Which Haven I supposed he hadd spoken idellie, but
that he eftsones repeted it, and wished to be brought to this poore
hovell before the gates, What thatt odde corner (saide I). Yes (quoth
he) that corner; and angerlie broke of with this sentence: Subsilire in
coelum ex Angulo licet.[62]

So we speedilie removed him hither, wher being softely layed he uttered these Speeches softelie: – Before I was olde, I desyred to lyve well, and now I am olde, I desire to die well: and to die well is to die willinglie. Manie there be that wish to lyve, yet wott not how to die: lett me be theire example yf they lyke not lyfe, to lyve, to die with lyking, who neither embraced Fortune when shee flew unto mee, nor ensued Fortune when she fled from mee, nor spared niggardlie, nor spent lavishlie, whatsoever she bestowed on me: but since it was my singuler hope to lyve beholding to the Crowne, I account it my speciall joye to dye beholding the Crowne. Holy Crowne! hallowed by the sacrament, confirmed by the fates; thou hast been the Aucthor of my last Testament. So calling for pen and inke (which were never far off) he drew a formall draught of his whole will, signed & subscribed by himselfe, but witnessed by us, the compassionate spectators of that lamentable action which he had no sooner entituled by wayes of truste, & geven me charge for the safe delivering thereof, but he fell soddenlye speecheles, & so continueth to this houre. The stile[63] runnethe thus: *To the most renouned Queene owner of the best Crowne & crowned with the best desertes, the lyving love of dying Loricus.* Now, most peereles Princes, sence there is none can laie challenge to this title, except they should also challenge your vertues, which were to complaine of Nature for robbing herselfe to do you right, accept I beseeche you the offer of him who dares not offer it to anie other; & one daie no doubt but the Knight himselfe, if happilie he recover (as what may not so sacred a Prince promise), will say it is in a good hand, & prove the best expounder of his owne meaning. In the meane season, thoughe myne endevors must be employed about your sick servant, yet my prayers shall not ceasse for your most gratiouse Majestie, that as you have over lived the vaine hope of your forraine enemies, so you may outlast the kinde wishes of your ioyall subjectes, which is to last to the last everlasting. Amen.

xii. To the most renowned Queene,
   Owner of the best Crowne, & Crowned with the best desertes, the lyving Love of dying Loricus.

   I Loricus, Bodie sicke,
   Sences sounde, Remembraunce quicke,
   Never craving, ever serving,
   Little having, lesse deserving.

Though a hartie true wellwiller
Of the Crowne & crowned Piller,
To that Crowne, my lyves content,
Make my Will & Testament.

Soule! goe first to heavenlie rest;
Soule the Bodies heavenlie gueste,
Where, both Host & Inn decaying,
Yeld the gueste no quiet staying.

Bodie! back againe, departe;
Earth thou wast, & Earth thou arte.
Mortall creatures still be jurneing,
From the earth to earth returning.

As for anie worldlie lyving
Nothing have I woorth the geeving:
Let the baser indeed take them,
We which follow God forsake them.

But if anie wishe to dwell,
As I did, in homely Cell,
Let him pull his Castells downe,
And as I did serve the Crowne,
Serve the Crowne, O Crowne deserving,
Better than Loricus serving.

In witness whereof I have set to my hande & harte.
Loricus, Columnae coronatae Custos fidelissimus.[64]

In presence of us whose names are underwritten,
Stellatus, Rectoriae Coronatae Capellanus.
Renatus, Equitis Coronati Servus observantissimus.[65]

xiii. The Page bringeth tydings of his Maister's Recoverie, &
      presenteth his Legacie:

The suddaine recoverie of my distressed Maister, whome latelie
you left in a Traunce (Most excellent Princes!) hath made me at one
tyme the hastie messenger of three trothes, your miracle, his
mending, & my mirthe. Miracles on the sicke are seldom seene
without theire mending: & mending of the good ys not often seene
without other mens mirth. Where your Majestie hath don a miracle,
& it can not be denied, I hope I may manifest, & it shall not be
disliked: for miracles are no miracles unlesse they be confessed, &
mirth is no mirth yf it be concealed.

May it therefor please you to heare of his life who lyves by you, & woulde not live but to please you; in whom the sole vertue of your sacred presence, which hath made the weather fayre, & the ground fruitfull at this progresse, wrought so strange an effect and so speedie an alteration, that, whereas before he seemed altogether speechles, now Motion (the Recorder of the Bodies Commonwealth) tells a lyvelie tale of health, and his Tongue (the Cocheman of the Harte) begun to speake the sweete language of affection. So tourning him selfe about to the ayre & the lyght, O wretched man (quoth he) callamities storie, lyfes delay, & deathes prisoner: with that he pawsed a while & then fixing his eyes on the Crowne, he sayd Welcom be that blessed Companie, but thrise blessed be her coming above the rest, who came to geve me this blessed rest!

Hereat Stellatus, his Chappelaine, besought him to blesse God onelie, for it was Gods spirite who recovered his spirites. Truthe (quoth he again) yet whosoever blesseth her, blesseth God in her: and ever blessed be God for her. – The conferrence continued long, but lovinglie, betwixt them; till at length upon question to whom the Will was directed, with knowledge how it was delivered, Loricus publiklie acknowledged the right performance of his true meaning unto your Royall Majestie, to whom he humblie recommended the full execution thereof, & by me hath sent your Majestye this simple Legacie, which he disposed the rather whilst he yet lyveth, than lefte to be disposed after his deathe, that you might understande how he alwaies preferred the deed.[66] Thus much your divine power hath performed to him, thus far his thankfulnes hath brought mee to your Majestie. As for anie other Accomplementes,[67] whatsoever Dutie yeldes to be debt, Devotion offers to be discharged; and if my Maister's best payment be onlie good prayers, what need more than the Pages bare woorde, which is allwaies – Amen.

xiv   The Legacye

Item. I bequethe (to your Highnes) THE WHOLE MANNOR OF LOVE, and the appurtenaunces thereunto belonging:
(Viz.)   Woodes of hie attemptes,
         Groves of humble service,
         Meddowes of greene thoughtes,
         Pastures of feeding fancies,
         Arrable lande of large promisses,
         Rivers of ebbing & flowing favours,
         Gardens hedged about with with private, for succorie,[68]

& bordered with tyme: of greene nothing but harte-
sease, drawen in the perfect forme of a true lovers
knott.[69]

Orchards stored with the best fruit: Queene Apples,
Pome Royalls, & Soveraigne Peare.

Fishing for dayntie Kisses with smyling countenances.

Hawking to springe pleasure with the spanniells[70] of
kindenes.

Hunting that deare game which repentance followeth.

Over & beside the Royaltie:[71] for

Weftes[72] of fearefull dispaire,

Strayes[73] of wandring conceiptes,

Fellons goods[74] of stolne delightes,

Coppie Holders[75] which allure by witte writinges,

Or Tennantes at will[76] who stand upon good behaviour.

The Demaines[77] being deepe sighes,

And the Lordes House a pittifull harte.

And this Mannor is helde in Knightes service,[78]

As may be gathered from the true Receavour[79] of fayre
Ladies, and seene in the auncient deedes of amorouse
Gentelmen.

All which he craveth may be annexed to his former Will,
& therewith approved in the Prerogative Courte[80] of
Youre Majesties acceptance.

In witnes whereof I have putt to my hande & seale;

LORICUS, Columnae coronatae Custos fidelissimus.

In the presence of us whose names are here under
written:

STELLATUS, Rectoriae coronatae Capellanus.

RENATUS, Equitis coronati Servus observantissimus.

Finis.

Notes

INTRODUCTION

1 But see below, p. 36, for an indication that it may be slightly earlier.
2 Strong, 1977, p. 119.
3 See MacCaffrey, 1969, passim.
4 Yates, 1947; reprinted Yates, 1975, pp. 29–87.
5 A list of these works will be found under the individual authors in the bibliography.
6 *Oberon, The Fairy Prince*, lines 252–288; lines 299–311, in Strong and Orgel, 1973, I, pp. 208–209.
7 *The Faerie Queene*, II.ix.22.
8 ibid, IV.x.49–51.
9 Douglas, 1966, *passim*.
10 Nichols, 1823, I, pp. 35–60.
11 Withington, 1918, I, pp. 174ff.
12 Withington, 1918, I, pp. 189ff.
13 Foxe: *Acts and Monuments*, 1563, quoted Withington, 1918, pp. 191–2.
14 Wilson, 1939, pp. 3ff.
15 Nichols, 1823, II, pp. 136–213.
16 *Judges* iv,4,–v.31.; *Judith*, passim; *Esther*, passim.
17 Goodman, 1839, I, p. 98: 'But after a few years, when we had experience of the Scottish government, then in disparagement of the Scots, and in hate and detestation of them, the Queen did seem to revive; then was her memory much magnified, – such ringing of bells, such public joy, and sermons in commemoration of her, the picture of her tomb painted in many churches, and in effect more solemnity and joy in memory of her coronation than was for the coming in of King James'.
18 See below, p. 153, n. 7.
19 Elizabeth never went further north than Stafford or further West than Bristol on her progresses (Chambers, 1923, I, p. 120), thus keeping to the parts of the country where there was little disaffection. The progresses were propaganda for the faithful, not gestures of goodwill to the potentially hostile.
20 Carey had participated in the Accession Day Tilts in 1585, 1586, 1589 and 1590 (Strong, 1977, Appendix I).

21 At least one of the score-keepers recognized him.
22 Carey, ed. Mares, 1972, pp. 28–29. Carey's plan in fact worked: when Elizabeth subsequently needed a messenger to the King of Scotland '. . . knowing (*though she would not know*) that I was in court, she said, "I hear your fine son that has lately married so worthily, is hereabouts; send him if you will to know the King's pleasure." My father answered, he knew I would be glad to obey her commands. "No (said she) do you bid him go, for I have nothing to do with him." My father came and told me what had passed between them. I thought it hard to be sent, and not to see her, but my father told me plainly, that she would neither speak with me nor see me. "Sir, said I, If she be on such hard terms with me, I had need be wary what I do. If I go to the King without her licence, it were in her power to hang me at my return, and for anything I see, it were ill trusting her." My father went merrily to the Queen, and told her what I said. She answered, "If the gentleman be so mistrustful, let the Secretary make a safe conduct to go and come, and I will sign it."' (ibid., p. 29).
23 Bacon: *Of Masques and Triumphs* in ed. Hawkins, 1972, p. 115.
24 The fact that the knights come to pay 'their annual vows' may be a reference to the Elizabethan Accession Day Tilts.
25 *Oberon*, ed. cit., I. p. 207.
26 Strong, 1977, p. 190, claims that James is 'cast as Arthur', but this is an over-simplification of a subtle text.
27 *Oberon*, in Strong and Orgel, 1973, I, p. 209.
28 Wedgwood, 1960, pp. 139–156.
29 See Strong and Orgel, 1973, I, Introduction *passim*.
30 Nichols, 1823, III, p. 577.
31 This is usually interpreted as the jealousy of an aged spinster of those young enough still to enjoy what she had missed. This is certainly an element of her opposition to the marriage of her ladies, but it may also be due to her desire to live out the cult of the goddess Diana, with whom she was identified, and who was notoriously opposed to any of her nymphs reneging on the vows of virginity they made when they joined her train.
32 Carey, ed. Mares, 1972, pp. 30–31.
33 The most recent editors of Robert Carey's *Memoirs* claim that Henry Carey was Mary Boleyn's only child (p. xiii). But he had an elder sister, called Catherine (Williams, 1974, p. 38) or Mary (Strong, 1977, p. 78), depending on the historian, who married Sir Francis Knollys, and was the mother of Lettice Knollys, Countess of Essex and subsequently of Leicester. The Earl of Essex was thus Elizabeth's cousin, and possibly her great-nephew.
34 Carey, ed. Mares, 1972, p. 60.
35 See above, n.22.
36 Elizabeth was not alone in disliking the match: all Carey's friends seem to have regarded it as unwise, only his father supporting him. The new Lady Carey had little money, and the Hunsdons were not wealthy – there was little for the youngest son – nor was she of particularly distinguished

birth, and because of their connection with Elizabeth the Careys could look very high for their spouses. Elizabeth might well have felt that a young relative for whom she had an affection had ruined his chances of acquiring wealth by marrying too poorly, and insulted her by marrying too low. In fact Lady Carey was responsible for the family's later spectacular success, by her wise and affectionate care of the Duke of York (later Charles I) during his sickly and unpromising childhood. She was evidently strong-minded and sensible, resisting all James I's attempts to have the Duke's late speech and walking corrected surgically, and insisting that he be properly fed. The marriage was happy, and justified Carey's decision to wed 'more for . . . worth than . . . wealth', but Elizabeth's disapproval of it should not be seen as the jealousy of an old woman determined not to let her young courtiers marry, but as the anger of one who sees a young relative for whom she feels some fondness throw away a good chance of improving his worldly prospects.

37 See bibliography under Strong and Yates. The links with Charlemagne in *Oberon* (see p. 12) may be a reflection of the pan-European imperial cult.
38 Strong, 1977, pp. 36.
39 Campion, ed. Davis, 1969, p. 7 (spelling modernized).
40 Campion, ed. Davis, 1969, p. 46 (spelling modernized).
41 Gorges, ed. Sandison 1953, p. 90.
42 Davies, ed. Krueger, 1975, p. 91.
43 Marie de France, ed. Ewert, *Laustic* 17–22.
44 Which actually took its plot from Byron's *Mazeppa*.
45 eg. ?Puttenham: *Partheniades*, quoted Wilson, 1939, pp. 243–4:

I saw marche in a meadowe greene
A fayrer wight than feirye Queene;
And as I would approche her neere,
Her head (yt) shone like Christall cleere;
Of silver was her forehead hye,
Her browes two bowes of Henevye;
Her tresses troust were to beholde,
Frizeld and fine as fringe of gold;
Her eyes, god wott what stuffe they arre,
I durst be sworne eche ys a starre: . . .
Twoo lippes wroughte out of rubye rocke,
Like leaues to shutt and to unlocke,
As portall doore in princes chamber;
A golden toonge in mouth of amber,
That oft ys hard, but none yt seethe;
Without a garde of yvorye teethe,
Even arrayed, and richelye, all
In skarlett, or in fine corrall;
Her cheeke, her chinne, her neck, her nose,
This was a lillye, that was a rose;
Her hand so white as whale's bone,

Her finger tipt with Cassidone;
Her bosome, sleeke as Paris plaster,
Held upp twoo bowles of alabaster: . . .
A slender grove, swifter than Roe,
A pretye foote to trippe and goe,
But of a solemne pace perdye,
And marchinge with a maiestye;
Her body shapte as strayghte as shafte,
Disclosed eche limbe with-outen craft;
Saue shadowed all, as I could gesse,
Vnder a vayle of silke Cypresse,
From toppe to toe ye mighte her see,
Timberd and tall as Cedar Tree,
Whose statelye turfe exceedeth farre
All that in frithe and forrest arre.

46 Strong, 1977, p. 67.
47 Jane Austen.
48 See below, p. 61.
49 Strong, 1969, p. 39.
50 Strong, 1969, p. 14.
51 Strong, 1969, p. 15.
52 eg. *Edi be thu, Hevene Quene*, Davies, 1963, no. 12, where Mary is asked,
  My swete Levedy, her my bene,
  And rew of me if thy wille is . . .
  Swete Levedy, of me thu rewe,
  And have mercy of thine knight.,
and has feudal submission made to her:
  ic am thy mon,
  Bothe to honde and to fote,
  On alle wise that ic con.
cf. also the sixteenth-century German armour in the Metropolitan Museum of Art which is engraved with a knight adoring the Woman clothed with the Sun, an adaptation of the shield of love device of the knight adoring a lady, such as that on the tournament display shield in the British Museum.
53 Ralegh, ed. Latham, 1951, p. 22.
54 See below, pp. 61ff.
55 Sir Hugh Platt, *The Garden of Eden* (1594), quoted Nichols, 1823, III, p. 441. The cherry was evidently associated with Elizabeth; it appears in the portraits. It was associated with the Virgin Mary, giving proof of her chastity: cf. Child, 1885 (1965), II, pp. 1–6.
56 Lydgate, ed. Bergen, 1924, III, p. 910 [Fall of Princes, VIII, 3112].
57 See Kendrick, 1950, passim.
58 Another, minor, factor in the visualization of the English golden age as high Gothic may have been the Robin Hood legend, referred to in AYLI, the subject of two plays by Munday, and lending itself well to incorporation in the forester-theme so often associated with pastoral, as

in *The Lady of May*. RH was also, as he still is, placed in an idealized-Gothic setting.

59 Segar, 1602, p. 197.
60 Schulze, 1933, p. 148.
61 For the question of the development and decline of jousting, see Clepham, 1919, passim, and Barber, 1974, pp. 159ff.
62 Segar is careful to give no more in his history of Arthur than is warranted by historians and antiquaries, and to separate fact (Arthur's battles) from surmise (the magical aid of Merlin) (1602, II, ch. 5). In the ten years between his books he changed his mind about the date at which Arthur lived, becoming more accurate in the process. In *The Book of Honor and Armes* he dates Arthur at c. 1020 (p. 11), in *Honor Military and Ciuill* at c. 500 (p. 53). It is tempting to ascribe Segar's greater accuracy to the appointment of Camden as Clarenceux Herald in 1597. His concern with the probable truth underlying the Arthur legend is shown in his affirmation:
'I verely thinke the Acts and enterprises of Vlysses, Aeneas, Hector, and other famous captaines (of whom Poets and profane Writers have written so many woonders) were indeed of notable men, and some part of their doings such, as writers haue made mention. Much lesse doe I doubt, that some egregious acts atchieued and written in the bookes of Amadis de Gaule, Ariosto, Tasso, King Arthure of England, and such others doe containe many things, which deserue not to be discredited'. (1602, p. 58).
For a discussion of Elizabethan antiquarianism see Kendrick, 1950.
63 Segar, ?1590, p. 90.
64 The length of the Christmas/New Year celebrations.
65 *A Letter of the Authors . . . To . . . Sir Walter Raleigh* in Spenser, ed. Roche, 1978, pp. 15ff.
66 Yates, 1975, p. 99ff.
67 Yates, 1975, p. 92.
68 For a differing view, see Axton, 1977, pp. 24–47.
69 Chambers, 1923, I, p. 143.
70 Yates, 1975, p. 92; Sidney, ed. Evans, 1977, p. 858.
71 Sidney, ed. Evans, 1977, pp. 353–355.
72 Yates, 1975, p. 90, claims the birds are phoenixes. Strong, 1977, p. 133, recognizes them as eagles, but does not explain the meaning implicit in the device.
73 See Dillon (ed.), Almain Armourer, 1905.
74 *Anglorum Feriae*, 319–322 in Peele, ed. Horne, 1952 p. 274. A portrait of Skydmore is reproduced in Strong, 1977, p. 158; and a suit of his armour is in the Metropolitan Museum of Art.
75 Strong, 1977, pp. 153–154.
76 Plumb, 1977, p. 75.
77 Strong, 1977, p. 131, gives Lee's age in the portrait as 33 but this must be a slip as he gives Lee's birthdate as 1533 and dates the portrait to 1568.
78 Strong, 1977, 139–140.

[79] Strong, 1977, p. 207, In *The Faerie Queene*, the future King Arthur acts as Gloriana's champion and representative, so it is appropriate that Elizabeth's champion should portray Arthur. The Royal Champion in a sense also stands in place of his master, and is an image of him, so it is again appropriate that Elizabeth's champion should be Arthur, who was, because of the tradition that he took the Virgin Mary as his badge, often seen as Her Champion: Cumberland's role thus links with both the Arthurian and the Marian aspects of Elizabeth's cult.

[80] Strong, 1977, p. 208.

[81] Chambers, 1936, pp. 271–2. Chambers says that this is not dateable, but I think that it is probably post–1590, the date of Lee's retirement, after which time his favourite guise was the knight-turned-hermit (based on Raymond Lull's explicator of chivalry). The hermit with whom the Black Knight had been would thus be Lee.

[82] Peele, ed. Horne, 1952, p. 244 (spelling modernized). Peele is the other candidate for authorship of the lyric.

[83] A motif which continues, the latest manifestation of the famous warrior turned holy recluse being Obi-wan-Kenobi in *Star Wars* (George Lucas, 1977).

[84] Malory, ed. Cowen and Lawlor, 1969, XVIII. Chs. 12–17.

[85] Printed by Caxton in 1483–5.

[86] Wind, 1967, p. 92n.

[87] Dowland, *Second Book of Airs*, 1600, reprinted Chambers, 1936, p. 143. Yates, 1975, p. 103 claims that this is a version of 'His golden locks', which it clearly is not.

[88] Nichols, 1823, I, pp. 315–6.

[89] For a discussion of the role of the Great House, see Girouard, 1978, chs. 1–4.

[90] Clarendon, 1840 II, p. 938. Another indication of the size of a nobleman's following is the number of retainers led by the Four Foster Children of Desire, see pp. 69ff.

[91] Sidney, ed. Evans, 1977, p. 71.

[92] In the above discussion I have benefited from a meeting of a Renaissance study-group held in Edinburgh in 1972, under the leadership of Professor Alastair Fowler.

[93] For Hatton's attitude to Holdenby see Brooks, 1946, p. 155.

[94] The visits were in fact, preceded by considerable notice, as the story of Sir Francis Carew's cherries shows (see p. 24).

[95] Kenilworth, 1575.

[96] Bisham, 1592.

[97] Kenilworth, 1575.

[98] Sudeley, 1592.

[99] Bisham, 1592.

[100] Woodstock, 1575.

[101] Kenilworth, 1575.

[102] Before Lee assumed it, this was a favourite role of Cecil's.

[103] Sidney, ed. Evans, 1977, pp. 69–70.

104 Either a reference to Pan's goat-legs, which denoted his sexuality, or to his traditional priapism.

105 A similar incident occurred in the Kenilworth entertainment, see p. 119.

106 A Wild Man with a club was traditional as a 'whiffler', or crowd-controller, in civic processions.

107 'Mouse' was a common term of affection at this date: Alleyn so addresses his wife, Henslowe, ed. Foakes and Rickert, 1961, p. 274 and cf *Hamlet*, III, iv, 184.

108 The girls' names are not given in full: presumably they are contractions of Sybil and Isabel, traditional names for shepherdesses. At the time of the entertainment Elizabeth Russell was eighteen, Anne about sixteen, and their mother was anxious to place them with the Queen as Maids of Honour, their small dowers making it imperative that they were given the greatest possible opportunity of meeting suitable husbands.

109 The Harvest King, either a man or a corn effigy, was carried in the wain at the end of harvest. This may refer either to the phallicism of the fertility figure, or to the habit of crowning the King with horns, to the accompaniment of lewd songs. Cf. Porter, 1974, p. 69.

110 OED: 'In old Anatomy, the tendons or nerves supposed to brace and sustain the heart'.

111 Embroidery of features may be seen on the Queen's robe in the *Rainbow* portrait.

112 These are all the Queen's flowers, and symbols, of virginity, cf. p. 24; double stitch and Queen's stitch are embroidery stitches.

113 A reference to the Astraea-theme of Elizabeth as the Virgin who brings fruitfulness and peace.

114 Elizabeth sent an expedition to aid Henry of Navarre against the Catholic League in 1591.

115 England had been openly helping the Dutch in their revolt against Catholic Spain since 1585.

116 This indicates that the two shepherdesses are Lady Russell's daughters; the printed account does not name them. For Lady Russell, see Strong, 1977, pp. 17–56.

117 Which evidently happened at this point.

118 Presenting the Queen with a jewel, possibly of little value, since it is not described.

119 Nichols, 1823, III, pp. 131–136; Barnes, 1592, sig. Aii–Aiiiiv.

120 Henry, Lord Norris.

121 The Queen had just come from Oxford, where she had been the object of much oratory.

122 The eldest son, William, was dead by 1592. The four writers of the letters all predeceased their parents; only the youngest, Edward, survived both his parents and the reign.

123 Elizabeth's nick-name for Lady Norris, who had dark colouring, was 'Crow'. She was the recipient of one of the few personal letters from Elizabeth to survive, written on the occasion of the death of her son

John in 1597.
124 Traditional.
125 The sense of 'Crow's nest' as the look-out point at the top of a ship's mast seems to be nineteenth-century, but the OED gives an early-seventeenth-century usage which seems to mean a fort on a hill. This would of course be an appropriate secondary meaning in connection with a soldier's household.
126 The Phoenix was a frequent emblem for Elizabeth, as it had been for the Virgin Mary.
127 "Which colour was dark, and now is the reverse".
128 Marginal note.
129 October 2nd.
130 The costume he probably wore may be seen in the portrait of Thomas Lee as an Irishman by Marcus Gheeraerts, in the Tate Gallery.
131 The dart was an Irish weapon. Here, as in the portrait of Thomas Lee, it is a light throwing-spear, not an arrow.
132 Elizabeth is not known to have had any knowledge of this language, but it is interesting that it was evidently well-enough known in England for the motto to be put in it. Suggestions that Spenser may have taught himself Irish are perhaps strengthened by this. cf. Smith, 1944, p. 473.
133 This may be a hint that he would welcome a posting nearer home.
134 The lackey is silent: whether out of a need for brevity or an inability to represent vocally an Irishman is not clear, but his silence was obviously felt to need some excuse.
135 The writer of this letter is supposed to be Sir Thomas Norris, Deputy to his brother John as President of Munster.
136 From Dutch *Schipper* and at this date almost always referring to a Dutch seaman.
137 The symbol of the Town of Ostend.
138 Elizabeth had some knowledge of Dutch, cf. Hentzner, 1901, p. 48.
139 A small sailing-vessel.
140 Supposedly from Sir Edward Norris, at that time serving in Flanders as governor of Ostend.
141 Coy or cold rather than easily nauseated.
142 The sword and the truncheon (the staff given to an officer as a symbol of authority, surviving as the swagger-stick) are both symbols of the soldier.
143 The seat of love and the passions: the darker its colour, the more intense the emotion.
144 The seat of melancholy.
145 Because all the blood is concentrated in the heart and liver.
146 ie. kiss, worship, their mistresses' hands with as much devotion as if they were the representation of the crucifixion (the pax) kissed by clergy and congregation at Mass.
147 In absolute possession, as opposed to a lease, which limits the time of the possession: another proof of the soldier's innate inconstancy.
148 The image is of eyes popping out on their stalks.
149 The writer of this comic letter (cf. the incident in LLL IV.i. where the

Princess reads a letter directed to Jacquenetta) seems to be the same as that of the following one, since it is supposedly opened by misreading of the superscription, and that is the only letter addressed to Lady, rather than Lord, Norris.

150 It is difficult to be certain which of the sons serving in France, John, Henry and Maximilian, is the supposed author of this, but if, as seems possible John (the model for Spenser's Artegall, see Bennett, 1940, pp. 191ff) was at Rycote for the entertainment, then Henry, the next in age, is probably the supposed writer.

151 vacillation.

152 A probable reference to the *Odyssey*, in which Odysseus of course fails to keep the winds in the bag in which he is given them.

153 The main shopping street in London.

154 This letter is presumably from Maximilian, who was killed in France in 1593.

155 Cause of rejoicing.

156 She was married to the governor of Jersey, Sir Anthony Paulet.

157 Listening to lovers seems to have been thought of as an amusement; cf. AYLI III.iv.48–v.34.

158 The Channel Islands were not yet luxurious tax-havens.

159 Nichols, 1823, III, pp. 168–72; Barnes, 1592, sigs. Cir–Ciiii.

160 Chambers, 1923, I, p. 112.

161 This was probably in response to the demands of cleaning: Later silk dresses had to be completely unpicked when they were cleaned, and those who deal with antique clothes have frequently remarked on the cobbled seams which contrast with the fine embroidery of the stuff: evidently the dresses were made up rather for ease of dismemberment than pride in stitchery.

162 Some idea of the various parts of the costume may be gained from the lists of Elizabeth's wardrobe printed in Strong & Oman, 1971, pp. 34–5.

163 See, for instance, the list of New-Year's gifts presented to the Queen in 1574–5: 'Item, a faire juell of golde, containing three personages, as Mars, Venus, and Cupido, fully garnished with sparcks of dyamondes and rubyes, with three emeraldes, one ruby bigger than the rest, and one round perle pendaunte with shorte cheynes of golde, all 2oz. scante. Geven by the Ladye *Cheyney*. The same faire jeull geven by her Majestie to the Ladye *Carye*, Sir *George Cary's* wife.' Nichols, 1823, I, p. 412.

164 Chambers, 1923, I, p. 11.

165 Chambers, 1923, I, p. 13.

166 For a general discussion of the costs, organization, and disruption involved see Chambers, 1923, I, pp. 106–126.

167 This lady was Surrey's 'fair Geraldine', and was unpopular with the staider members of the Elizabethan establishment, Archbishop Parker writing to Burleigh in 1561 that 'she ought to be chastised in Bridewell'. (Strong, 1969, p. 26.) This perhaps explains why, at the age of 55, she was lodged up two flights of stairs, among obscure officials and very junior

courtiers, rather than with the other great nobles near the Queen. Burleigh's explanation would no doubt be the chimney in the room, which would provide warmth for an old lady.

168 Blanche Parry, by now aged 75, had been with Elizabeth since her babyhood. She had charge of the Queen's jewels.

169 'Evidences' seem to be documents, and the provision of 2 document chambers in the Queen's and Burleigh's suites is a reminder that the business of government had to be transacted, even on progresses.

170 Nichols, 1823, II, pp. 400–404. For the building of Theobalds, see Summerson, 1959, and Girouard, 1978, 111ff.

171 Chambers, 1923, I, pp. 117–8.

172 Chambers, 1923, I, p. 117.

173 Chambers, 1923, I, p. 115.

174 Nichols, 1823, I, pp. 131–2.

175 Nichols, 1823, II, p. 370.

176 Chambers, 1923, I, p. 119.

177 Kenilworth, 1575. See Gascoigne, ed. Cunliffe, 1910, I, p. 106ff.

178 Chambers, 1923, I, p. 114.

179 Chambers, 1923, I, p. 117ff.

180 Chambers, 1923, I, pp. 114–5.

181 Chambers, 1923, I, p. 109ff.

182 Most recently by Axton, 1977, pp. 24–47, who sets it in the context of other Dudleian entertainments.

183 Sidney, ed. Duncan-Jones and Van Dorsten, 1973.

184 Furnivall, 1907; Gascoigne, ed. Cunliffe, 1907–10, II, pp. 91–131. Also described by Scott, loc cit, and Bradbrook, 1960.

185 Cunliffe, 1911, Gascoigne, ed. Cunliffe, 1907–10.

186 For example, see Old Fortunatus in Dekker, ed. Bowers, 1953, I, p. 114.

187 Girouard, 1978, p. 25.

188 See below, n. 197.

189 Notably Orgel & Strong, 1973.

190 See, for instance, the Lady in fancy dress by Marcus Gheeraerts the Younger, reproduced Strong, 1969 b, p. 70.

191 The title-page of Sidney's *Arcadia*, 1593 (subsequently re-used for other works) shows Musidorus and Pyrocles in their disguises as Amazon and shepherd, and may well be close to such costumes in entertainments.

192 For instance, the Burford Indians: cf. Piggot, 1976, p. 25ff.

193 The decorated tree at Cowdray, or the lake at Elvetham.

194 Both types can be seen in the pictures of the seventeenth-century Dutch pageant by Denis van Alsloot in the Victoria and Albert Museum. Laver, 1947, passim.

195 Shown in Strong, 1973, p. 195.

196 Strong, 1973, p. 135ff.

197 The Unton picture is in the National Portrait Gallery. The masque portion is reproduced Girouard, 1978, p. 95.

198 Not, pace. Girouard, red paint on their faces. 1978, p. 89.

199 See Strong, 1973, passim.

200 For the best examination of this, see Greenblatt, 1973, passim.

THE FOUR FOSTER CHILDREN OF DESIRE: 1581

Introduction

1 Wickham, 1959, I, pp. 191ff.
2 Cf. Strong, 1973, pp. 121–169; Yates, 1975, pp. 121–207.
3 See p. 9ff.
4 Yates 1959, passim.
5 Sidney, ed. Duncan-Jones and Van Dorsten, 1973, pp. 33–57. Both Sidney and Walsingham had been in Paris at the time of the St. Bartholomew's day Massacre, and remained implacably anti-Valois.
6 Sidney, ed. Duncan-Jones and Van Dorsten, 1973, p. 34.
7 Sidney, ed. Duncan-Jones and Van Dorsten, 1973, pp. 34–37.
8 Sidney, ed. Duncan-Jones and Van Dorsten, 1973, p. 14. Connell, 1977, claims *The Four Foster Children* as Sidney's (pp. 56, 69, 120) (as does Wallace, 1915, p. 264), but does not treat it at any length.
9 Sidney, ed. Ringler, 1962, pp. 345–6; pp. 518–9.
10 For these arguments, see Sidney, ed Ringler, 1962, pp. 518–9; Fogel, 1960, passim.
11 Sidney, ed. Ringler, 1962, pp. 343–4.
12 See the summary of the contents of the Ditchley MS in Chambers, 1936, Appendix D.
13 See Yates, 1975, p. 102.
14 Sidney, ed. Evans, 1977, pp. 353–55.
15 Printed in Sidney, ed. Duncan-Jones and Van Dorsten, 1973, pp. 13–32.

Text

1 Goldwell does not claim to have had a hand in writing the entertainment.
2 Sic, but it should surely be 'asleep'.
3 Boast.
4 Admonishing.
5 Either a military officer (OED 3) or a manager of business, etc. (OED 5).
6 One who has general management of a design (OED 1).
7 This presumably refers to the schedules distributed at the various jousts. Philip Gawdy sends to his father "ij small bookes for a token, the one of them was gyven me that day that they rann at tilt, divers of them being gyven to most of the lordes, and gentlemen about the court, and one especially to the Quene." Chambers, 1923, I, p. 145.
8 Whitsun, or Pentecost, was the traditional high feast at Arthur's court, when challenges and other marvels were eagerly expected at Camelot, so

the choice of Whitsun for this entertainment may be related to the Arthurian element in the cult of Elizabeth.

9 Philip Howard, 1st Howard Earl 1557–1595. Son of Duke of Norfolk. Succeeded as Earl of Arundel (through grandfather) 1580. 1584 became Catholic. 1586 committed to Tower, where he remained.

10 4th Lord Windsor, son to the Catholic 3rd Baron, who died in Venice in 1575, and had befriended Sidney on his visit there in 1574.

11 Sidney's constant friend since their schooldays.

12 Simple, innocent.

13 Wean. The dry nurse succeeded the wet nurse as the child grew older.

14 Suspect may be the case.

15 Raise.

16 As it was highly unlikely that the Four Foster Children would overcome all that came against them, the odds are intrinsically weighted against them.

17 This presupposes that the Foster Children will be defeated.

18 It is unclear whether this was supposed to represent a siege engine or, more likely, part of the earthworks thrown up around a besieged town.

19 ie. felt hats, as opposed to the velvet hats of the higher-ranking retainers.

20 The unicorn (a badge of chastity) appears in the background of a portrait of the 5th Lord Windsor and on his armour. Cf Strong, 1969, p. 30. May this in fact be of 4th Baron, and a commemoration of Four Foster Children?

21 Sidney's extravagance meant that he died massively in debt and that his father-in-law, Walsingham, bankrupted himself to pay it off. (See Sidney, ed. Duncan-Jones and Van Dorsten, 1975, p. 143ff). This was partly a result of his determination to live out an ideal life, courtly and chivalric, in which *largesse* was one of the principal virtues, and partly a result, despite his father's cautions (he advised his sons 'that if they meant to live in order, they should ever behold whose sons, and seldom whose nephews they were.' Sidney, ed. Duncan-Jones and Van Dorsten, 1973, p. 124) of his expectations of inheriting the vast wealth of his uncle, the Earl of Leicester. It is noteworthy that the trains of the gentlemen, Sidney and Greville, are much smaller than those of the peers, Arundel and Windsor.

22 'Blue' armour was unengraved or plated polished steel.

23 Probably elaborately slashed and shaped knee-high boots, such as may be worn by Pyrochles on the title-page of the *Arcadia*, but it can refer to the thick soled boots worn by tragic actors.

24 So are we not our own.

25 In front of, or opposite.

26 That is, they behaved like the commanders of an army besieging a castle.

27 Sic, but it should be 'parlie'.

28 Not in BM2.

29 Not in BM2.

30 Sic, but it should probably be 'these'.

31 There was a strong element of private personal reference and esoteric symbolism in all the Elizabethan Tilts. After his retirement in 1590 Lee wore a device and motto embroidered on his clothes which no-one except himself seems to have understood. Cf. Strong, 1977, p. 153.

32 In fact, of twenty-two defenders, only seven are accounted for in this narrative (and Lee, as Unknown, would presumably not have had a device).

33 As becomes apparent, Parrott and Cooke were dressed as Adam and Eve, hence their page's representing an Angel.

34 There is a Frozen Knight in the Iberian jousts in the *Arcadia*, see p. 34. It is not clear whether this refers to a previous defendant (which would have to be Henry Grey) or a contestant at a previous tilt, who did not attend this one, or whether it was a previous disguise of Parrott or Cooke (the text seems to suggest that Adam and Eve are the Frozen Knight's substitutes).

35 Twinkling here means rapidly blinking, rather than bright.

36 Since sexual desire is often assumed to be the sin first awakened after the Fall, it is appropriate that the Four Foster Children should be said to be sprung from Adam and Eve.

37 This seems to be a reference to the game of hide-and-seek, with its cries of 'warm' and 'cold' (OED says it was known before 1672), but also carries on the idea of Elizabeth as the sun.

38 This seems to be a reference to a cloud hiding Christ from the disciples' sight.

39 A reference to Icarus.

40 This, and the rest of the speech, reiterates Lee's favourite interpretation of the Elizabethan knight's relationship to her: love and service with no hope of reward. See p. 121ff.

41 The giants Otus and Ephialtes piled mount Pelion on mount Ossa in an attempt to scale Olympus and overthrow the gods.

42 A reference to Ovid, Metamorphoses II, 327–28, Phaeton's epitaph: "Here Phaeton lies; in Phoebus' car he fared, And though he greatly failed, more greatly dared."

43 Sic, but should read 'this'.

44 This passage applies to Elizabeth the imagery of the Virgin Mary, which formed an aspect of her cult (Mary was the second Eve who did not fall). See Yates, 1975, pp. 34ff, 78ff; Warner, 1976, p. 48.

45 Sic but should be credulitie.

46 His disguise as a mossie knight (his shield was covered with moss, and his armour may have been) recalls Artegall's disguise in FQ IV.iv.39, see above p. 41.

47 There may well be an element of parody in this speech: the extremeness of the attitudes, the occasional descents (as here) into bathetic practicality, may indicate a comic intention.

48 Sea-coal, washed on to the beach, another indication of the comic intent of this speech (it might possibly refer to coal-fish, but would still be comic).

49 The mossie knight is a type of the knight maddened by love, who becomes a wild-man, suffering from love-melancholy (cf. FQ. IV.vii.38ff; Malory, ed. Cowen, 1968, XI, chs. 8ff), rather than a knight-turned-hermit.

50 This seems to mean that he was taking exercise to keep fit, and would if so be another comic element. If 'lim' is a misprint for 'time', it seems to mean that he may not have been there a long time but that he was so miserable that all time seemed long.

51 Twilight.

52 Misprint for 'scrowle' = scroll.

53 This may be another explanation of the eagle and the sun image used by Lee (see p. 35), implying that he was blinded by the Queen's beauty, but the renewal of youth explanation seems more probable (both meanings may of course be intended).

54 Misprint for 'more'?

55 Misprint for 'once'.

56 This is the pasteboard shield that was presented to the Queen, and subsequently displayed in Whitehall, not the shield used in jousting.

57 These were Elizabeth's cousins (see p. 144, n. 33) and were frequent participants in jousts (three of them are mentioned in *Anglorum Feriae*, 261ff, where they are compared to King Arthur's Knights. Peele, ed. Horne, 1952). There is at least one Knollys in every tilt list printed by Strong, 1977, Appendix 1.

58 The enchantress Medea was responsible for Jason's achieving the golden fleece.

59 Otos and Ephialtes, see p. 155, n. 41.

60 Icarus.

61 This may be a misprint for 'gate' meaning station, rather than 'gale' = wind.

62 Misprint for 'woo'?

63 Misprint for 'or necessary'.

64 Either a misprint for 'sorts' = lots or destinies, or referring to the Fortress of Beauty, to be tested by the assault of the Four Foster Children.

65 That is, they are the opposites of the Four Foster Children.

66 N omits 'is'.

67 Nod.

68 N omits 'then with'.

69 N: than is.

70 N reads, 'Night, the ordinary truce maker, though no truce be treated, (if at least your presence make it not lightsome) will wrap all in his blacke and mourning weedes, perchance mourning for that the noblest Desire hath bene . . . .', which makes better sense.

71 N omits parenthesis, inserts 'To conclude'.

72 Cf. *The Golden Ass*, IV.35.

73 Cupid.

74 N omits 'their . . . . them', inserts 'your eies may be brightened'.

75 N 'and therewithall'.

76 N inserts 'so'.

[77] N reads: 'This said, and all the triumphant shewes ended, the Knights in verie comelie and convenient order (as they came) departed:'.

[78] N inserts: 'And they relaxed their tired bodies, and enjoyed great peace, and they pampered their limbs with sweet relaxation'.

[79] Probably a misprint for 'above'.

[80] In fact, what the four foster children's entry represents is a Triumph of Desire. Cf. Fowler, 1970, passim.

[81] Pressed out, exhausted.

[82] N: scarselie.

[83] N inserts 'their'.

[84] That is, the four sons of Sir Francis Knowles.

[85] Fighting on foot, across a low wooden barrier.

[86] The archetypal motivation of romance-knights.

[87] In contrast to the flame colours in which the knights first entered, indicating the heat of their passion.

[88] N 'Fortune'.

[89] N 'tytle'.

[90] N 'captivated'.

[91] N inserts: 'And thus ceassed those Courtlie Triumphes, set foorth with most costlie braverie and gallantnesse, whereof I maie saie as the Academicall Poet sometime said at the gratious entering of hir Majestie into Cambridge:

Hic cocco murex, aurem superatur ab auro,
Naturam certant vincere quaeque suam:
Nil ibi sat pulchrum, quamvis pulcherrima quaeque,
Et quamvis vincant omnia, victa jacent.' ⚑

*See Nichols, 1823, I, p. 160. The verse is not transcribed in the account of the Queen's visit to Cambridge (1564) but it is probably part of the verse 'Oration gratulatory' delivered to her at the gate of Queens'.

So purple here is conquered by scarlet
and gold overcome by gold.
All things strive to master their own nature.
There, nothing is sufficiently beautiful
Even though all things are beautiful
and although all things should prevail, they lie defeated.

(*aurem* in line 1 seems to be an error for *aurum*).

[92] Good words.

COWDRAY 1591

Introduction

1 These might well have been supplied through the office of the Revels, whose resources were available to Elizabeth's hosts. See Chambers, 1923, I, p. 116.

2 eg. Drummond, Earl of Perth.

3 In the miniature of George Clifford Earl of Cumberland as Queen's Champion he has hung his shield in a tree and thrown his gauntlet down to challenge the Queen's enemies, and it is traditional for a challenging knight to hang his shield in a tree for his opponent to beat (Malory, ed. Lawlor and Cowen, 1969, VII, ch. 6). The tree hung with shields may, however, signify that Elizabeth has overcome all the knights who have hung their shields in it, since this is a method of displaying the arms of the vanquished.

4 Cooper, 1968, pp. 29ff.

5 Lyly, ed. Bond, 1902, I, pp. 404ff.

6 See p. 153, n. 7.

Text

1 l. 'Sussex by the Lord'.

2 l. 'August 14'.

3 l. 'The Queens Maiesty came . . .'

4 l. 'the 14'.

5 Cf. the giant porters at Kenilworth, 1575, see p. 166, n. 3.

6 l. Omits 'August 15'.

7 Amphion built the lower city of Thebes by the music of the lyre given him by Hermes.

8 l. 'none such'.

9 A reference, presumably, to Lord Montague's Catholicism.

10 Virgil, *Aeneid* i.80–1.

11 Elizabeth was showing Lady Montague great favour, so she may have been weeping from relief.

12 l. 'Wherewithall . . . geese' omitted.

13 This suggests that Lord Montague used the court musicians who travelled in Elizabeth's train, rather than his own from Cowdray.

14 It is interesting that this is the same sport offered to the ladies in LLL, IV, i.

15 Not in 2; l reads 'under the which were placed her Highnes Musitians, and this dittie following song while her Majestie shot at the Deere . . .'

16 Participation in this more strenuous sport was presumably beyond the Queen at this date.

17 An open meadow.

18 'All the hunting . . . . forest' not in l.

[19] The Montague family had evidently vacated the house itself to make way for the Queen and her household.

[20] Dinner at this date was eaten at mid-day.

[21] The Pilgrim's dress is of rather richer materials than any real pilgrim would be likely to wear. The scallop-shell, originally a sign that the wearer had been to Compostella, was by now a general indication of a pilgrim.

[22] 'After dinner . . . sort following' not in 1, which has the heading, The Pilgrimes speech.

[23] At this stage a branch of study that included heraldry, genealogy and topography as well as the first scratchings of archaeology.

[24] Accessible to all because it was in open country.

[25] Blows.

[26] Shrewish; ill-tempered.

[27] Place of confinement, from hawking; or perhaps mute, as in trumpeting.

[28] 1. 'that what'.

[29] Perhaps the earliest example of 'hearts of oak' used as a synonym for loyalty and for ships.

[30] Ramparted; defended – the 'true hearts' may refer to the ships that defend the coasts, as well as the loyal men of the shire.

[31] A great height.

[32] In the Queen's merciful treatment of him as a Roman Catholic.

[33] Pilgrims were entitled to free passage and protection.

[34] 'one' 1.

[35] 'by them, yet we' not in 1, which reads 'by you we . . .'

[36] God made this peace for us through Elizabeth.

[37] The Phoenix, a common symbol for Elizabeth.

[38] Song not in 2.

[39] 1. '. . . crie of hounds, with whom her Maiestie hunted and had good sport'.

[40] 'at a table . . . long' not in 1.

[41] 'euening' 1.

[42] Ie. going westward along the Thames (towards Westminster, the Queen's centre, from the City). Cf the plays *Eastward Ho* and *Westward Ho* whose titles are taken from bargemen's cries.

[43] Sets baited traps, as for mice.

[44] Excessively high rents.

[45] Presumably by drugging or poisoning the water: obviously as illicit a method of fishing as using dynamite.

[46] 1. 'the'.

[47] Maids: Skate and Thornback when young, and also the Twait Shad.

[48] A compliment to the Queen, who is attended by Maids of Honour.

[49] 1. 'Envie blush, and Envie stands amazed . . .'

[50] 1. 'states'.

[51] 'To peake over the perch; lit. to topple or tumble off the perch, fig. to die' OED.

[52] 1. 'excellent'.

53 1. 'worthie of the greatest good'.

54 'That ended . . .' end of poem not in 2. From the end of the poem 1.
continues; 'For the rest of the Entertainment, honorable feasting, and
abundance of all things that might manifest a liberall and a loyall heart,
because I was not there, I cannot set downe, thus much by report I heare,
& by the words of those that deserve credite, that it was such as much
contented her Majestie, and made many others to wonder. And so her
Majestie well pleased with her welcome, & he throughly comforted with
her Highnesse gracious acceptance, she went from thence to Chichester.'

55 Compare the country dance at Kenilworth, which was presented purely
for the mockery of the Court. See Nichols, 1823, I. p. 423.

ELVETHAM 1591

Introduction

1 Nichols, 1823, III, 586–595.

2 See, for instance, Nichols, 1823, III, 241–45.

3 Katherine Grey was the younger sister of Lady Jane Grey, and in the
event of Elizabeth's death without an obvious heir might have been one
of the claimants to the throne. She had died in 1568.

4 See Strong, 1973, 195–6.

5 See Bond, 1902, I, 404ff.

6 Cf. Jonson's *To Penshurst*, discussed on pp. 41ff.

7 Where she lives as Queen of the dead.

8 The importance of this ceremony still survives: the name of the ship
presages its fortune and a careful choice is important (those who named
the Titanic might be thought to have doomed the ship by their choice
of a name so rich with associations of futile strength and inevitable
defeat).

9 The Fairy Queen was, of course, a common figure at entertainments, cf.
p. 122.

10 Sidney, ed. Duncan-Jones and Van Dorsten, 1973, 13–32.

11 Orgel and Strong, 1973, I, 405ff. In some ways the Bisham entertainment
is like an ante-masque to which Elizabeth herself provides the masque.

12 See p. 119.

13 For Catherine de Medici's entertainments, see Yates, 1959, *passim*,
and Strong, 1973, 121–167.

14 VI.ix. *passim*.

Text

1 No large income from rents and surrounding lands.

2 score, 20 paces: OED (A pace for a man 5ft 9in tall is about 2ft 9in).

[3] It is not clear whether this decoration was of real boughs and nuts, or whether they were painted on the walls. The ivy of the ceiling seems to have been carved or painted.

[4] Place for storing candles.

[5] For storing ewers and towels for washing at table.

[6] 1. Officers.

[7] 1. inserts here 'An other to entertaine all commers, suiters and such like'.

[8] Here the food which had not been eaten by the Court and their servants would be handed out to anyone who turned up. Cf. Girouard, 1978, p. 12.

[9] ie. these were all temporary buildings, like those of the Field of the Cloth of Gold.

[10] 1. 'My Lords'.

[11] A reference to Elizabeth's role as Diana, goddess of the moon.

[13] 1. '40', which seems a more plausible measurement.

[13] Privet. A mount like this may be seen in the gardens of Packwood House, Warwickshire.

[14] 1. omits 'the'.

[15] A small, light vessel, often part of the equipment of a man-of-war. (Hence the guns).

[16] 'Here follows . . . . companie issued' and illustration omitted 1.

[17] 1. 'auoiding tantiloqies (sic) [tautologies], or reiterations'.

[18] Finally in execution what it was first in conception.

[9] 1. 'twentith'.

[20] 1. 'my Lord of Hertford'.

[21] 1. 'after dinner, when every other . . .'

[22] 1. . . . 'entertainment, about three of the clocke his Honor seeing all his Retinew well mounted and ready to attend his pleasure, hee drew them secretly into a chief thicket . . .'

[23] 1. '. . . few words, but well couched to the purpose, hee put . . .'

[24] 1. omits 'the'.

[25] The gold chain was a favourite symbol of service in a great, or royal, household, indicating both the allegiance of the wearer and the wealth of the employer who bestowed it.

[26] 1. . . . 'favour towards them. This done, my Lord with his traine (amounting to the number of 3. hundred, and most of them wearing chains of gold about their necks, and in their hats Yellow and Black feathers) met with her Maiestie two miles off, then comming to Eluetham from her owne house of Odiham four miles from thence. As my Lorde in this first action . . .'

[27] The poet as *vates* is discussed in Sidney's *Apologie*. See Sidney ed. Duncan-Jones and Van Dorsten, 1973, 76ff.

[28] To presage or prognosticate. Here to prophesy.

[29] Elizabeth carries an olive branch in William Roger's engraving, *Eliza Triumphans*, among other pictures.

[30] He wears the high boots of the tragic actor.

[31] 1. Cannea.

[32] 1. casses.

33 This indicates the intention to use this account as propaganda, to celebrate the entertainment as a popular, not an elite, exercise.

34 The image is of the hassock used for praying in church.

35 ie. on mount Parnassus, another assurance that this is a true poet.

36 The family name of Hertford was Seymour.

37 This ostensibly refers to the simplicity of Elvetham: so poor a house cannot offer the deceitful luxury of the court, but in view of the suspicion with which Elizabeth regarded Hertford, it must have an underlying irony.

38 Elizabeth as a goddess of fertility and increase. There may be a suggestion that she is combining the fruitfulness of autumn (the season of her visit) with a restored fruitfulness of Spring. A combination of continual spring and autumn (both fruitful and moderate seasons, which avoid the extremes of summer and winter) was a quality both of Eden, or the Earthly Paradise, and the Golden Age.

39 The Astraean and Golden Age imagery is continued in this picture of Elizabeth as the bringer of Peace and Temperance.

40 This reinforces the suggestion of the Poet's speech that Elvetham has been transformed into Paradise by Elizabeth's arrival.

41 Another example of Elizabeth's readiness to exercise her personal charm while on progress.

42 Here it seems that a distinction is being made between the song, or music, and the ditty, or words; a distinction made clearer in the heading of the song in 1., which reads 'The Dittie of the six Virgins Song'.

43 London was traditionally Troynovant, built by Brutus, grandson of Aeneas, and other Trojans, cf. FQ III.ix.44ff.

44 The Satyrs here seem to be representatives of nature, as well as traditional participants in unrestrained celebrations.

45 In *England's Helicon*, 1600, this is ascribed to Thomas Watson. See also his *Italian Madrigals*, 1590 (the setting is possibly by Byrd, or possibly Francis Pilkington, see *Avis*, 1605). See Brennecke, 1968, pp. 39ff.

46 Hertford's second wife, Frances Howard, daughter of Lord Howard of Effiingham.

47 1. omits 'and her Majesty . . . hir Majestie's entrance'.

48 Chambers are small pieces of ordinance, especially small pieces without carriages, standing on the breech, used to fire salutes. (NED). Pieces are probably small cannon here. 1. omits 'and two brasse peeces'.

49 1. 'my Lord'.

50 These seem to be musicians specially provided for the occasion, neither part of the staff, of Elvetham (although they may have been from the Earl's household) nor the Queen's own musicians. The general enthusiasm of the Queen's response to the music provided suggests that they were performers of high calibre.

51 Christopher Hogwood suggests that this may possibly be the pavan 'The Sacred End', pub. 1609.

52 1. omits 'there was in the morning . . . contented hir Highnesse'.

53 1. omits 'a variety of consorted music at dinner time'.

54 1. 'my Lord'.

55 With a pelmet.

56 A canopy like this may be seen in the picture of *Queen Elizabeth Carried in Procession.* See Strong, 1977, p. 36.

57 1. 'by foure of my Lordes chiefe Gentlemen'.

58 Elizabeth's consent to the entertainment provided was probably, in fact, obtained on all such occasions.

59 Ugly.

60 1. omits 'Phorcus and Glaucus'. It is not clear whether two sets of Sea-gods are implied, or whether Phorcus and Glaucus are alternative names for Neptune and Oceanus. Neptune was the Roman equivalent of Poseidon, son of Rhea and Kronos; Oceanus a river god, who alone of the older gods was allowed to retain his power under Zeus. Phorcus was a Titan, and Glaucus a son of Minos who became a sea-god. It is possible that the second pair of names is an inept attempt to give Greek equivalent for the supposedly Latin names in the first pair. The illustration does not help as it shows six Tritons, not five, Nereus pulling the pinnace, and omits the other pair or pairs of gods altogether.

61 It seems that the musicians in this entertainment were female, and not boys dressed as girls.

62 This was a favourite device in the entertainments, being used (without music) at Kenilworth, and later at Ditchley (see page 132).

63 1. 'Summerset'. This is fairly common in the sixteenth century for 'somersault', and may be a faulty etymology linking the exercise with the county. Here, it no doubt ties in with the five-a-side lawn tennis players (see p. 114) who are all from Somerset. Hertford's father was, of course, Lord Protector Somerset.

64 Nereus, one of the aspects of 'the Old One of the Sea', was a particularly appropriate god to pay homage to Elizabeth: as the moon-goddess Diana, she controlled the seas (cf. Ralegh's *The Love of the Ocean to Cynthia*).

65 A reference to the defeat of the Spanish Armada in 1588.

66 Elizabeth did not make many visits to the coast, and she seems to have kept away from the South coast in particular during the period when there might have been some danger of a Spanish invasion. Nereus is saying that since she has been unable to come to the sea, he has brought the sea to her.

67 'Gold-breasted' indicates that this is the New World, not the Indian sub-continent.

68 Since it was left by India, it must have been of gold.

69 In theory, the monarch held the whole kingdom, and allotted lands to nobles to hold under her. Elizabeth was touchy on this point, see p. 166, n. 9, for her exchange with Lady of the Lake at Kenilworth in 1575.

70 Spain. (England was still at war with Spain in 1591).

71 A snail is of course proverbial for its slowness and cowardice.

72 Thetis was a sea-goddess, the female equivalent of Nereus.

73 Spring.

[74] Sorrow.

[75] 1. has a different version of this song:

> The Sea nymphes Dittie.
> How haps that now, when prime is don,
> An other spring time is begun?
> Our hemisphere is overrunne,
> With beauty of a second Sunne.
> *Eccho*. A second Sun.
> What second Sun hath raies so bright?
> To cause this unacquainted light?
> Tis faire Elisaes matchlesse Grace,
> Who with her beames doth blesse the place,
> *Eccho*. Doth blesse the place.   The music is not known.

[76] It is difficult to imagine what these looked like, but one may be represented at the bottom right-hand corner of the picture.

[77] 1. 'reproche'.

[78] omits 'all'.

[79] These are probably instruments fashioned to look like shells, rather than real conch-shells.

[80] 'Let it be given to the most worthy'.

[81] A reference to the proverbial licentiousness of the satyrs, of whom Sylvanus was the leader.

[82] Two antiphonal elegiac couplets, each expressing the notion 'You take precedence over the Muses and the nymphs of Ida, and are more beautiful than the goddesses of the deep sea'.

[83] 1. 'the land'.

[84] 1. 'then Sylvanus with his followers retired . . . .'

[85] An anti-Hapsburg reference. The Order of the Golden Fleece, founded in Philip the Good. Duke of Burgundy, in 1430, was the chief order of chivalry of Philip II, the equivalent of the English Garter.

[86] 1. 'I Now . . .'

[87] Presumably these resembled those worn by the shepherds in the illustrations to Spenser's *Shepheardes Calender*.

[88] 1. 'The Plowmans Song'.

[89] In *England's Helicon*, 1600, this is ascribed to N. Breton. Phillida being made the Lady of May is a reflection of her acceptance of love: May was the traditional month for fulfilment of love. Hellenore's being made the Lady of May in FQ.III.x.44. is an indication of her sexual laxness, but it is doubtful if such an implication is intended here. There is music for this by John Baldwin (BM MS RM 24.d.2). See Brennecke, 1968, pp. 49ff, where it is printed.

[90] 1. 'my L.'

[91] See note 62, above.

[92] Chambers points out (1923, I, p. 123) that this is the first recorded game of a form of lawn tennis.

[93] These may be our modern Catherine-wheels, golden rain, and roman candles.

94 Not a full meal, but dessert.
95 1. continues:
   To saisfie the curious, I will here set downe some particulars in the banket.
   Her Maiesties Armes in sugar-worke.
   The seuerall Armes of all our Nobilitie in sugar-worke.
   Many men and women in sugar-worke, and some inforst by hand.
   Castles, Forts, Ordinance, Drummers, Trumpeters, and soldiors of all sorts in sugar-worke.
   Lions, Vnicorns, Beares, Horses, Camels, Buls, Rams, Dogges, Tygers, Elephants, Antelops, Dromedaries, Apes, and all other beastes in sugar-worke.
   Egles, Falcons, Cranes, Bussardes, Heronshawes, Bytters, Pheasants, Partridges, Quailes, Larkes, Sparrowes, Pigeons, Cockes, Oules, and all that flie, in sugar-worke.
   Snakes, adders, vipers, frogs, toades, and all kind of wormes in sugar-worke.
   Mermaides, whales, dolphins, cungars, sturgions, pikes, carps, breams, and all sortes of fishes, in sugar-worke.
   All these were standing dishes of sugar-work. The selfe same devises were also there in flat-worke. Moreover these particulars following, and many such like, were in flat sugar-worke, and sinamond.
   March – panes, grapes, oisters, muscles, cockles, periwinckles, crabs, lobsters.
   Apples, peares, and plums, of all sorts.
   Preserves, suckats, jellies, leaches, marmelats, pasts comfits, of all sorts.
96 1. 'siluer'.
97 Aureola here seems to be identified with Aurora, the dawn.
98 Music by Edward Johnson. In BM MSS Add. 30480-84. See Brennecke, 1968, pp. 52ff, where it is printed.
99 1. 'that shee desired to see and hear it twise ouer'.
100 1. omits 'It was . . . the whole action'.
101 1. omits 'all'.
102 The device of those who greeted the Queen lamenting her departure in black costumes is used again at Harefield. Nichols, 1823, III, pp. 586–595.
103 1. omits 'he being attire . . . signifie sorrow'. The text is a little confused here: the Poet should presumably have been mentioned with the Graces and Hours.
104 A reiteration of the theme of Elizabeth as the fruitful virgin, but the sun is also an emblem of monarchy.
105 1. omits 'then Nereus . . . greater sorrow'.
106 Ladies almost always wore masks when riding on horseback or in coaches, to protect their complexions.
107 1. '. . . two, that were cunning'.
   O Come againe faire Natures treasure,

Whose lookes yeeld joyes exceeding measure.
O come againe heav'ns chiefe delight,
Thine absence makes eternall night.
O come againe worlds starbright eye,
Whose presence doth adorne the skie.
O come againe sweet beauties Sunne:
When thou art gone, our joyes are done. Music by Edward Johnson in
BM MSS Add 30480-84. See Brennecke, 1968, pp. 54ff., where it is printed.

[108] 1. '. . . openly protested to my Lord of Hertford'.

[109] 1. '. . . was so honorable, as hereafter hee should finde the rewarde thereof in her especiall favour'.

[110] 1. 'manie and most happie . . .'

DITCHLEY 1592

Introduction

[1] eg. Malory, ed. Cowen, 1969, I. p. 25. For a more detailed, and different interpretation of the Kenilworth entertainment, see Axton, 1977, passim.

[2] The Eccho was a fashionable device in both poetry and song. Sidney includes an Echo-poem in the *Arcadia* Eclogues (Sidney, ed. Ringler, 1962, pp. 62ff.) and there was an Echo-song at Elvetham (see p. 110).

[3] There were figures of giant porters on the walls at Kenilworth as Elizabeth first approached the castle.

[4] Nichols, 1823, I, p. 495.

[5] This interpretation of the entertainment was first put forward by Cunliffe (1911). Chambers (1936) and Prouty (1942) attempted to rebut it, but do not seem convincing.

[6] The common confusion of Delphi and Delos.

[7] So in the text, but it should surely by Contarenus.

[8] *The Hermit's Tale at Woodstock* in Nichols, 1823, I, pp. 557ff.

[9] At her approach to the castle, Elizabeth was welcomed by the Lady of the Lake with a speech ending,

'Passe on, Madame, you need no longer stand;
The Lake, the Lodge, the Lord, are yours for to command'.
(Nichols, 1823, I, p. 492).

to which Elizabeth answered, 'We thought indeed the Lake had been oours and doo you call it yourz noow? Well, we will herein common more with yoo hereafter'. (Nichols, 1823, I, p. 431).
This was a miscalculation, as it indicated Elizabeth's willingness to listen to more arguments for the alliance with Leicester.

[10] Chambers, 1936, p. 88. Chambers thinks that this is the first appearance of the Fairy Queen in Elizabethan literature, while Baskerville, 1920, suggests that this entertainment may be the genesis for the concept of Elizabeth as the Fairy Queen.

[11] Chambers, 1936, p. 89.

[12] See Gascoigne, ed. Cunliffe, 1910, I. pp. 106ff.

[13] Yates, 1975, p. 95.

[14] This is, of course, the formula used by Spenser as the framework of *The Faerie Queene*.

[15] I am grateful to Professor Thomas Roche for drawing this to my attention.

[16] Dekker, *Old Fortunatus*, Prologue at Court 40–49. In Dekker, ed Bowers, 1953, I, 114.

[17] See Yates, 1975, p. 79.

[18] Malory, ed. Cowen, 1969, XIX. ch. 10.

[19] Malory, ed. Cowen, 1969, XVII. ch. 21.

[20] *St. John* x, v. 38.

[21] See, for instance, Davies, 1963, nos. 27, 51, 147.

[22] Chambers, 1936, 276.

Text

[1] Side heading '1592 September 20'. This is the first day's entertainment, September 20. The guardian of the grove must have stopped the Queen as she approached it.

[2] This ominous note is frequently struck by the guardians of the perils which confront brave knights: see, for example, Malory, ed. Cowen, 1969, VI. ch. 10.

[3] The Queen evidently responded as she should, ignored the warning, and progressed into the grove, where she is addressed by an arboriform Knight.

[4] Was thwarted.

[5] The knights and ladies in tree-form may owe something to the Fradubio episode in *The Faerie Queene*, I.ii.30ff, which is itself paralleled in Virgil, Dante, and Ariosto, to one or all of which it must owe its inspiration. See Spenser, ed. Roche, 1978, 1081, n. 31 1ff.

[6] These are, or is one of, the ladies who have been transformed to leaves.

[7] Chambers's speculation, illegible in MS.

[8] Addressed to the Queen, in comparison with whom the ladies perceive their imperfections.

[9] That is Elizabeth, the only constant woman.

[10] Another knight-transformed.

[11] Looked for, expected.

[12] eares MS: Chambers's reading.

[13] one.

[14] pun on 'grave'.

[15] one.

16 Who must have conducted the Queen through the grove.

17 Elizabeth was evidently accompanied by a train.

18 It is not clear whether the grove was inside or outside: references to its darkness and the fresh air to follow suggest that it may have been in a building, or a temporary structure.

19 'you' MS. Chambers's speculation.

20 ? spring.

21 Echo, tell an unhappy man what it is to love? E: the sea, what are the waves? E: grief/who sails on it? E: Life/what is a river? E: light/Tell me what crime is? E: (?) Coldness/What are terrors? E: Errors/what would an error be, I ask? E: The heart/If it be the heart, then is there no hope in love? E: to die.

22 The Queen has by now been led to a ?pavilion, hung with some cryptic pictures, where an old knight is in an enchanted sleep, attended by his page, who now speaks.

23 These are the allegorical pictures which the Queen must interpret.

24 Presumably the Fairy Queen here is Elizabeth, in another aspect, who must release the knight from the consequences of his offence against herself, but the imagery of this entertainment is cryptic.

25 Elizabeth interprets the pictures, the sleeping knight wakes, and, as becomes apparent later, the knights and ladies in the grove are restored to human shape.

26 Apparently a reference to the Woodstock entertainment. See p. 122.

28 *The Hermit's Tale at Woodstock* described the bulk of the entertainment. See p. 119ff.

29 suited, appropriate to each other.

30 This whole passage is difficult to interpret. Presumably the one 'who should not be denied' was Elizabeth, who asked for the pictures from the Fairy Queen, and she, wishing to keep them, cheated ('was fayne to juggle') and moved them by supernatural means to Ditchley. This may suggest that the Fairy Queen is distinct from Elizabeth, her rival, almost her opponent, and that her undoing of the Fairy Queen's spell indicates her superior power. In this case, the sleeping knight would still have been guilty of inconstancy, but not inconstancy to Elizabeth.

31 For the device of the crowned pillar and its significance in the cults of Elizabeth, see Strong, 1969, 46; 1977, 154; Yates, 1975, 58.

32 That is, the Ladies in the leaves are those who have attempted to interpret the pictures and failed.

33 That is, the knight's sin is inconstancy.

34 penalty.

35 Here he presents her with a gift.

36 May she bless both heaven & sun.

37 These are supposed to be two of the Ladies imprisoned in the leaves. N. reads 'The Songe after Dinner at the two ladies entrance'.

38 Printed in *The Phoenix Nest* 1593.

[39] 'the late'.

[40] Hamper and Nichols both assume this to be Liberty (*The Phoenix Nest* has 'Inconstancie', but 'Lightness' might be possible).

[41] Ph N inserts, prob. correctly.

[42] 'Faithfull' in Ph. N.

[43] Motion ceases when an end has been achieved.

[44] Chambers: 'Now Love ys dull without feare of loosing, which can not be where there are no rivalls'.

[45] Chambers: 'to please'.

[46] Pygmalion made a statue which came to life.

[47] All in the whole and all in any part of it.

[48] A gift of some form of embroidered garment.

[49] Chambers: 'woorthie'.

[50] Another gift of apparel: it seems possible that the gifts might have been complementary; perhaps a smock, and a girdle or busk.

[51] Always the same, one of Elizabeth's favourite mottos, referring to her virginity, her triumph over time, and her unchangeability.

[52] Not in Ditchley.

[53] Give me all you have, soul and faith and hand: if you give me these three, you give me all you have.

[54] Both voice and tongue speak Elizabeth's praises. Ditchley: 'Diva tuas laudes et nox, ligna loquuntur'.

[55] Lee himself: this was the persona he had used at the Woodstock entertainment.

[56] Copse

[57] This is the attitude that Lee consistently held that Elizabeth's servants should have to her.

[58] Not in Ditchley.

[59] There is a tension between the 'King's highway' (the route to God in heaven), and the 'Queen's highway', both the route to Elizabeth, worshipped as a goddess, and the route to God which the saintly Elizabeth follows.

[60] Shattered, damaged (cf. crazy paving).

[61] Ditchley continues here:

Your Majestie this simple legacie which he disposed the rather whilst he yet liveth, then left to be disposed after his death, that you might understand how he alwayes prefered the deds of the livinge, before the hops of the ded; Thus much your devyne power hath performed to him, thus far his thanck fulnes hath brought me to your Majestie; as for any other accomplishments, whatsoever dewtie yealds to be debt, devotion offers to see discharged: And if my Master his best payment be only good prayers, what needs more then the pages bare word wich is Always: Amen?

and breaks off.

[62] It is permitted to leap into heaven from a corner.

[63] Address.

[64] Most faithful guardian of the crowned pillar.

65 They are Chaplain of the crown's guardian, and most faithful servant of the Knight of the crown, possibly two of Lee's retainers.

66 This is, of course, a pun on the expression, 'take the will for the deed'.

67 'Anything that completes or perfects; that adds grace or ornament to body or mind': OED.

68 shelter.

69 The idea is of an Elizabethan formal garden, cf. Hyams, 1977, p. 147.

70 A springer spaniel was used for hawking to flush out the game, rather than to chase it (rather like some gun dogs now – which may still be springers).

71 Rights over certain commodities, granted by the Crown.

72 A piece of property which is found ownerless, and which, if unclaimed within a fixed period after due notice given, falls to the lord of the manor: OED.

73 A domestic animal found wandering away from the custody of its owner, and liable to be impounded and (if not redeemed) forfeited: OED.

74 Either stolen goods, forfeit by the thief, or that thief's goods, forfeit to law.

75 Those who hold lands 'at the will of the lord according to the custom of the manor' by copy of the manorial court-roll: OED.

76 A tenancy at will is where the land is held by the tenant so long as lessor and lessee please that the tenancy should continue: OED Tenancy 1b.

77 Here, probably the land of an estate actually held by the owner, and not rented out.

78 Tenure of land under the condition of performing military service: OED.

79 OED 2c: 'the Reiceiver of Fyffes, . . . receveth the mony of all such who compound with the King . . . for the buying of any lands, or tenements houlden in *Capite*'.

80 The court of an archbishop for the probate of wills and trial of testamentary causes . . . its jurisdiction was transferred in 1857 to the Court of Probate: OED.

Bibliography

An Almain Armourer's Album, ed. Viscount Dillon, 1905, London.

Axton, Marie, 1977, 'The Tudor Mask and Elizabethan court drama', in *English Drama: Forms and Development* ed. Axton and Williams, Cambridge, 1977, 24–27.

Bacon, Francis, 1972, *Essays*, ed. M. J. Hawkins, London.

Barber, Richard, 1974 (2nd ed.), *The Knight and Chivalry*, Ipswich.

Barnes, Joseph, 1592, *Speeches delivered to her Majestie thus last progresse, at the Right Honorable the Lady Russels, at Bissam, the Right Honorable the Lord Chandos at Sudley, at the Right Honorable the Lord Norris, at Ricorte*, Oxford. BM. C33e7 (19).

Baskerville, C. R., 1920. 'The Genesis of Spenser's Fairy Queen', *MP* XVIII, 49–54.

Bennett, J. W., 1942, *The Evolution of 'The Faerie Queene'*, Chicago.

Bergeron, David, 1971, *English Civic Pageantry*, London.

Bradbrook, Muriel, 1960, *Drama as offering: the princely pleasures at Kenelworth*, Rice Institute Pamphlet XLVI.

Brennecke, Ernest, 1968, 'The Entertainment at Elvetham, 1591', in: John H. Long (ed.) *Music in English Renaissance Drama*, Lexington, Ky.

Brooks, Eric St-John, 1946, *Sir Christopher Hatton: Queen Elizabeth's Favourite*, London.

Campion, Thomas, ed. W. R. Davis, 1969, *Works*, London.

Carey, Robert, ed. F. H. Mares, 1972, *Memoirs*, Oxford.

Chambers, E. K., 1923, *The Elizabethan Stage*, 4 volumes, Oxford.

Chambers, E. K., 1936, *Sir Henry Lee: An Elizabethan Portrait*, Oxford.

Child, F. J. (editor) 1882–1898 (1965), *The English and Scottish Popular Ballads*, 5 volumes, New York.

Clarendon, Edward Hyde, Lord, 1702–4 (1840), *A History of the Rebellion and Civil Wars in England*, 2 volumes, Oxford.

Clepham, R. C., 1919, *The Tournament; its periods and phases*, London.

Connell, Dorothy, 1977, *Sir Philip Sidney: The Maker's Mind*, Oxford.

Cooper, John R., 1968, *The Art of 'The Compleat Angler'*, Durham, N.C.

Cunliffe, J. W., 1911, 'The Queenes Majesties Entertainment at Woodstocke', *PMLA*, XXVI, 92–141.

Davies, Sir John, ed. Robert Krueger, 1975, *Poems*, Oxford.

Davies, R. T. (editor), 1963, *Medieval English Lyrics*, London.

Dekker, Thomas, ed. F. Blowers, 1953, *Works*, 4 volumes, Cambridge.

Douglas, Mary, 1966, *Purity and Danger*, Oxford.

Fogel, E. G., 1960, 'A Possible Addition to the Sidney Canon', *MLN* LXXC, 389–394.

Fowler, Alastair, 1970, *Triumphal Forms: Structural Patterns in Elizabethan Poetry*, Cambridge.

Foxe, John, 1563, *Actes and Monuments* . . . , London.

Furnivall, F. J. (editor), 1907, *Robert Laneham's Letter*, London.

Gascoigne, George, ed. J. W. Cunliffe, 1907–10, *Complete Works*, 2 vols, Cambridge.

Girouard, Mark, 1978, *Life in the English Country House*, New Haven and London.

Goodman, Godfrey, Bishop of Gloucester, ed. J. S. Brewer, 1839, *The Court of King James I*, London.

Gorges, Sir Arthur, ed. H. E. Sandison, 1953, *Poems*, Oxford.

Greenblatt, Stephen, 1973, *Sir Walter Ralegh: The Renaissance Man and his Roles*, New Haven and London.

Henslowe, Philip, ed. R. A. Foakes and R. T. Rickert, 1961, *Diary*, Cambridge.

Hentzner, Paul, ed. H. Morley, 1901: *Travels in England During the Reign of Queen Elizabeth*, London.

Hyams, Edward, 1977, *A History of Gardens and Gardening*, London.

Kendrick, T. D., 1950, *British Antiquity*, London.

Laver, James, (editor), 1947, *Isabella's Triumph*, London.

Leech, Clifford, 1935, 'Sir Henry Lee's Entertainment of Elizabeth in 1592', *MLR*, XXX, 52–5.

Lydgate, John, ed. H. Berger, 1924–1927, *Fall of Princes*, 4 volumes, London, EETS.

Lyly, John, ed. R. W. Bond, 1902 (1967), *Works*, 3 volumes, Oxford.

MacCaffrey, Wallace, 1969, *The Shaping of the Elizabethan Regime*, London.

Malory, Sir Thomas, ed. Janet Cowen and John Lawlor, 1969, *Le Morte D'Arthur*, 2 volumes, Harmondsworth.

Marie de France, ed. A. Ewert, 1963, *Lais*, Oxford.

Nichols, John, 1823, *The Progresses, and Public Processions, of Queen Elizabeth*, new ed., 3 volumes, London.

Peele, George, ed. D. H. Horne, 1952, *Minor Works*, New Haven.

Piggot, Stuart, 1976, *Ruins in a Landscape: Essays in antiquarianism*, Edinburgh.

Plumb, J. H., 1977, *Royal Heritage*, London.

Porter, Enid, 1974, *The Folklore of East Anglia*, London.

Prouty, C. T., 1942, *George Gascoigne, Elizabethan Courtier, Soldier and Poet*, New York.

Ralegh, Sir Walter, ed. Agnes Latham, 1951, *Poems*, London.

Schulze, I. L., 1933, 'Notes on Elizabethan Chivalry and *The Faerie Queene*', *SP*, XXX, 148–159.

Scott, Sir Walter, 1821, *Kenilworth, a romance*, 3 volumes, Edinburgh.

Segar, William, 1590, *The Booke of Honor and Armes*, London.

Segar, William, 1602, *Honor Military and Civill*, London.

Sidney, Sir Philip, ed. William A. Ringler, Jr., 1962, *Poems*, Oxford.

Sidney, Sir Philip, ed. K. Duncan-Jones and J. Van Dorsten, 1973, *Miscellaneous Prose*, Oxford.

Sidney, Sir Philip, ed. M. Evans, 1977, *The Countess of Pembroke's Arcadia* (1593) Harmondsworth.

Smith, Roland M., 1944, 'More Irish Words in Spenser', *MLN* lix, 472–477.

Spenser, Edmund, ed. Thomas P. Roche, 1978, *The Faerie Queene* (1590, 1596), Harmondsworth.

Strong, Roy C., 1962. *Elizabethan Pageantry as Propaganda*, University of London Ph.D. thesis (unpublished).

Strong, Roy C., 1969, *The Elizabethan Image: Painting in England 1540–1620*. London.

Strong, Roy C., 1969 (b), *The English Icon*, London and New York.

Strong, Roy C., and Oman, Julia Trevelyan, 1971, *Elizabeth R*, London.

Strong, Roy C., 1973, *Splendour at Court: Renaissance Spectacle and Illusion*, London.

Strong, Roy C., and Orgel, Stephen, 1973, *Inigo Jones; the Theatre of the Stuart Court*, London.

Strong, Roy C., 1977, *The Cult of Elizabeth*, London.

Summerson, Sir John, 1959, 'The Building of Theobalds, 1564–1585', *Archaeologia* xcvii, 107–126.

Wallace, Malcolm William, 1915, *The Life of Sir Philip Sidney*, Cambridge.

Warner, Marina, 1976, *Alone of All Her Sex: The Myth and Cult of the Virgin Mary*, London.

Wedgwood, C. V., 1960, 'The Last Masque', in *Truth and Opinion*, 139–156, London.

Wickham, Glynne, 1959, *Early English States 1300 to 1660: Volume I: 1300 to 1576*, London.

Williams, Neville, 1967, *Elizabeth Queen of England*, London.

Williams, Neville, 1974, *All the Queen's Men*, London.

Wilson, E. C., 1939, *England's Eliza*, Cambridge, Mass.

Wind, Edgar, 1967 (revised), *Pagan Mysteries in the Renaissance*, Harmondsworth.

Withington, Robert, 1918, *English Pageantry: an historical outline*, Cambridge, Mass.

Yates, Frances A., 1947, 'Queen Elizabeth as Astraea', *JWCI* x, 27–82.

Yates, Frances A., 1959, *The Valois Tapestries*, London.

Yates, Frances A., 1975, *Astraea*, London.

Index